CRUCIBLE *of* FAITH

CRUCIBLE
of FAITH

The Ancient Revolution That
Made Our Modern Religious World

PHILIP JENKINS

BASIC BOOKS
New York

Basic Books
Hachette Book Group
1290 Avenue of the Americas, New York, NY 10104
www.basicbooks.com

Printed in the United States of America

First Edition: September 2017

Published by Basic Books, an imprint of Perseus Books, LLC, a subsidiary of Hachette Book Group, Inc.

The Hachette Speakers Bureau provides a wide range of authors for speaking events. To find out more, go to www.hachettespeakersbureau.com or call (866) 376-6591.

The publisher is not responsible for websites (or their content) that are not owned by the publisher.

Print book interior design by Jeff Williams

Library of Congress Cataloging-in-Publication Data
Names: Jenkins, Philip, 1952– author.
Title: Crucible of faith : the ancient revolution that made our modern religious world / Philip Jenkins.
Description: New York : Basic Books, 2017. | Includes bibliographical references and index.
Identifiers: LCCN 2017010045| ISBN 9780465096404 (hardcover : alk. paper) | ISBN 9780465096411 (ebook)
Subjects: LCSH: Christianity—Origin. | Cosmogony, Ancient. | Judaism—History—Post-exilic period, 586 B.C.-210 A.D. | Judaism—History—Talmudic period, 10–425.
Classification: LCC BR166 .J465 2017 | DDC 200.9/014—dc23
LC record available at https://lccn.loc.gov/2017010045

LSC-C

10 9 8 7 6 5 4 3 2 1

To Byron Johnson, with thanks.

CONTENTS

MAPS

TABLES

OF DATES, NAMES, AND PLACES

HISTORIANS USE VARIOUS METHODS for presenting dates in the distant past. The traditional system of BC/AD has a Christian bias, as it explicitly refers not just to Christ but to "the Lord," and in the interests of objectivity many writers prefer the term "Common Era," or CE, instead of AD. That is not without problems, as the basis for Common Era dating is still the supposed date for Christ's birth. Nevertheless, this book will use BCE and CE throughout.

I will refer often to the text that Jews know as the Tanakh or the Bible and Christians refer to as the Old Testament. Jews naturally dislike the latter term because it suggests that their scriptures are outmoded or surpassed, and many modern Christians respect these sensitivities by themselves adopting the term "Hebrew Bible" or "Hebrew scriptures." For various reasons, though, it is difficult to find a neutral or wholly accurate term for this collection because the Hebrew Bible and the Old Testament are not quite identical in their contents.

This point requires some explanation. The Jewish Bible—the "Hebrew Bible"—has three sections, the *Torah (Law)*, *Nevi'im (Prophets)*, and *Ketuvim (Writings)*, which gives us the acronym *Tanakh*. In the books that it treats as approved or canonical, that collection corresponds exactly to the Protestant Old Testament. However, the precise number of books differs somewhat in each version, because works that are treated as a unity in the Hebrew (such as Ezra and Nehemiah) are distinguished in the Protestant text.

In its attitude to the canon—that is, in its choice of approved works—the "Hebrew Bible" represents one approach, but it is not necessarily the only one. During the third century BCE, Jewish scholars translated biblical texts into the Greek version known as the Septuagint. Because it is a translation, one would assume that its readings are inferior to those of the

Hebrew or Aramaic, but that is not always so. In many cases, the Septuagint preserved readings that are older and arguably more authentic. Also, the Septuagint reflects the choice of books prevailing in the ancient era and is thus considerably wider in scope than what is found in the Tanakh. The fact that certain books were accepted within the canon while others were rejected was based on critical and historical assumptions that were not always sound—for instance, deciding which books might be genuinely ancient.

In creating their own canon, most Christian churches from early times through the Reformation relied on the Septuagint and thus included in their Old Testaments several works absent from the Hebrew Bible. This meant 1 and 2 Maccabees, Sirach (Ecclesiasticus), Tobit, Baruch, Judith, and the Wisdom of Solomon; in addition, they knew more extended versions of books like Daniel and Esther. During the sixteenth-century Reformation, Protestants demoted these books to the inferior level of *Apocrypha*, "hidden things," but that division was not observed by Roman Catholic or Orthodox Christians or by many other smaller churches around the world. For non-Protestants these *Deuterocanonical* books (literally, the "Second Canon") are canonical rather than merely apocryphal, and they are unequivocally part of the Old Testament. Orthodox churches use the category *anagignoskomena*, "those which are to be read," which includes the Deuterocanonicals, but also 1 Esdras, 3 Maccabees, and Psalm 151.

It is therefore difficult to know how to refer to texts that are canon for some but not for others. To illustrate the problem, how should I refer to the influential book of Sirach, which was originally written in Hebrew around 190 BCE, although historically it was mainly known in Greek? Portions of the Hebrew original survive among the Dead Sea Scrolls (together with the Book of Tobit), although that does not necessarily say anything about the canonical status of either work. In later times, Sirach did not form part of either the Hebrew Bible or the Protestant Old Testament, but it is canonical for Catholics, Orthodox, and other groups. It thus forms part of (some) Old Testaments, but not the Hebrew Bible.

Complicating the matter further, some sizable churches have long operated in isolation from other Christian communities and they are still more expansive in their definitions. The most significant is the Ethiopian Orthodox Tewahedo Church, which counts an impressive forty million members. Besides the familiar books of the Protestant Bible plus the Deuterocanonical works, they also use and canonize other significant writings that once circulated widely but have since been forgotten in most of the Christian world. These include 1 Enoch and the book of Jubilees, both of which will be discussed at length in these pages. Various churches worldwide also accept additional books under the general name of "Maccabees."

With all due caveats, then, I will use both the terms "Hebrew Bible" and "Old Testament" where they apply, sometimes with additional detail to explain how I am using the words in a particular context.

Also potentially sensitive is the name given to the region in which so much of the action of this book occurs. In my usage "Palestine" refers to the geographical area west of the river Jordan that is today covered by the state of Israel, the Palestinian territories, and the Gaza Strip. That reflects the historical usage prior to the twentieth century. (During the British mandate era that ended in 1948, the term was extended for administrative convenience to cover what is today known as the nation of Jordan.)

Some dislike the term "Palestine" because it was imposed by the Romans after the crushing of the Jewish revolt in 135, and they believe that it deliberately and insultingly recalls the Philistines, who were deadly enemies of the Jews. In modern times the word is associated with the Arab inhabitants of the land rather than Jews. Some critics, indeed, believe that to speak of "Palestine" is a deliberate attack on Zionism, which is certainly not my intent.

But other terms are equally thorny as historical signifiers, and that includes "Israel." Depending on the period in question, the term "Israel" has three meanings, namely, the Jewish people, the state of that name founded in 1948, or the Northern Kingdom during the ancient Hebrew period from roughly 900 to 600 BCE. None of those usages is helpful in supplying an accurate and objective geographical term. During the second and first centuries BCE, for instance, there was indeed a Jewish kingdom, but it was centered in the land we call Judea rather than in the former Northern Kingdom of Israel. Similar reasons of geographical limitation prevent us from using the term "Judea" for the larger geographical entity.

For lack of an objective alternative, then, "Palestine" is the best available descriptor, and it has often been used by Jews themselves. Even the Jerusalem Talmud, the *Yerushalmi*, is alternatively titled the Palestinian Talmud, and much of it is written in the dialect known as Jewish Palestinian Aramaic. In modern times "Palestine" is the standard preference of most mainstream historians and archaeologists of the region, both Jewish and others. It is, for instance, the usage found throughout the respected *Cambridge History of Judaism*.

INTRODUCTION

Then shall he say also unto them on the left hand, Depart from
me, ye cursed, into everlasting fire, prepared for the Devil and
his angels.

MATTHEW 25:41

ACCORDING TO MATTHEW'S gospel, Jesus told the frightening parable of a man sowing good seed in a field. In the night an enemy sows
tares (weeds) among the wheat, and the two kinds of plants grow up
together. The farmer tells his servants not to try purging the tares
immediately, lest they damage the wheat. Jesus explains his meaning:

> He that soweth the good seed is the Son of Man; The field is the
> world; the good seed are the children of the kingdom; but the
> tares are the children of the wicked one; The enemy that sowed
> them is the devil; the harvest is the end of the world; and the
> reapers are the angels. . . . The Son of man shall send forth his
> angels, and they shall gather out of his kingdom all things that
> offend, and them which do iniquity; And shall cast them into
> a furnace of fire: there shall be wailing and gnashing of teeth.
> Then shall the righteous shine forth as the sun in the kingdom
> of their Father. (Matt. 13:37–43, KJV)

The rigorous determinism of this passage—the implication that
humans are born good or wicked, with no ability to change their

destiny—together with its hellfire imagery, makes it unpopular among modern-day Christian preachers.

As with so many such stories credited to him, Jesus used commonplace rural imagery. He framed it, though, in a worldview that made many assumptions about spiritual realities as well as the universe and its hierarchies. Forces of good and evil, light and darkness, contend in the world until God's final victory. People must be urgently concerned about these conflicts because their conduct in the present world affects their fate in the afterlife. Although this parable is unusually explicit in its imagery, the basic ideas are quite unsurprising to anyone who knows the West's religious heritage. Angels and Judgment, Messiah and Satan, Hell and demons—these are the familiar building blocks of Western religion. They are also staples of two millennia of Christian art. All are integrated into a complex mythological system.[1]

What few modern readers will understand from such a passage is just how new the themes were at the time Jesus preached. Clearly, we assume, the source for these ideas is "the Bible," but however pervasive they are in the New Testament, they are not firmly rooted in the Old. During the period covered by the Hebrew Bible, up to around 400 BCE, few of those ideas existed in Jewish thought, and those that did were not prominent. By the start of the Common Era, these motifs were thoroughly integrated and acclimatized into the Jewish religious worldview. They have shaped Western faith and culture ever since.

So much of what we think of as the Judeo-Christian spiritual universe was conceived and described only *after* the closure of the canonical Old Testament text. Virtually every component of that system entered the Jewish world in the two or three centuries before the Common Era, and we can identify a critical moment of transformation around the year 250 BCE. These centuries constitute a startlingly little-known historical era that has seldom received the attention it deserves. It was in these years when the heavens and hells became so abundantly populated and when the universe was first conceived as a battleground between cosmic forces of Good and Evil. With the rise of Christianity, such Jewish-derived themes spilled forth into the wider world, becoming transcontinental. In the seventh century, Islam fully absorbed and incorporated these religious components as well. Today, these beliefs are the shared cultural inheritance of well over half the world's people.

During the two tempestuous centuries from 250 through 50 BCE, the Jewish and Jewish-derived world was a fiery crucible of values, faiths, and ideas, from which emerged wholly new religious syntheses. Such a sweeping transformation of religious thought in such a relatively brief period makes this one of the most revolutionary times in human culture. These years in effect created Western consciousness. In terms of its impact on human culture, the Crucible era is at least as significant as the celebrated Axial Age, which had been identified several centuries earlier and produced great intellectual leaps in societies as diverse as Greece, India, and China.[2] Just over two thousand years ago, a new universe was created, one that we still inhabit today.

THAT EMERGING BELIEF system—this new universe—was not the creation of isolated thinkers or writers who designed their religious system according to literary whim. On the contrary, these new ideas developed in direct response to cultural crises and political events of that era, and they can be understood only in that context.

The period began with the Hellenistic kingdoms that ruled the Middle East during the third century BCE, a Jewish encounter with globalizing modernity that produced both social tumult and effervescent creativity. These centuries were marked by such themes as the massive expansion of cities and of commercial economies, persistent conflict between native peoples and foreign rulers, and the growing importance of Diaspora communities. Throughout this period, Jews were in intimate contact with powerful religious and intellectual influences, from Mesopotamian religions and Persian Zoroastrian beliefs to the multiple philosophical currents of Hellenism.

Such intoxicating ideas could not fail to leave their impact on Jewish thinkers, but these new directions were not merely a response to foreign influences and imports. Yes, the Zoroastrian faith taught ideas of a Last Judgment and of something like the Devil and angels, while Jews and Christians borrowed from Greek terminology. But the picture is not as simple as scholars might once have believed. In the Zoroastrian case, we are much less confident than we might once have been about exactly when such religious themes emerged in the Persian setting and how they were transfused into the Jewish worldview. Similarly, with the Greeks, multiple schools of thought affected the Jewish world. Some—such as Platonism—were vastly more significant than others, such as Cynicism or materialist skepticism. It was not a question of *whether* external influences were available, but rather which of them appealed most to the needs and tastes of the potential recipients at a given time. The demand side of the equation mattered as much as supply.[3]

And the demand was high. These foreign currents flooded into a Jewish world that was, quite independently, in the course of its own religious reconstruction, a natural and logical outgrowth of strict monotheism. The growth of pure monotheism during the seventh and sixth centuries BCE raised troubling questions about the means by which God could act in history. Monotheism created an intellectual need for intermediary figures who enacted the divine will in his stead, and that necessitated a fast-growing belief in the reality and power of angels. Meanwhile, attempts to explain the existence of evil in a divinely ordained system inspired an obsessive interest in dark angels and in Satan himself. The need to see justice in the divine order inspired a vital new belief in concepts of the afterlife and resurrection, in ultimate rewards and punishments. (The study of the End Times—of Judgment, Heaven, and Hell—is called eschatology.) Persian and Greek worldviews were welcomed into a Jewish system that was already in headlong transformation, accelerating changes already in process.[4]

Jews were in frequent contact with other groups, and they had to decide how those strangers related to their own world and their own God. If there was one God, then he must in some sense be the God of the whole world. But universalism itself raised many questions. Was truth designed for only one racial group, or could others adopt it? Most daringly, might the spiritual universe expand to include other beings who could be understood as being godlike? Could Jewish rulers dare to appropriate Greek and foreign styles of authority, which raised kings to near-divine status (and sometimes not just "near")?[5] Such questions became acute when so many Jews lived outside Palestine, in a widespread Diaspora. Judaism was founded on the principles of one God and of one holy people in a sacred land. How far could the people sing the Lord's song in the strange countries of the Diaspora?

Believers faced daily debates over exclusivism and universalism, and issues of ritual purity proved especially divisive. Some responded by stressing ethnic particularism, condemning the Gentile world as the realm of Darkness. Other thinkers, though, followed the implication of doctrines of God's transcendent authority to preach a bold universalism. That view was symbolized in these years by a new emphasis on Adam, the parent of all humanity, whether Jewish or Gentile. At the same time, the ancient pre-Flood (and thus pre-Covenant) patriarchs became the subjects of extensive pseudoscriptural writings. So bitter did debates between various factions become that from the second century BCE onward, some thinkers whom we would undoubtedly call Jews were attacking others (who were no less certainly Jewish in our eyes) to the point of rejecting their religious identity altogether. Universalist approaches reached a new height in the early Christian world, when the apostle Paul extended to all believing Gentiles membership in a new Israel, under a New Covenant.[6]

I HAVE SPOKEN of a "revolution," and the word demands definition. Over any period of several centuries, any culture will experience some changes, unless it is wholly cut off from other societies. No era should ever be labeled a "time of transition." After all, what historical period was ever so moribund as to lack alteration or innovation altogether? In matters of belief or culture, ideas develop naturally over time, and they might be expressed through new literary genres or artistic forms. Of themselves, those changes would not constitute a revolution. That comment is all the more true of very lengthy periods like the sprawling Axial Age of ca. 800–200 BCE, which supposedly spanned some six centuries.

By "revolution," then, I mean a fundamental shift in assumptions that affects most or all of the belief system, and one that occurs within a relatively short historical period. Those changes echo through the culture or faith in question, transforming belief and practice at all levels, for ordinary followers as well as elite thinkers. As Thomas Paine famously wrote, the American Revolution meant that "our style and manner of thinking have undergone a revolution. . . . We see with other eyes; we hear with other ears; and we think with other thoughts, than those we formerly used." A new consciousness takes hold. After the transformation has occurred, it simply becomes impossible to revert to the old order or even to comprehend it. So sweeping are the changes in their impact, so seemingly inevitable, that later generations cannot even imagine a time when matters had ever been different. Without any attempt to deceive, those later heirs to revolution commonly rewrite and reinterpret older texts and stories in light of the newer orthodoxies.[7]

In the case of the Crucible era, the events occurred within about two centuries. Both the pace and the intensity of change were at their height during a generation or so at the heart of this period, roughly between 170 and 140 BCE. We can without hesitation, then, describe these profound changes as a thoroughgoing cultural and religious revolution.

At first glance, this idea of a revolution might seem to contradict the notion presented earlier of a prolonged evolution from earlier trends. Theorists of biological evolution, though, deploy the idea of *punctuated equilibrium*, which offers many analogies to patterns of historical transformation. According to this theory, changes occur over long periods, but at very unequal rates. For long periods, biological changes are slight and gradual, to the extent that conditions appear almost static. That seeming stability masks the gradual changes that are accumulating powerfully below the surface, however. Under various external forces, such as a sudden dramatic climate crisis, the pace of change then accelerates intensely, with rapid and obvious development and diversification. As the crisis fades, conditions once more resume something approaching stasis or equilibrium. However short-lived those transformative eras might appear in the full span of historical time, their influence is profound and enduring. In mainstream history, they are called times of revolutionary change, of which the Crucible era is a prime example.

THE WORLD IN which these religious debates occurred was anything but one of tranquil intellectual exchange. So turbulent was this age, in fact, and so often scarred by political and social upheaval, that the older spiritual equilibrium could not have remained intact.

To illustrate this point, we might consider an era that at first glance looks like a near golden age of order and stability. Between about 215 and 185 BCE, the Jewish high priest was Simon II, who was probably identical with the legendary sage and moral exemplar Simon the Just, or Shimon haTzaddik. (Some link that title to an earlier incumbent of the high-priestly office, but the chronology fits this man vastly better.) Although later rabbis regarded him as one in a long line of scholars and thinkers who theoretically traced back to Moses, Simon's rule effectively marked the beginning of a sequence of renowned pupils and successors. He even occupies a prestigious place in the beloved collection of ethical and moral teachings known as the *Pirkei Avot* (Chapters of the Fathers). On several occasions, his career touched on major events. His first cousin Joseph was a secular magnate in the region under the Ptolemaic Empire, one of the imperial superpowers of the day. Simon is even a named character in at least some versions of the Bible. As a revered spiritual ruler and an ambitious builder, Simon was the subject of a fulsome and near-messianic tribute in the Deuterocanonical book of Sirach, where he is "like the sun shining upon the Temple of the Most High, and like the rainbow gleaming in glorious clouds." Simon features in heroic guise in the fictitious work 3 Maccabees, which describes the attempts of an Egyptian king to force his way into the Temple. According to this legend, Simon's noble prayer persuades God to intervene and strike the king with paralysis (Sirach, chap. 50, RSV).[8]

On closer examination, this period of untrammeled glories looks much shakier and more perilous. Simon's predecessor as high priest was his father, Onias II, who so infuriated the Ptolemaic king who then ruled Palestine that the king seriously considered displacing the Jews altogether and resettling the land with Greek military colonists. In the 190s, Simon himself led his people through a vicious civil war as well as a major clash between the Ptolemaic Empire and its deadly rival, the Seleucid realm. He had two sons, both of whom held the high priesthood but whose careers ended in disaster. One son, another Onias, was deposed and subsequently murdered as a result of plots and conspiracies among Seleucid officials. Simon's other son, Jason, was an extreme Hellenizer whose accommodation with pagan and Greek practices threatened to subvert Judaism altogether. Jason's actions provoked the nationalist revolution led by the Maccabees in the 160s, and he died in exile. (Simon and Onias will be discussed in Chapters 2 and 5.)

Such turmoil forces us to look again at the literary and religious heritage of Simon's era, a cultural explosion that we would never guess from the bland adulation expressed in Sirach. It was during his tenure, in the late third and early second centuries, that there appeared some momentous texts that differed starkly from the traditions of the Hebrew Bible, such writings as 1 Enoch and the book of the Giants and possibly the book of Noah. The greatest of these was 1 Enoch, a sprawling collection of visions and meditations attributed to Noah's great-grandfather. Seemingly without warning or precedent, Enoch's visions suddenly plunge us into a phantas-magoric universe of angels and demons, judgment and apocalypse, Heaven and Hell. These wildly innovative works were the first to present those ideas in any detailed or systematic form in a Jewish context. They were the first to list the names of the great archangels, to imagine hellfire, to map the phases of the apocalypse, to depict evil figures very much like the later Satan in his demonic court. The book of 1 Enoch and its contemporaries also point to a current of Jewish thought deeply suspicious of the Jerusalem Temple and pay-ing scant attention to such fundamental themes as the Covenant and Torah. (For the Enochic writings and their distinctive tendencies, see Chapter 3.)

Simon might have seen such works as poisonous or seditious. The circumstances of their writers remain wholly obscure—not just their identity, but whether they lived in any kind of sect or reli-gious community. By some interpretations, the famous Essene sect commonly associated with the Dead Sea Scrolls emerged during Simon's high priesthood, and that group almost certainly had some connections with the new speculations. But whatever their origins, Enochic ideas persisted for centuries and had a profound impact on both Judaism and later Christianity. Those writings are over and above the more orthodox scriptures of Sirach and the book of Tobit that themselves reflect the fresh currents reshaping Jewish thought. Whether Simon actually knew what was happening under his aus-pices, he was presiding over a critical moment in the religious history of the region and ultimately of the world.

ALL SOCIETIES HAVE their conflicts and unrest, and especially in the ancient world, these struggles often became violent. What was unusual in the Jewish context was the extreme frequency and sever-ity of violence as well as the wearyingly persistent record of coups, riots, and massacres. To adapt the wry saying of the English writer Saki, the Jewish world in this era produced far more history than it could consume locally.[9]

The revolution of the 160s culminated in the establishment of rule by the Maccabean family, which history recalls as the Hasmonean dynasty and which endured until the establishment of Roman power in 63 BCE. Although the Hasmonean regime won major external victories, it was also marked by frequent civil wars and factional feuds. Making conflicts still more emotive, the family also held the high priesthood. Thus, the Hasmoneans were religious authorities as well as secular, and all protests against the regime therefore occurred in a sacred context. It was in protest against the Hasmonean priest-kings that the famous Qumran sect that produced the Dead Sea Scrolls abandoned the world, awaiting the imminent day of God's Wrath.[10]

For centuries, Jerusalem was the setting for recurrent acts of conquest and civil war, as the Temple itself regularly witnessed political bloodletting. The historian Josephus reports one such incident of savage repression in the Temple precincts themselves, around 90 BCE. The king was Yannai (Jonathan), who had also taken the auspicious Greek name Alexander and is known to history as Alexander Jannaeus. As high priest, the king was celebrating the feast of Sukkot or Tabernacles. Protesters insulted the king and pelted him with the palm branches and citron fruits that they carried as part of the festival. Jannaeus responded by calling in his (Gentile) soldiers, who reputedly killed six thousand within the Temple precincts. The exact numbers are uncertain, but this was appalling bloodshed in the holiest of places.[11]

As scholars and thinkers tried to make sense of such convulsions, they developed the literature of apocalyptic. In their revelations, divine messengers used symbolic imagery to show how worldly events fitted into God's plan, offering hope in desperate times. That apocalyptic genre encouraged a terrifying new eschatology, with the End Times understood in terms of cosmic warfare. From the second century onward, internecine battles repeatedly led sects to identify their heroes and leaders as messianic figures, while enemies were portrayed as servants of Belial or Satan. We can trace the kings who became the models for early concepts of Antichrist and the Beast, the priests and monarchs who supplied the blueprints for future messiahs, and the crises and catastrophes that inspired hopes of millennial kingdoms. In an era when so many thousands were being slaughtered in struggles against tyranny, new theologies sought to explain and justify the death of the righteous. Ideas of martyrdom became widespread, alongside audacious new concepts of the afterlife and the Last Judgment.

The sense of pervasive crisis did not end with the fall of the Hasmonean dynasty. In the century following 50 BCE, contemporaries found it difficult not to interpret the pagan Roman occupation and the Herodian tyranny in terms of supernatural evil and imminent apocalypse. Even before the start of the Common Era, what were once revolutionary religious ideas and expectations became commonplace, moving from the world of elite thinkers and priests to become the vernacular of ordinary people. Ideas of cosmic warfare and apocalyptic drove believers to militant and revolutionary action. They inspired radical sects and would-be messiahs and ultimately in the 60s CE provoked full-scale insurrection against the Roman Empire. This Jewish revolt resulted in national cataclysm and the fall of the Second Temple in 70.

The construction of the new Other world was anything but an otherworldly process.

SCARCELY LESS INNOVATIVE than the new insights about the worlds beyond were the means by which humanity learned such truths, namely, through the sacred texts and scriptures that presented divine revelations. Even if living teachers and charismatic prophets still mattered enormously in the Crucible years, religious belief was chiefly conveyed through scriptures, some of which enjoyed special status. Obviously, texts had played a sanctified role in previous centuries, but much closer attention was now paid to specifying and controlling the limits of approved scripture. Creating the concept of the Bible had a profound impact on the character of religious authority and the people or institutions qualified to exercise it.[12]

The new role of texts and scriptures also meant that religious debate and speculation would proceed through writings modeled on canonized Bible books. Although Christians call this period intertestamental—that is, lying between Old and New Testaments—it has left extensive records in the form of many texts presented in scriptural format, but nevertheless excluded from the scriptural canons of either Jews or (most) Christians. It was not that writers after 250 BCE ceased producing spiritual treatises. Rather, at least some religious groups made the gradual (and arbitrary) decisions to exclude these writings from the new category of scripture. Some of these texts are celebrated today because of their spectacular discovery among the Dead Sea Scrolls, but many others also exist. (See Table 1.) The sheer volume of such writings in the second century BCE alone is impressive.

TABLE I.I   MAJOR TEXTS AND SCRIPTURES
_____

This table gives the dates and canonical status of selected ancient texts referred to in the present book. The dating attributed to particular works is often controversial, and equally credentialed experts might offer a wide range of likely time periods. That is especially true when a book is composite in nature, with different sections being composed many years apart from each other. Where such disagreements exist, I have tried to give the best consensus date. Dates that are particularly controversial are marked with a question mark, but similar punctuation could in fact be attached to a great many more of the statements and attributions here. The canonical status of a text is reflected as follows:

C   canonical in Jewish biblical tradition and in the modern Protestant Old Testament

DC   Deuterocanonical: fully canonical in the Old Testaments of Catholic and Orthodox Christian churches, but apocryphal in Protestant versions

OTP   Old Testament pseudepigrapha and apocrypha, not canonical in Jewish or most Christian traditions (although the highly distinctive Ethiopian church sometimes provides exceptions)

Q   Dead Sea Scroll material found at Qumran

Text	Likely date of composition	Canonical status
Zechariah	Early portions are late sixth century BCE, but "Deutero-Zechariah" is later, possibly late third century or early second century BCE	C
Malachi	Mid- to late fifth century BCE	C
Job	Fifth to fourth century BCE?	C
Ruth	Fifth to fourth century BCE?	C
Jonah	Fifth to fourth century BCE?	C
Ezra/Nehemiah	Ca. 420–320 BCE?	C
Books of Chronicles	Fourth century BCE	C
Proverbs	Fourth to third century BCE?	C
Ecclesiastes	Third century BCE	C
Aramaic Levi Document	Third century BCE	Q
Treatise of the Two Spirits	Third century BCE	Q
Noah	Third century BCE; original text lost, but fragments survive in other works	OTP
Esther	Third to second century BCE	C
1 Enoch	Different sections range from mid-third century BCE through first century BCE	OTP
Tobit	Late third century to early second century BCE	DC
Book of the Giants	Early second century BCE	OTP
Sirach/Ecclesiasticus	Early second century BCE	DC
Baruch	Mid-second century BCE	DC
Jubilees	Mid-second century BCE	OTP
Judith	Second century BCE	DC
Daniel	First chapters are early second century BCE?; chapters 7–12 are from the 160s BCE	C
Daniel (additions)	Bel and the Dragon is probably second century BCE	DC
Sibylline Oracles	Ca. 200 BCE–600 CE, but the earliest oracles are second century BCE	OTP

TABLE I.I   MAJOR TEXTS AND SCRIPTURES *(continued)*

Text	Likely date of composition	Canonical status
Letter of Aristeas	Second century BCE	OTP
Testaments of the Twelve Patriarchs	Composed and edited over a lengthy period, but the earliest materials are second century BCE	OTP
Thanksgiving Hymns	Mid-second century BCE	Q
Damascus Document	Mid-second century BCE	Q
Community Rule (1QS)	Mid-second century BCE	Q
1 Maccabees	Late second century BCE	DC
2 Maccabees	Mid- to late second century	DC
The War of the Sons of Light Against the Sons of Darkness (War Rule)	Second to first century BCE	Q
4QInstruction	Second to first century BCE?	Q
Pesher Habakkuk	Second to first century BCE?	Q
Testament of Amram	Second to first century BCE?	Q
3 Maccabees	First century BCE?	OTP
The War of the Messiah (Qumran)	First century BCE	Q
Testament of Job	First century BCE	OTP
Psalms of Solomon	Mid-first century BCE	OTP
Wisdom of Solomon	50 BCE–50 CE	DC
Assumption of Moses/ Testament of Moses	First century BCE	OTP
Testament of Abraham	First century CE	OTP
Life of Adam and Eve	First century CE	OTP
Joseph and Aseneth	First century CE	OTP
Lives of the Prophets	First century CE	OTP
2 Enoch	First century CE	OTP

Political events and culture wars called forth literary responses, often framed in terms of visions credited to ancient prophets and sages. Enoch, Ezra, Baruch, and Isaiah were all reliable names to whom works could be credited. Contemporary writers also greatly expanded the already available biblical accounts of patriarchs like Adam, Seth, and Melchizedek. These texts are sometimes called pseudepigrapha, that is, falsely titled works, as opposed to being "false" in their nature or deficient in quality.[13]

Such works were very influential. Any attempt to understand the range of ideas available to Jews of the first century CE, and to the circle of Jesus himself, means reading not just such Deuterocanonical works as Sirach and Tobit, but also pseudepigrapha like 1 Enoch, the Psalms of Solomon, and the Testaments of the Twelve Patriarchs. In terms of their subject matter, these works cover a huge spectrum. Some writings are political manifestos, others contain polemical material on the vices of a particular king or dynasty or high priest, while still others have no discernible relationship to current events. Taken together, they constitute a substantial written universe, demonstrating the enormous range of ideas in contemporary discourse.[14]

MANY OF THE motifs in these pseudepigraphic writings are familiar to us through the Abrahamic religions, while others now seem eccentric, even shocking. Certainly, such "marginal" or "sectarian" ideas do not fit in the established orthodoxies of any mainstream faith today. But the fact that they seem so strange and exotic is significant for what it suggests about how and why some of those Crucible-era themes triumphed, while others faded into obscurity.[15]

Judaism as we know it historically is the complex of religious beliefs and practices that were formulated and proclaimed by rabbinic scholars in the early centuries of the Common Era and developed over a long period in the Talmud. Those scholars were working after the great revolt and the loss of the Temple in 70 CE. As such, they were profoundly suspicious of apocalyptic, messianic, or millenarian ideas of the kind associated with political militancy. In consequence, many once popular texts and themes vanished from the Jewish heritage. A period of intense cultural rethinking fundamentally redefined the limits of acceptable religious faith, closing many of the intellectual avenues that had been so avidly explored during the Crucible years.

Any history of the Jewish world in the Crucible era itself must avoid hindsight in using such terms as "mainstream" and "marginal," "normative" and "sectarian," "orthodox" and "heretical." Only retroactively were some "sectarian" movements and motifs consigned to the fringes of that broad cultural universe. That comment applies to many of the themes of the Dead Sea Scrolls. Early Christianity itself was an authentic heir of the speculations and obsessions of the Crucible years. And through both rabbinic Judaism and Christianity, such ideas shaped the nascent faith of Islam. All three were heirs of the same religious revolution and shared very similar beliefs about the spiritual universe. So also, indeed, was the now extinct dualist faith of Manichaeanism.

Even some of the ideas from the Crucible era that strike our modern eye as bizarre and extravagant proved remarkably durable. Still today, with some awe, historians are continuing to discover just how widely these concepts cast their influence. That process of historical development has affected our understanding of the relationship of emerging Christianity to its Jewish environment. Earlier generations of scholars sought to distinguish between "Jewish" and "Gentile" themes in early Christianity, arguing (for instance) that the gospel of Matthew was distinctly Jewish, whereas John's gospel supposedly betrayed its Greek and Gentile biases. In fact, any such attempt to separate Jewish and Gentile elements is necessarily doomed. By the first century CE, ideas that originated in Hellenistic sources had already been long integrated into Jewish thought. Any sense of the religion in that era must take into account the spectrum of ideas and influences in a Judaism that displayed such polyphonic diversity. Actually, the range of influences was even broader than this would suggest, as both the Jews and the Greeks of this era had through the centuries borrowed so heavily from still other traditions, especially from Mesopotamia. That pattern especially applies to the Enochian literature that displays so many signs of its Mesopotamian character and origin. So what exactly was "Jewish" in the time of Jesus and Paul, and what was "Greek"?

THE CRUCIBLE ERA was incredibly fertile both in generating new spiritual concepts and in naming them. The rise of new spiritual and political worlds created an urgent need for new words, many of which remain at the core of the Western religious vocabulary. Even offering a brief list of such words in English gives a sense of how much we owe to this era, and some European languages include even more examples.

These centuries needed a term for the new and pervasive concept of "apocalypse" and also popularized the concept of "Armageddon." Even when older Hebrew terms were translated more or less laterally into Greek, they could not fail to acquire many new trappings from Hellenistic thought and philosophy. Those additional meanings have been passed on to us today. Although the Jewish world had its notion of subdivine spiritual beings, it borrowed from Greek the terminology of "angels" and "demons," with their elaborate hierarchies that included "archangels." And although the concept of the Lord's Anointed, the "messiah," dated back at least to the sixth century BCE, its meaning was transformed into the later End Times image of the *moshiach*, or *Christos*—the Christ. That in turn generated other names for new things, such as for "Christians" and for the "Antichrist." Both Christ and Antichrist would play their roles at the final "crisis," the Greek word co-opted to portray the final Judgment. So would "Satan," an old Hebrew word for "adversary." The title in these years, however, applied to a specific and vastly threatening spiritual entity.

We observe the invention of the Bible itself and the idea of Scripture. It was the Crucible age that specified that certain texts should be defined as the definitive holy scriptures of the Jewish people. Moreover, these books (and no others) constituted "the Books" (Greek: *ta Biblia*). Only in this same era do we find a specialized word for those writings that made up scripture or the scriptures (*he graphe*, singular, or *tes graphes*, plural). Several books of the Bible composed long before the Crucible era bear Greek names that reflect their translation during these years, commonly the third and second centuries BCE. We think of works like Genesis, Exodus, and Deuteronomy. The list of approved texts was the "canon," whereas other works were "hidden," or "apocryphal." Those Greek Bible translations gave us many religious terms, including "blasphemy," "diaspora," "idol," "paradise," "holocaust," and "proselyte." The Septuagint Greek word *diabolos* gave us "devil."

Although the Hebrew Bible includes the word "Yehudi," it is only in our period, in the book of Esther (written during the third or second century BCE), that it comes to mean "Jew" in the historic ethnoreligious sense. A few decades later, the second book of Maccabees invented the word "Judaism" (with "Hellenism" thrown in for good measure to define its rival). Some words, like "rabbi" and "synagogue," were invented to describe the new institutions of a developing faith. Some partisan or sectarian labels, such as "Zealots" and "Pharisees," also entered general usage.

In other cases, words in general parlance came to be applied to particular religious concepts and innovations. This happened within Judaism at first, but it was soon adopted by Christianity. Examples included "apostle" (messenger), "baptism," "disciple," and "martyr" (witness). Jewish sects had their "episkopoi" before Christians did, and long before English speakers corrupted that title into "bishops." The Greek term for "good news" was "evangelion," which in turn gave rise to "evangelist" and "evangelical." Translating that "good news" title into Old English gave us the word "gospel." Jewish sectarians called the Therapeutae had a "monasterion," a room for contemplation, which developed into the later concept of the "monastery."[16] We can scarcely imagine a time when religion lacked such foundational terms.

THE CRUCIBLE YEARS spanned a period of two centuries, from the mid-third century BCE through the mid-first. Of course, long-term cultural developments rarely coincided neatly with decades or centuries, and trends and ideas overlapped substantially.

Chapter 1 gives the essential background of the Jewish world from the monotheistic developments of the seventh and sixth centuries BCE to the Greek encounter of the late fourth century.

Chapters 2 and 3 describe how Greek, Jewish, and Eastern worlds interacted and began the process of cross-fertilization, with a clear cultural watershed around 250 BCE. Chapter 4 is devoted to the great surviving legacy of this encounter: the book of 1 Enoch.

The most intense and transformative period began with the Maccabean revolt. Chapters 5–9 address the critical revolutionary years between roughly 170 and 50 BCE and the maelstrom of bold ideas and worldviews that emerged in this time.

Chapters 10 and 11 show how these new insights and attitudes acquired mainstream status. They also gave rise to religious structures, including Christianity, rabbinic Judaism, and Islam, as well as other movements that had a major impact in their time, such as Manichaeanism.

THOSE TWO CRITICAL centuries made the religious world the West has known ever since. Without this spiritual revolution, neither Christianity nor Islam would exist, and Judaism itself would have been unimaginably different. Just how thoroughgoing was the change in religious sensibility can only be understood if we look at the Hebrew Bible, which later faiths so often claimed to be following scrupulously.

Chapter 1

THE OLD WORLD

Living with Radical Monotheism

———————

Understand that I am He: before me there was no God formed, neither shall there be after me. I, even I, am the LORD; and beside me there is no savior.

ISAIAH 43:10–11, KJV

THE OLD TESTAMENT offers many unequivocal proclamations of monotheism. According to the book of Deuteronomy, Moses himself recites the wonderful deeds of the Lord, YHWH, who alone is God: "There is none else beside him" (4:35). Yet however uncontroversial such words may sound today, they stand in marked contrast to other biblical verses that situate YHWH in the company of other deities. Psalm 82 depicts God taking his place among the council of gods, ready to pronounce judgment. Other verses likewise have God speaking in the plural ("Let us make man in our own image" [Gen. 1:26]). Even in Deuteronomy, one passage shows YHWH being allocated Israel as his own people, the implication being that other deities had their own nations (32:8–9).

With varying degrees of success, scholars through the centuries have struggled to reconcile such texts with a monotheistic view. The most likely interpretation is that in early times, YHWH was seen as one deity among several, and only gradually did his followers claim his unique and exclusive divinity. God was many before he was One. Over time texts were edited to eliminate embarrassing contradictions, but many older passages and hymns were simply too well established and too cherished simply to be discarded.[1]

But monotheism had implications that went far beyond the editing of texts. The shift from multiple gods to one absolute deity transformed attitudes toward belief and practice, which provide the essential foundation for developments in the ensuing Crucible era.[2]

JEWS AND CHRISTIANS alike believe their doctrines derive from "the Bible," however they define the limits of that term. Through the centuries, Christians and Jews alike have ransacked the Old Testament for passages and texts to justify their beliefs. They claim, for instance, that some particular verse describes the origins of human sinfulness, or defines Satan, or foreshadows the Messiah. Christians have regularly read Christ back into the Old Testament, sometimes by means of optimistic mistranslation. In practice, such exegesis demands a great deal of special pleading, of varying degrees of plausibility, and many such conclusions would have baffled Hebrew writers of the First Temple era (ca. 950–587 BCE).

However much later believers claim continuity from the sacred text, the differences of belief and practice are at least as marked as the similarities. Mainstream religious life in biblical times was very different from most later concepts of Judaism. Some themes were constant, including dietary laws and the practice of circumcision, but the older religion was grounded in sacrifice and firmly rooted in the land.

No less striking are what seem to us to be puzzling omissions from biblical-era religion. The biblical view of the divine world was, by later standards, quite limited, and the heavens were relatively depopulated. Angels do feature in the Old Testament as divine envoys and as mighty figures in the celestial court, but most references are plain and even curt. Angels played no discernible role in the divine plan, they had no individual identity, nor were they given specific functions, such as guardianship over regions or natural phenomena. Satan, likewise, enjoyed no independent existence, nothing like his later role as a rebellious leader of evil forces. We can readily supply a list of negatives for other concepts that in retrospect appear central to the Judeo-Christian tradition, including Heaven, Hell, the afterlife, and the final Judgment, to say nothing of the Messiah or resurrection.[3]

Even in the fifth century BCE, when the Hebrew Bible was theoretically closed, few of those ideas were present in Jewish thought— but they assuredly were by the mid-first century, and they utterly dominate the world of the New Testament. What had happened in the meantime—the crucial difference that permitted those plots and characters to enter fully into the action—was a tectonic theological shift that has left its indelible mark on the scriptures.

THE BIBLE TELLS a story. In fact, it tells an abundance of stories, often in multiple versions that clash with each other. I will present the familiar account found in the Bible as we know it before offering some alternative interpretations.

The biblical story begins with the origin of humanity and the making of civilization. Through successive generations, YHWH made covenants with different people and, through them, their descendants. With Noah, after the Flood, he made a covenant applicable to all humanity. With Abraham, he made the pact from which the Hebrew people emerge, ordaining the law of circumcision. In Moses's time, around 1200 BCE, the Sinai Covenant established the strict monotheistic law to which the Hebrew people would thereafter be subject, as the foundation of faith and practice.[4]

Much of the biblical text describes the kingdoms that emerged in the land of Canaan after the Hebrews invaded and occupied it in the twelfth century, and the principle of monotheism is central to that narrative. Hebrew kingdoms rose and fell between roughly 1000 and 587, beginning with the mighty sovereigns David and Solomon and the foundation of the First Temple. Again according to the received history, those regimes varied in their faithfulness to divine ordinance. Some obeyed the one God and followed his Law, while others permitted and even welcomed foreign deities, polluting the sacred land with polytheism and improper sacrifices. From the ninth century BCE, prophets regularly arose to denounce the abuses of their time. To use a common prophetic metaphor, Israel was pledged to God as a faithful spouse, but time and again it betrayed monogamy by whoring after foreign gods. Persistent infidelity had real-world consequences, as God punished the erring with invasion and disaster. From the end of the eighth century, a sweeping revival urged a return to stark monotheism and the laws of the Mosaic covenant. Even so, that proved inadequate to stay God's wrath, and the Babylonians conquered Jerusalem in 587, taking the people into exile.[5]

However familiar the story may be, it must be approached in terms of how and why it was constructed and written. Although some isolated biblical sources may date to the eleventh and twelfth centuries, much of the narrative was composed between the eighth and fifth centuries, and some material is later than that. The writers at that time were not only recording history but using it as an ideological weapon in ongoing struggles in which they were passionately engaged. They were activists at least as much as recorders of sober fact, and it is futile to expect objectivity.

Many of the biblical writers lived during the seventh-century religious revival that so earnestly preached monotheism and the Mosaic covenant, and they back-projected those values into history—arguably into periods in which such values and institutions had scarcely existed. To take an example, one of the best-known biblical stories is that of the Covenant at Sinai, with Moses's encounter with God, and the giving of the Ten Commandments. How can we imagine the biblical story without such a linchpin? But an ancient creedal statement preserved in Deuteronomy (26:5–10) tells how God rescued the Hebrew people from Egypt and brought them into the land of Canaan, without once mentioning the Sinai story. In itself that absence does not mean that the story was not known or believed in that early era, but it does imply that over time the account of the Sinai Covenant became much more significant than it had once been.[6]

An alternative view of the nation's religious history would suggest that originally, it was much more akin to that of its neighbors, including the Canaanites, and Israel had emerged from that people. Instead of monotheism—belief in one God alone—we should speak rather of henotheism, the belief in a God who is supreme but by no means alone among deities, or of monolatry, the conscious decision to worship one particular God among many. The God of the Hebrews was YHWH, just as their Moabite neighbors followed Chemosh, and both deities were equally valid in their respective homelands. Even in the Ten Commandments, God does not declare that he is the sole Lord, but rather demands, "You shall have no other gods before me." Only a God concerned about potential rivals would be portrayed as "jealous." A common biblical word for God is *elohim*, used in the singular, but it originally referred to plural beings.[7]

The Hebrew God had once been one deity among several who was worshipped together with his goddess consorts. Only from the end of the eighth century did militant reformers develop the now familiar idea of implacable monotheism, a rigid creed to be demanded of all true members of Israel. Those reformers earned the support of various kings, whom the Bible remembers as noble heroes, leaders like Hezekiah (ca. 720–686) and Josiah (ca. 640–610).[8] A key moment in the great reform occurred about 620, when priests claimed to have found in the Temple an ancient book of the Law (2 Kings 22–23). When the king, Josiah, read it, he was appalled to see the differences that existed between this divine blueprint and the actual society of his own day, and he launched a sweeping (and bloody) reform. Supported by his clerical allies, he sacked and desecrated pagan temples and shrines, slaughtering their priests. Such activities focused on the veneration of ancestors, leading to the disruption of tombs and shrines. Josiah struck especially at the images of the Asherah, the goddess.[9]

THE TEXT THAT inspired Josiah's actions was all but certainly what is today called Deuteronomy. Rather than being an authentic ancient rediscovery, this text was actually written not long before Josiah's time. Scholars today link the work with a group or movement pledged to a stern reformist agenda, and this school of thought was political in nature, as well as literary and historical. That Deuteronomistic movement is credited with much of the historical writing presently found in the Bible, as well as the work of prophets like Jeremiah.[10]

Throughout the ensuing struggles, the revolutionaries asserted that they were introducing no innovations; rather, they were restoring things to the way they should have been, and they produced scriptures to prove it. In the century after 650 BCE, priests and scribes engaged in a massive revision of the Jewish religion, writing and reediting many scriptures that today constitute the core of the Hebrew Bible. Among other changes, tales of Moses and the Exodus were rewritten to become far more central to the religious narrative.[11]

Later generations read the earlier history of Israel through the histories created by those revolutionaries. That retroactive attitude extended to lived Hebrew religion, which had once covered a much wider range of beliefs and practices than the existing biblical text might reveal. When reformers denounced the pagan shrines and sacred groves, they were in fact attacking ancient manifestations of their own religion of the land and people. As history was rewritten, those aspects of ordinary everyday religion had to be reinterpreted as syncretistic borrowings from foreign paganism. During the Babylonian captivity, scholars and prophets sustained the religious project begun in the previous century and gained an intellectual hegemony over the nation's religious life. The sixth century was the era of such celebrated prophets as Jeremiah, Ezekiel, and Second Isaiah. That process continued unchecked when, in the 530s, the new Persian Empire of Cyrus permitted the Jewish people to return to Palestine, where a Second Temple arose. The land remained under Persian rule for a full two centuries, until the 330s. The books of Ezra and Nehemiah tell us about the attempts to restore "normality" in the new Persian order. The holy people were back in their land, their religious life was concentrated in the Second Temple, and strict monotheism was the order of the day.[12]

THE NEW MONOTHEISM of the Second Temple era—and it was new—demanded a frontal attack on older religious traditions, which in turn sparked a wide-ranging cultural transformation. I will focus here on five critical aspects of the change, namely, the growth of intermediary spiritual beings, the decline of classical prophecy, the quest to explain the origins of evil, a growing belief in an afterlife, and the rise of belief in a Last Judgment. In rudimentary form, those changes were already emerging in a series of innovative biblical texts written after the return from Exile in Babylon. These late-written ("post-Exilic") books included Zechariah, Joel, and Job.[13]

Monotheism profoundly affected patterns of worship. Not only should one god alone be worshipped, but there were strict limitations to how he could be imagined and portrayed. True worship could not involve visual or material depictions of the deity; it must be imageless, "aniconic." God could not even, properly, be named. Although the dating of the change is uncertain, at some point in this era it became strictly prohibited so much as to pronounce the once commonly used four-lettered name of God, YHWH. The book of Ruth (3:13) implies that the term was still spoken at the time that text was written, in the fifth or fourth century, but by the second century Jews were increasingly using euphemisms like "Heaven." Early in the Common Era, rabbinic scholars declared an absolute prohibition on uttering so sacred a name, except by the high priest himself. In later centuries, pious Jews have commonly referred to God only as "the Name," *haShem*. Even God's name became inaccessible and perilous.[14]

But exalting one deity in such an unprecedented way posed multiple intellectual difficulties for believers. If God was in fact so transcendent, how could he interact with his Creation? In most ancient societies, the idea of such interactions is commonplace. Pagan deities converse directly with humans, and they issue commands. Gods intervene directly in human affairs; they fight on battlefields, often against rival deities; and they speak through chosen seers or prophets. But is such mundane behavior feasible for the Lord of the whole universe? Only in eliminating the multiplicity of gods do we realize how useful a pantheon can be in explaining many otherwise mysterious aspects of reality.

Theophanies, divine appearances, had once been common in the Hebrew tradition, but in the new environment they had to be treated very cautiously and selectively. Just how sensitive the matter might be is apparent from a story in chapter 13 of the book of Judges, in which Manoah and his wife are told of the greatness of their unborn son, who would become the legendary hero Samson. As the surviving story tells us, the message is carried by an angel, who ascends to Heaven when the couple carry out a sacrifice. At that point, and for no reason apparent to modern readers, Manoah suddenly realizes that he has actually been talking directly with God and fears immediate death. The inconsistencies arise from merging different versions of an ancient story. In an original version, God himself presumably visited the couple, but any hint of such a personal and intimate divine encounter was unacceptable in Deuteronomistic times, when the story was revised and edited. In this instance, as in many others, God's presence has been camouflaged by substituting an angelic figure.[15]

The Second Temple period, then, was marked by an ever-growing emphasis on intermediary figures who serve God and transmit his commands. Yet they did not partake directly of his nature, because any such sharing of divinity would violate his absolute quality. Angels increasingly formed a complex heavenly hierarchy and came to serve many of the functions that would earlier have been served by God personally. (I will discuss this trend more in Chapter 8.)[16] If there was one God, then of necessity he must have a great many messengers.

How, THEN, COULD a mere mortal dare claim to have spoken with or for God? In early tradition, humans often conversed with God. Moses did so, and the prophets boldly prefaced their remarks by saying, "Thus says the Lord," or confidently announcing, "The Word of God." Over time, though, claims of direct contact with deity became troubling.

Prophecy had to change over time. During the great age of Hebrew prophecy, between the ninth and sixth centuries, God inspired the prophet to speak on his behalf, in order to guide and correct his people. His goal was not so much to foretell the future, but rather to highlight failings of the nation and community and to urge the people to return to the ways of righteousness in a public act or declaration. Prophetic books were associated with named individuals, whether any particular person authored part or whole of the work attributed to him or not.[17]

In this classic format, prophecy became much scarcer after the fifth century BCE. One critical source on these matters is the historian Josephus, and as I will often have cause to cite his works, it will be useful here to describe the man and his background. Josephus (37–100 CE) was an insurgent commander in the Jewish revolt of the 60s, but a timely defection allowed him to survive the catastrophe. He then reconstructed himself on Roman lines as Flavius Josephus. He published his account of *The Jewish War* around 75, and by 94 he published *Jewish Antiquities (Ioudaike Archaiologia)*. That work reported and summarized biblical history, presenting it in the most favorable and benevolent manner for a cultured Greco-Roman audience. He devoted careful attention to the Hebrew scriptures and to claims for their authority. On the issue of prophecy, he dated the end of the legitimate sequence of prophets to the fifth century, specifically around the time of the Persian king Artaxerxes (465–424). That did not mark the end of prophecy as such, but rather concluded the social consensus surrounding the legitimate claimants.[18]

Later writers accepted that true prophecy had become rare and even consigned it to the distant past. The book of 1 Maccabees reports Jewish leaders in the 160s tabling decisions on some issues until a true prophet should appear, with the suggestion that such a development was not expected anytime soon. The same book records that "there was great distress in Israel, such as had not been since the time that prophets ceased to appear among them" (9:27). Later rabbis remained firm on this question of termination, largely in reaction to early Christian claims that the prophetic tradition continued in that community.

In fact, prophecy of the old kind can be traced throughout the Second Temple period and beyond, but it changed in both substance and format. As I will show, prophecy merged into the strikingly different mode of apocalyptic, that is, End Times visions that gave cosmic significance to earthly struggles. (The word "apocalyptic" comes from the Greek for "revelation," as in the New Testament book of that name.) Of course, the Old Testament contains a lot of prophetic passages that look somewhat like the apocalyptic literature we know, but those later apocalyptic works differed in certain key ways from this classic model. In the new world, writers reported insights received not from God directly but from intermediary figures, either angels or else patriarchs of former times. The newer form is also distinguished by the question of authorship. While prophets like Amos or Isaiah spoke through their own names, apocalyptic works are anonymous or pseudepigraphic, that is, attributed to some mighty sage of bygone centuries, such as Enoch or Daniel.[19]

Nor do apocalyptic writers address the whole community in the mode of the old prophets. The newer literature was fundamentally a revelation of a secret, in declarations passed through an inspired seer. Instead of being ringing public declarations, these texts are cryptic, ambiguous, and of necessity open to debate and interpretation. The fact that something was "revealed" of itself implies concealment, further suggesting that the world's great truths are hidden from the masses. This is bookish, esoteric literature, and it is designed to be read, not proclaimed.[20]

The transition from classical prophecy did not occur at any one historical moment, but one text in particular signals the change in progress, namely, Zechariah. This book is generally divided into two sections, which were written by separate individuals at some distance in time; just how far they were separated is a matter of lively debate. Respectively, they are known as First Zechariah, which was written at the end of the sixth century BCE, and Second or Deutero-Zechariah, which is probably three centuries younger.

In its way, each section of Zechariah marked a critical religious transition. First Zechariah (c.520 BCE) offers a curious mixture of old and new styles, with some portions looking back to the earlier prophets, while others foreshadow later genres. Angelic themes predominate, and the twenty references to "angels" in this one short book constitute almost a fifth of all such citations in the whole canonical Old Testament. The text begins conventionally enough for prophetic works, as the Word of the Lord tells Zechariah of his displeasure with Jerusalem. Soon, though, Zechariah is receiving his messages from an angel, together with the first recorded examples of the conversations characteristic of the later apocalyptic genre. Typically, the angel asks whether the prophet recognizes the meaning of some sign, the prophet declares his ignorance ("No, my lord!"), and the angel then explains (6:12–14). For the reader, the lesson is to underscore the lack of direct inspiration claimed by the prophet. Adding to later resonances, Zechariah sees a vision of the angel of the Lord together with Satan, that centerpiece of much later religious writing. In its highly allusive and symbolic content, First Zechariah looks forward to countless successors, from Daniel through the book of Revelation and beyond. There are four horsemen as well as flying scrolls and four mysterious horns that symbolize nations or rulers. As read by later generations, one passage about the coming of a future "Branch" points to messianic ideas (6:12–13).[21]

From the third century BCE onward, apocalyptic became a hugely popular genre of religious literature, which had a very long afterlife.

In terms of the nature of religious authority, the shift from prophecy to apocalyptic signified a restriction of popular access to the
divine and a new emphasis on formal channels, whether priestly or
scriptural.

GIVING SUCH AN absolute and solitary role to one God raised
other problems in terms of explaining injustice or evil. If God was
only one deity among many, then evil acts or misdeeds were easily
explained in terms of the malice of powerful rival forces. When his
people were suffering in Egypt, YHWH had to struggle against the
gods of that country who presumably were to blame (Exod. 12:12).
But how was such suffering possible under the rule of an omnipotent
deity, who lacked either colleagues or foes? Why did the righteous
suffer on earth, while the wicked self-evidently prospered? This is
the classic issue of theodicy, of understanding God's justice in the
face of the gross evils in the world he supposedly created. Now, not
all believers saw an impenetrable mystery in these matters. Generations of prophets explained the evils suffered by the Hebrew nation
in terms of the sinfulness of the people. In that vision, outside enemies like the Babylonians became divine scourges, whips used to
beat and punish stubborn sinners. Fathers whipped their disobedi-
ent sons, and God chastised his rebellious people. But that was not
the only conceivable solution, nor was it the most attractive.[22]

Yes, God was all-good and all-powerful, but the same could not
be said of those subdivine intermediary figures who now proliferated. Belief in angels was quite acceptable, so was it legitimate to
blame some of them for worldly evil and the existence of human
sinfulness? No later than the mid-third century, speculations about
rebel angels were becoming commonplace. Increasingly, too, one
particular intermediary was being identified as an evil overlord, under
various names that included Satan, Mastema, and Belial. If that figure was not (yet) an evil counterpart of God himself, then writers
were well on their way to such a construction. Such speculations

were already beginning to appear in the book of Job, which probably dates from the fifth or fourth centuries BCE. (We will return to
that work shortly.)[23] In the centuries following the "closing of the
Bible," then, not only was there an upsurge in the number of angels
and other intermediary figures, but those figures spanned a whole
spectrum of morality and malice.

ANOTHER APPROACH TO divine justice was to relocate to another life
the vindication of the righteous and the punishment of the wicked.
That in turn demanded a much stronger belief in the afterlife.

In the canonical Hebrew Bible, concepts of the afterlife are pallid
and indistinct. In the pre-Exilic Jewish world, individuals who died
survived at best as shades who had little distinct identity, and in the
grim words of Psalm 115, "The dead praise not the LORD, neither
any that go down into silence" (17). The Bible refers often to Sheol,
the place of the dead, but this miserable place was not reserved for
notorious sinners or wrongdoers. Regardless of one's virtue or piety,
the ultimate fate of humanity was the grave, with its maggots and
worms. In the third century BCE, the author of Ecclesiastes reflected
the traditional view when he wrote that the same fate ultimately
came to righteous and evil alike, to the pious and blasphemous. All
go down to the dead, to Sheol, where "the dead know not any thing,
neither have they any more a reward; for the memory of them is
forgotten. Also their love, and their hatred, and their envy, is now
perished; neither have they any more a portion for ever in any thing
that is done under the sun. . . . [T]here is no work, nor device, nor
knowledge, nor wisdom, in the grave, whither thou goest." Hence,
"to him that is joined to all the living there is hope: for a living dog is
better than a dead lion" (9:5–10). The fact that the book was notionally credited to King Solomon helped ensure that such a materialist
manifesto remained within the biblical canon.[24]

Escape from Sheol was not a realistic possibility. The book of
1 Samuel (28:3–25) tells how King Saul used a medium or witch to

summon the spirit of the deceased prophet Samuel, but even such a glorious figure had not been granted anything like heavenly rest or bliss. He was a pathetic shade. Given such dreary prospects, biblical authors could never use the afterlife as the solution to the dilemma of why many good people died miserably, while the evil enjoyed their splendor and comfort until their last moment. Some passages portray Sheol as an entity or even a deity, but these statements are metaphorical rather than theological. As a state of nonexistence, Sheol is not an enemy whom God will someday defeat or subdue.

Only a few statements in the Hebrew Bible itself point to any more optimistic outcomes, and they were isolated outliers or literary metaphors rather than statements of doctrine. Although they are difficult to date, two psalms (49:15 and 73:24) both imply that good and evil had different destinies after death, so that the righteous went to God, while the evil descended to Sheol. The psalmist could even hope that "God will redeem my soul from the power of the grave; for he shall receive me." A few texts hint at resurrection, albeit communal rather than individual, but again these are outliers. The prophet Ezekiel reported the baffling vision of the valley of bones and skeletons, who would one day be raised from their graves and returned to the house of Israel (37:1–14). A Christian reads this in terms of the resurrection at the Day of Judgment, but in context the passage refers to a national restoration and revival without any suggestion of individual postmortem continuity. Such passages raise an issue that we will encounter repeatedly, namely, that Hebrew thinkers sometimes used the image of a person or a man to represent a whole community or nation, commonly Israel itself. It is tempting, but misleading, to understand such accounts as if they refer to individuals rather than communities.[25]

The older view of the afterlife changed utterly in the centuries following the Bible's supposed "closure" during the Second Temple era. Sheol is a major theme of the book of Job, which was written during the Persian rule over Palestine, and that Persian connection might have contributed to a new interest in the afterlife. Whatever its origins, Job is by far the most direct and sustained consideration of theodicy in the whole Bible, using a dramatic story to frame weighty questions of moral vindication and divine righteousness. Job begins the work possessed of great riches and happiness. In order to test Job's faith, God allows his servant or minister Satan to destroy Job's family and belongings and to inflict terrible diseases on him. Most of the book comprises Job's attempt to comprehend what has happened to him and to reconcile that with a belief in God's goodness.

Those meditations involve discussions of the afterlife. In an extraordinary passage, Job expresses the hope for survival after death and even for resurrection:

> *If a man die, shall he live again?*
> *All the days of my appointed time will I wait, till my change come.*
> *Thou shalt call, and I will answer thee. (14:13–15, KJV)*

The exact meaning of the text is controversial, but a later passage has Job proclaim:

> *For I know that my redeemer liveth,*
> *and that he shall stand at the latter day upon the earth:*
> *And though after my skin worms destroy this body,*
> *Yet in my flesh shall I see God. (19:25–26, KJV)*

The text can be translated in many ways, and I am deliberately here using the King James version, which unabashedly brings out Christian resonances. But implications of resurrection are clearly present in the text. Christians love these words and have no problem in identifying the redeemer as Christ. "I know that my redeemer liveth" is a beloved hymn, while the second part seems to confirm the idea of resurrection. Unlike in Ezekiel, moreover, this expectation is expressed in the first person, suggesting an individual resurrection.[26]

But if such ideas were not yet official doctrine, at least they were being contemplated as a necessary solution to the quandaries of monotheism. By the third and second centuries BCE, visions of Heaven and Hell became commonplace, with holy figures and sinners consigned to their appropriate eternal destinies. In both cases, heavenly and hellish, angels served as custodians as well as messengers. For most Jews (if not all), the afterlife became a natural expectation, to the point that a text like the book of Wisdom (first century BCE) offers a telling parody of the Ecclesiastes text we noted earlier. As the author of chapter 2 of Wisdom asks: So you believe that we are shadows that just fade away and nobody returns after death? So what is to prevent you from committing every form of sin and exploitation?[27]

In the third century CE, Jewish oral traditions were collected and transcribed in the Mishnah, a text that became a foundation of rabbinic Judaism. When it listed the deadliest errors that could separate a Jew from the world to come, it specifically condemned "one who says that [the belief in] resurrection of the dead is not from the Torah." How could anyone ever have doubted so fundamental a belief?[28]

REWARDS AND PUNISHMENTS could take many forms, but commonly they were associated with a special Day of Judgment, the grand climax of history. As in the case of resurrection and the afterlife, such ideas grew steadily in significance from the fifth century BCE onward.[29]

The theme was not wholly new. Later readers could authentically look back to biblical passages that warned of a Day of the Lord, when God's justice and power would break into human affairs and overwhelm human arrangements and power structures. The image drew on the ancient mythology of YHWH, the warrior king, conquering and defeating his enemies. Such an idea already appeared in the eighth century in the prophecies of Amos and Isaiah. Isaiah warns of a time of imminent battles and catastrophes, the mighty Day of the Lord, when sinners will be destroyed and the heavens will tremble. It is a day of wrath and reckoning, "to make the earth a desolation, and to destroy its sinners from it" (13:9–11).

But the differences with later images are also striking, especially Isaiah's concentration on how divine wrath will strike one particular place, in this instance Babylon. Despite some universal language, it is not obvious that Isaiah is referring to anything like the Day of Judgment as known in later religions. The identity of those being rewarded and punished is also critical, as there is no sense of individuals being sorted and certainly not of the dead being summoned to answer for the misdeeds they committed during their lives. As in most such early accounts, the beneficiary of God's intervention is the nation of Israel as a whole rather than singularly moral or righteous individuals. What had made Amos so subversive in his day was that he actually challenged Israelites to ask themselves if they would survive a day of righteous judgment that might claim sinful Jews alongside wicked Gentiles.[30]

The most compelling biblical vision of judgment is found in the prophet Joel, whose well-developed scenario for the End Times meshes readily with later apocalypses: "And I will shew wonders in the heavens and in the earth, blood, and fire, and pillars of smoke. The sun shall be turned into darkness, and the moon into blood, before the great and terrible day of the LORD come" (2:30–31, KJV) Nations that had maltreated and exploited Israel would be subjected to a formal trial. Even so, salvation would still be available to a remnant of true believers, those who called on God's name. So well did this text harmonize with later views that it formed the basis for the first recorded Christian sermon preached in Jerusalem after Jesus's death and resurrection, on the Day of Pentecost. Joel is very difficult to date, but the most probable setting is the fifth century, after a captivity affected Judah and Jerusalem and "Greeks" were a known part of the Jewish world.

Like Job, Joel stands at a point of transition, reflecting ideas that were stirring and gaining in popularity but as yet held nothing like mainstream status. By the third century, that transformation was complete, and visions of judgment are central to the works of that period attributed to Enoch.

FOR CHRISTIANS, JEWS, and Muslims alike, religious practice assumes individual behavior and individual responsibility. Individual people pray, they commit sins, and they are rewarded and punished accordingly, in this world or the next. That idea seems so obvious that it is difficult to imagine any alternative approach, but such was not always the case. The book of 1 Samuel depicts a woman praying silently in the sanctuary of Shiloh, in a scene set around 1000 BCE. As she was "speaking in her heart," with her lips moving, the priest naturally assumed that she was drunk and rebuked her accordingly (1:13). True worship, he knew, was public, communal, and sacrificial, leaving no room for private or individual devotions.

The reform era of the seventh century BCE witnessed a steady movement toward concepts of the individual in religion and a consequent decline in collective and communal identity. Such notions were novel at a time when guilt and sin were seen as a collective matter for the family and the clan. In older scriptures, God punished whole communities and the descendants of wrongdoers. In later texts, rewards and punishments fell to individuals alone, with no ramifications for their heirs. No, said the prophets, each individual must bear full responsibility for fulfilling God's covenant. In the 580s, Ezekiel mocks the traditional idea that the child will suffer for the sins of his ancestors. Why, asks God, do you quote the proverb "The fathers eat sour grapes, and the children's teeth are set on edge"? "Behold, all souls are mine; as the soul of the father, so also the soul of the son is mine: the soul that sins, it shall die" (18:1–4). That doctrinal change had a material side as well, as people increasingly received individual burial rather than merely being laid in the tombs of clans or tribes, "gathered to his ancestors."[31]

Individual humans confronted a solitary God, who judged their individual sins. Such an unprecedented concept subverted all older religious notions and opened the door for revolutionary change. Ultimately, it would allow the individual the prospect of eternal life, when he or she might be rewarded or punished according to the principles of cosmic justice.

WHILE RELIGIOUS IDEAS were changing, so too were the forms in which religious knowledge was being developed and passed on. The growing role of sacred scripture in these centuries did not necessarily follow from the growth of monotheism, but it closely accompanied that trend and reinforced it. In the story of Josiah's reformation, the crucial moment occurred with the alleged finding of the ancient scripture and the king's decision to value this above any and all tradition or conventional practice. The monotheistic program was asserted in a body of writings collected and collated during the sixth century or no later than the fifth. Increasingly, a division was being drawn between what was and was not sacred scripture. Religion was becoming textualized and scripturalized.[32]

Later tradition declared that the broad outlines of the canonical Bible had achieved some degree of consensus by the fifth century, specifically the time of Ezra and Nehemiah in the restored Jerusalem.[33] Theoretically at least, the canonical Bible/Old Testament was "closed," or finished. That statement needs to be qualified, though, because several books were added after that date and earlier books were revised and expanded (see Table 1). At the Qumran settlement, probably founded in the 150s BCE, sect members voraciously explored scriptural texts with little sense of dealing with a closed canon. But if the formal limits of scripture remained quite fluid for centuries, closure was coming. The process of canonization was well under way no later than the third century BCE, when Egyptian Jews realized that translating the sacred books into Greek (the Septuagint) was essential to preserving their religion, and they had to decide exactly which texts belonged to this collection. At the start of the second century, the book of Sirach refers to a biblical canon very much like what would be known in later centuries and lists the great patriarchs and prophets found in it. Later in that century, the Letter of Aristeas first refers to the Hebrew scriptures as the Books, *ta Biblia*, and, indeed, as scripture (Sirach 44–50).[34]

But whatever the exact limits of the Bible might be, scriptural authority as a concept was acknowledged and respected. When Ezra and Nehemiah reconstructed the Temple and purified the religion of the land (as they saw it), they consecrated their action by a mass public reading of the Law. Scripture became the criterion by which to assess popular ritual life and devotion—in this instance, in the harshest possible manner.

The rise of scripture reflected a wider transformation of sensibility, a new proclamation of the means by which holiness could be explored and expressed. The main expression of religious worship continued to be sacrificial, but beyond that there was a new emphasis on the internal and spiritual rather than material or sensual forms. If it is too early to use the later Protestant criterion of religious authority as *sola scriptura* (scripture alone), then the concept was at least recognizable. And as in later Reformation times, the growth of reading in the ancient world contributed to new patterns of private devotion and of individual religiosity. No later than the second century, the Hasidim were "pious" individuals who lived by what they found in the scriptures and organized their lives around the commandments and rules of purity they found there. Some of their heirs became famous as the Pharisees, others as the Essenes.[35]

The emphasis on text contributed to the decline from the charismatic guidance claimed in earlier centuries, as the rise of scripture established a body of divine truth that any would-be prophet contradicted at his peril. It seemed outrageously bold, if not blasphemous, to offer anything that might be taken as a new scripture or pseudo-scripture, and any such act demanded subterfuge. Biblical scholar

Ronald Hendel speaks of "the textualization of prophecy," which encouraged new generations to attribute their own would-be revelations to already established heroes or prophets of bygone days.[36]

Reading could of itself be a holy act, and texts might be sacred objects. The written word revealed the divine Word. That principle opened the way to new forms of religious inquiry, including seeking sacred truths in the text itself, in the patterns of written letters. Whole new areas of mystical contemplation now became possible. The emphasis on reading placed a whole new premium on literacy and on offering the educational means necessary to achieve it. Scribes and schools gained a whole new importance. In the early second century, Jesus ben Sira, author of Sirach, ran an academy for young members of the Jerusalem elite. Religion became at once more literate and more literary.[37]

The movement toward text had potent political implications. As Protestant Christians have long known, a book-based faith is likely to be both diverse and sectarian. In sacred books—in the "Bible"— the faithful read, meditated, and found explanations for the evils that they saw around them (among other things). This increased the likelihood of sectarian division, as different groups read scriptures differently. They found independent justifications and interpretations and wrote their own religious texts. By the second century, schools of interpretation were evolving into sects, with some entering into formal schism and declaring themselves the true core of faith.

THE NEW APPROACH to reading and text opened the door to literary creativity. The grandson of Ben Sira recorded that his ancestor, "when he had much given himself to the reading of the Law, and the prophets, and other books of our fathers, and had gotten therein good judgment, was drawn on also himself to write something pertaining to learning and wisdom" (Sirach/Ecclus. prologue, KJV). Reading begat new writing. Authors used the process of narrative writing to explore religious ideas and dilemmas, commonly for the purposes of improvement, but also to tell good stories. Authors situated their stories in the acknowledged world of sacred history, during the time of a particular known king or prophet. The book of Tobit was written around 200 BCE, but it situates its action in the time of "Shalmaneser of the Assyrians" (1:2), who lived a half millennium before and is recorded in the biblical book of 2 Kings. Other second-century texts, such as Judith and Daniel, placed their action in the time of the Babylonian Exile, some four centuries previously. Such authors were assuming the existence and significance of scripture and slotting their own works into that canonical tradition. Instead of consciously writing history, then, authors sought to fit their stories into an established historical record that they already knew from reading, and they did so by giving their works a spurious antiquity. Historical fiction was born.

Even if the canon was closed (or closing), that did not prevent later writers from expanding and commenting on established texts in order to present new stories that, over time, came to be regarded as de facto part of the original scripture. The Bible is taken as a given and used as a springboard for development and elaboration. To take one example, the book of Genesis tells us very little about Terah, father of Abraham, except that he lived in the Mesopotamian city of Ur. No later than the 160s BCE, the expansion of Genesis known as the book of Jubilees (chap. 12) records that Terah was by profession a maker of idols and that early in his career Abraham burned those images as a rejection of idolatry. That story subsequently became a mainstay of rabbinic tradition, and in later centuries it has often been cited as if it was part of the original Genesis narrative. In that form, Terah's story found its way into the Qur'an.[38]

In Jubilees the Terah story was a mere chapter in a much larger work, but similar curiosity about the unexplored reaches of scripture inspired full-length freestanding accounts. Between the fifth and second centuries BCE, there appeared such inspired fiction as the books of Job, Ruth, Judith, Tobit, Esther, and Daniel, all of which were accepted as canonized scriptures in at least some Bibles. That tradition of religious fiction continued prolifically for a millennium afterward.

Such texts never admitted their fictional quality, and the quest to assert authenticity was intimately linked to new constructions of the heavenly hierarchy. Just why should readers accept the spiritual credentials of a recently written book that lacked any claim to respectable antiquity? One common solution to that question lay in claiming angelic guidance or inspiration. We have already seen the significant role that angels played as conveyers of heavenly truths in First Zechariah. Later visionaries usually claimed to have truths from writings or tablets that were revealed to them in Heaven or via angels, who were lovingly described. And once the scriptural canon was closed and venerated, later authors needed special warrants to justify their own literary and theological contributions. Angels and heavenly messengers became a rhetorical necessity to demonstrate how and why those writers had obtained the religious texts and messages they were revealing to the world.[39]

WHEN RELIGIOUS FORMS and practices changed, so did the definition of the people following that distinctive way of life. New concepts and definitions of ethnicity transformed the meaning of such basic terms as "Jew" and "Israelite."

In earlier times, the Hebrew people had been divided into the two kingdoms of Israel and Judah. After the Exile, the southern land of Judah confronted the Samaritans, with their rival cult and Temple. Much has been learned about the Samaritans in recent years, and we now have a stronger sense of their significance. The canonical Bible states that the Assyrian invasion of the eighth century BCE devastated the northern land of Israel, so that most of the inhabitants were killed or exiled, to be replaced by newer pagan migrants. These, allegedly, were the ancestors of the half-breed Samaritan people, and any reader of the New Testament knows the bitter hostility that separated Jews and Samaritans in Jesus's day. What a miracle that there could be a *good* Samaritan![40]

In reality, that historical picture reflects later polemics and myth-making. The people of Samaria never lost their basic Hebrew and Yahwistic heritage, the same sense of inheritance from Moses and Aaron, and always upheld their claim to be the true Israel. They continued to share cultural and religious affinities with the Jews of Judea, and Jews and Samaritans communicated and interacted with each other. And far from being reduced to a marginal minority, Samaritans usually outnumbered Jews, at least from the seventh century BCE through the second. In the mid-fifth century, Samaritans built their own Temple on Mount Gerizim, which they understood to be the true intended site of the institution ordained in the Torah.[41]

The people of Judah acquired their own ethnic label. In the Persian Empire, they belonged to Yehud Medinata, the province of Judah, and increasingly the term "Judah/Judea" came to mark the territory of a religion rather than merely an ethnic group. In anything like its modern sense, the word "Jew" appears as an ethnic or religious term in the fifth and fourth centuries BCE. The classical world was well used to the idea of particular nations or peoples with their characteristic customs and their known homeland, so it made excellent sense to refer to a *Ioudaios*, which might mean a Jew or Judean. Soon, the distinctively religious elements of this label were emphasized, and in the second century BCE the second book of Maccabees coined the word "Judaism" to describe a package of religious customs and beliefs in a sense we can recognize today. And if Judaism was a distinct thing, then a new concept was needed for those groups and characteristics that did not belong to it. The term "goyim" shifted its meaning from the "nations" and their inhabitants to the nations that did not follow Judaism: the Gentiles.[42] Jews, as newly defined, assuredly traced their inheritance through the biblical patriarchs and prophets, but their religious system was nothing like a simple continuation of those older patterns.

ALREADY DURING THE Persian period (539–332 BCE), religious life was being transformed through the sweeping internal changes we have already noted. In the 330s Alexander the Great conquered and absorbed that older empire, including Palestine. Globalization and imperial rivalries posed alarming questions of resistance or assimilation. The revolutionary cultural consequences added vastly to internal conflicts and debates and sped the religious transformation.

Chapter 2

THE YEARS OF THE GREEKS

The Jewish World Confronts Greek Empires

———————

So Alexander reigned twelve years, and then died. And his servants bare rule every one in his place. And after his death they
all put crowns upon themselves; so did their sons after them
many years: and evils were multiplied in the earth.

1 MACCABEES 1:7–9, KJV

IN 164 BCE, the Maccabean insurgents captured the Jerusalem Temple, which had been desecrated by pagan Greeks. The joyous reded-
ication is recorded at length in an unabashedly triumphant history
called the first book of Maccabees: "On the twenty-fifth day of the
ninth month, which is the month of Chislev, in the one hundred and
forty-eighth year, they rose and offered sacrifice, as the Law directs"
(4:52–53). That is the origin of the feast of Hanukah, but the author
dates the event in a curious way. He gives the exact date in terms
of the traditional calendar still followed today by Jews, who begin
Hanukah on the twenty-fifth day of the month Chislev. But "the one
hundred and forty-eighth year" is based on the dating system of the
"kingdom of the Greeks," that is, the Seleucid era, which marked
time from the conquest of Babylon in 312 BCE by the Greek general
Seleucus I. Although that specific act of conquest is now largely forgotten (and who remembers the foes from whom he conquered it?),
the long shadow it cast points to the lasting impact of those Greek
dynasts. Well into the Middle Ages, many scholars in the Arab and

Middle Eastern worlds continued to date by the Year of the Greeks, which was the practice of the great Syriac Christian churches. Even when a society attempted to secede from the Greek political order, as did the Maccabean revolutionaries, the wider cultural hegemony was almost inescapable. Jewish nationalists might retake Jerusalem, but the Greeks still owned time.

From the end of the fourth century, the Jewish world faced the challenge of Hellenization. New contacts with Greek culture at any stage would have been provocative, but the Jews were encountering a dazzling golden age of science and culture. Some of these influences proved highly attractive to Jewish thinkers, while others inspired resistance. And the exchange went both ways: Jews now had to present their religion to the wider world, and that act of interpretation forced a rethinking of basic categories. By no means were all the changes of the next 250 years a response to Hellenization, but that movement does provide the essential context and environment for what did occur. Greek was the language in which new developments were proposed and discussed.[1]

Alexander's conquests began centuries of interaction between Greek and Jewish cultures, out of which would emerge most Western religious thought.[2]

HISTORIANS PROPERLY PAY attention to the world-conquering career of Alexander the Great but far less to the enduring and significant changes he sparked. If one story is vastly famous, the other is little known to nonspecialists. From the 330s through the mid-second century BCE, Jews were subject to one or other of the great Hellenistic empires that claimed Alexander's heritage, the Ptolemaic and Seleucid realms. These empires battled for control over the region, which changed hands repeatedly: Palestine itself changed ownership seven times just between 323 and 301. Relative stability followed when the Ptolemies secured the area for most of the third century. The Seleucids then dominated from 200 through much of the second century. (Contrary to legend, only very slowly did the

Maccabean revolt end the Greek dominance of Palestine.) Later regimes, including the Herodians and Romans, were suffused with those Greek-derived cultural and political ideas.[3]

The story of the two empires goes back to Alexander's time and his refusal to name an heir on this deathbed. That left his Macedonian generals to fight for power, and fight they did. These were the *Diadochi*, the Successors. One of the clique was Seleucus Nicator, the Victor, a great general who campaigned as far east as India and inherited much of the vast eastern territory conquered by Alexander. Seleucus married a Persian princess, and their son succeeded him as Emperor Antiochus I. The next sovereign, Antiochus II, took the title *Theos*, "the god."[4]

Through the third century BCE, the Seleucid Empire was a superpower, which in its extent recalled the ancient Persian Empire (see Table 2.1). Well into the second century, the core territories of this "Greek" empire comprised Syria, Mesopotamia, Babylonia, and western Iran. The empire was still a mighty force under Antiochus III, also termed the Great, who ruled from 222 to 187. Born in what is now Iran, this Antiochus reasserted his family's rule over Parthia and Bactria and used war elephants to stage a new invasion of India. He invaded Greece and won historic victories against Ptolemaic Egypt. At first sight, his realm looks almost as grand as that of Alexander a century previously, although his reign ended in disastrous conflict with Rome. Antiochus's son and eventual heir was Antiochus IV, who is notorious in Jewish history as a fanatical advocate of Greek culture and religion. Indicating the transnational quality of the empire's power, that younger Antiochus originally bore the Iranian-derived name Mithridates.[5]

The other great Middle Eastern power was the Ptolemaic realm, which was centered in Egypt but at times extended its power into Cyprus and Asia Minor. Insofar as that empire is recalled today, it is usually as yet another Egyptian dynasty, the successor to its thirty native predecessors. We may imagine them in the stereotypical patterns of dress and appearance that we associate with the term

TABLE 2.1 THE HELLENISTIC DYNASTIES
(SELECTED RULERS; ALL DATES BCE)

Seleucid dynasty	*Ptolemaic dynasty*
Seleucus I Nicator (312–281)	Ptolemy I Soter (323–285)
Antiochus I Soter (281–262)	Ptolemy II Philadelphus (285–246)
Antiochus II Theos (262–246)	Ptolemy III Euergetes (246–221)
Antiochus III the Great (223–187)	Ptolemy IV Philopator (221–204)
Seleucus IV Philopator (187–176)	Ptolemy V Epiphanes (204–181)
Antiochus IV (175–164)	Ptolemy VI Philometor (181–145)
Demetrius I Soter (161–150)	Ptolemy VIII Physkon Euergetes (169–116)
Alexander Balas (150–145)	•
Demetrius II Nicator (146–139 and 129–126)	•
Antiochus VII (138–129)	•

"ancient Egyptian," a timeless world with its pharaohs and pyramids, its hieroglyphic inscriptions and animal-headed deities. Yet the Ptolemaic ruling class was thoroughly Greek in language, culture, and personal names: Ptolemy is a Greek name that means "warlike." The cultural mixing of the time is symbolized by the celebrated Rosetta stone, which was produced in 196 BCE under Ptolemy V Epiphanes. This stone is most famous today for containing a single text translated into multiple languages, allowing modern scholars for the first time to use Greek to comprehend hieroglyphic inscriptions. But the Rosetta text is a curious amalgam of traditions. It offers a barrage of Greek names (Alexander, Pyrrhides, Demetria, Arsinoë), but all in the context of ancient Egyptian ritual formulae and religious concepts. King Ptolemy himself is "Son of the Sun, beloved of [the Egyptian god] Ptah." At his death in 181 BCE, he became the first royal Ptolemy to be mummified in the Egyptian mode rather than cremated in Homeric Greek style. Although the empire's famous last ruler is sometimes depicted today in African guise, Cleopatra is a purely Greek name, which means "glory of the father." She was the first of her dynasty who bothered to learn the Egyptian language.[6]

The Ptolemaic dynasty, or Lagids, was at its height in the first half of the third century. Ptolemy I was a companion of Alexander who took the title of Soter, "the Savior." His best-known monument was the Great Library of Alexandria, one of the world's foremost cultural centers for centuries to come. His son was Ptolemy II Philadelphus, a prestigious ruler whose diplomatic contacts extended to India. He even received Buddhist emissaries from the Indian court, as did his Seleucid contemporary Antiochus II. Ptolemy's son in turn was Ptolemy III Euergetes, "the Benefactor." Just six successive Ptolemies spanned the era from 323 to 145. Such long reigns imply stability, although later members of the dynasty were notorious for acts of tyranny, interfamily feuds and violence, and truly bizarre behavior. In the second century, the empire suffered from internecine court politics at its worst. Ptolemy II began the practice of kings marrying their sisters, and it is not surprising that their descendants often showed signs of mental illness and instability.[7]

Palestine had the ill fortune to find itself on the borders between these two superstates. The so-called Syrian Wars entangled the Ptolemies and Seleucids sporadically between 274 and 168. At the worst moments in these struggles, Palestine was squeezed between the twin imperial grindstones. The book of Daniel offers a knowledgeable summary of regional history and dynastic doings between 330 and 168, presented in the form of retroactive prophecy concerning the kings of the North (Seleucids) and the South (Ptolemies). One typical section tells how "the king of the South will march out in a rage and fight against the king of the North, who will raise a large army, but it will be defeated. When the army is carried off, the king of the South will be filled with pride and will slaughter many thousands, yet he will not remain triumphant" (11:11–12). The reference is to the rivalry between Ptolemy IV and Antiochus III in 217 as well as Ptolemy's victory at the Battle of Raphia, one of the largest conflicts in the whole of ancient history. It was no mere antiquarian curiosity that made Jews care about these transactions. For almost two centuries, the political and cultural fate of the Jewish people depended on the successes and failures of those kings of the North and South.[8]

THE COMING OF the Hellenistic empires vastly expanded the geographical scope of the Jewish world, and raised Jewish awareness of distant lands and kingdoms scattered over three continents. Such interactions inevitably had their cultural impact. One convenient symbol of that wider world is the elephants that Hellenistic empires regularly used as vital weapons of war at Raphia and elsewhere, where the animals played a role equivalent to modern tanks. The kings obtained their elephants from India (attempts to use the more aggressive African elephants went disastrously wrong) and then deployed them across the known world. Quite regularly, the people of Palestine would have witnessed elephants either in action or en route to campaigns. Such animals were a vital and much-feared component of the Seleucid forces fighting the Maccabean rebels. The wide-ranging travels of the elephants suggest the global cultural synthesis that grew from Alexander's achievement, into which Jews now entered.

The vast scale of that world is indicated by the hundreds of cities across the region named for the various Greek overlords. Alexander himself was an enthusiastic founder of cities, Egypt's Alexandria being the most famous. But so were the various rulers called Seleucus and Antiochus, and Seleucias and Antiochs appear across the Hellenistic world. Six kings bore the name Seleucus, and there were thirteen Antiochi. Numerous Laodiceas and Philippis commemorated other royal kin, and names like Philadelphia recalled royal titles. (Philadelphus signified "brotherly love.") Sometimes these cities were new foundations, but in other cases the kings granted their names to existing sites, to which they granted special favors. These cities were scattered from North Africa into India and throughout central Asia. Some of those Alexandrias, Antiochs, and Seleucias vanished or were annihilated, but others lasted into the Middle Ages or beyond, and they stubbornly continued to date their history according to the Year of the Greeks. (Some Christian tombstones in central Asia still used this dating as late as the fourteenth century CE.)

Jews spread widely across this world, which defined the limits of urban civilization for early Christians. Much of early Christian history concerns the great cities of Egyptian Alexandria and Syrian Antioch on the Orontes, where Jesus's followers were first called Christians. The Seleucid Empire originally had its center at Babylon, but about 275 the kings built their new capital at Seleucia on the Tigris. Under later Parthian rule, that metropolis was merged into the new twin city of Seleucia-Ctesiphon, which at its height might have been the world's most populous city. Seleucia-Ctesiphon in turn was the predecessor of Islamic Baghdad.[9]

Culturally and symbolically, Palestine during the Crucible years stood in a Hellenistic triangle, formed by imaginary lines joining the three great cities of (Syrian) Antioch, (Egyptian) Alexandria, and (Babylonian) Seleucia-Ctesiphon. Each, in its day, was one of the centers of the ancient world. Together, they exercised an overwhelming influence on non-Greek peoples. That triangle retained its pivotal role for a full millennium, until after the rise of Islam.

THE RULERS OF the Persian Empire had devoted themselves to spreading their culture, but Greeks were still more vaultingly ambitious in these matters. Indeed, they made culture a central ideological component of their rule and of the authority claimed by particular rulers and dynasties.

The modern word "Hellenistic" might suggest that this era was somewhat inferior to that of classical, Hellenic, Greece: it was only "Greek-ish." But in terms of culture and scholarship, this was one of the greatest ages of human history, with few parallels before the European experience of the Renaissance and the scientific revolution.

This era produced innovators and thinkers in an awe-inspiring range of fields, some of which were only now defined as scholarly disciplines. Beyond the work of individual pioneers, once separate cultures flowed together under the auspices of the Greek overlords to create new syntheses. Babylonian, Persian, and Indian cultural currents entered Greek thought and vice versa. Meanwhile, ideas and individuals spread rapidly through empires and across continents. The sheer pace and energy of innovation in these years, roughly between 300 and 100, are breathtaking. For anyone who cared about learning, science, or culture, whatever their race or religion, these were heady times.[10]

Listing just a few of the outstanding figures from these two centuries gives a sense of the range of accomplishments during this cultural explosion. The process of discovery and speculation continued apace long after my arbitrarily chosen terminal date of 100 BCE. The most celebrated thinkers of this era included Euclid the mathematician and the many-sided genius Archimedes. In astronomy, Hipparchus built on Babylonian precedent to map the stars; Aristarchus of Samos presented a heliocentric view of the solar system that prefigured Copernicus. Eratosthenes, the third-century librarian of the royal collection of Alexandria, was an astronomer, philologist, poet, and mathematician who founded the discipline of geography. Among other accomplishments, he was the first to calculate the circumference of the earth, which he did with high accuracy.[11]

At the core of the new science was a fascination with astronomy and cosmology, the study of the heavens, an area that also held enduring appeal for Jewish thinkers. This concern went far beyond a general interest in one single aspect of nature, penetrating as it did many other fields of thought. The religious implications were pervasive. Through studying stars and planets, scholars were addressing such key questions as the origin and creation of the world, the nature of heavenly hierarchies, and the spiritual forces or beings that governed these realities. That in turn shaped attitudes toward fate, determinism, and free will. The study of the heavens was also critical to such practical matters as the calendar and timekeeping. No hard-and-fast boundaries separated astronomy from astrology, and as such, it touched on many other disciplines, especially medicine. The human body, after all, was believed to reflect the structures of the heavens. Cosmology was no less intimately linked to political ideologies and concepts of power. The fact that Hellenistic kings wore solar diadems and radiate crowns was no mere fashion choice: they were the suns at the center of the political universe.[12]

Beyond theoretical speculation about the wider universe, Greek scholars of this time were prolific inventors. In the first century BCE, Hero of Alexandria became the world's most prolific and versatile practical inventor until the time of Thomas Edison. This tradition is exemplified by the long mysterious object found on a shipwreck at Antikythera in the Aegean Sea, dating from the second century BCE. This find is now recognized as a strikingly sophisticated analog computer designed to calculate the motions of the sun and moon for both calendrical and astrological purposes. In its spectacular original condition, before its long immersion under the sea, this Antikythera mechanism would have given observers a visually stunning illustration of the workings of the heavens as recognized by the best scholars of the day. Both Hipparchus and Archimedes have been credited as designers. Scarcely less amazing is what it implies about the technology of the time. Although the mechanism is unique, it must have formed part of a much larger tradition of sophisticated design and execution, of which it is presently the sole survivor.[13]

Other fields of knowledge advanced similarly. Herophilus of Alexandria pioneered the study of medical anatomy, while other scholars theorized about the role of the heart and the circulatory system. This was quite apart from the intense activity in the humanities—in literature, drama, and the newly founded genre of the novel.

Scholars of the time knew nothing of modern disciplinary labels. Much of what we would call science was incorporated under the general title of philosophy, the love of wisdom: the Greek word may date back to Pythagoras, around 500 BCE. In terms of their intellectual influence at the time, speculative philosophers were at least as prestigious as scientists or other scholars. Several great philosophical schools flourished in this era, and their ideas provided the essential matrix for civilized thought. The ideas of Plato and Aristotle were the most widely influential, but major new schools emerged from around 300. These included Stoicism, as well as the ideas of Epicurus, whose followers preached a daring materialism, grounded in atomic theory.[14]

Historians of the European Renaissance world often address the deeply destabilizing effects of all the new science and learning. New continents were being discovered, as were new substances and planets; even the size and location of the earth itself were being reimagined. As John Donne wrote around 1600, "New philosophy calls all in doubt. . . . 'Tis all in pieces, all coherence gone." No point of knowledge or culture seemed firm or dependable; all was in flux, everything open to debate and challenge. Yet every word of that description would apply precisely to the Hellenistic world in the golden age of Archimedes and Hipparchos—a proto-Enlightenment, yet in a world still suffused in ideas of the supernatural. Or according to the maxim proclaimed by the sage Thales in the sixth century BCE, it was a world in which "all things are full of gods."[15]

MORE THAN JUST bringing disparate cultures into contact, the far-reaching power of the Greek regimes drove those conquered territories to present their ideas to a global audience. Egypt and Mesopotamia were two of the world's oldest cultures, but it was in the third century BCE that representatives of each wrote widely influential accounts of their origins. In the 280s, Babylonian scholar Berosus wrote a Greek-language account of that culture's history, mythology, and religious heritage, and he expounded matters of cosmology and astrology. Sometime during that same century, Egyptian priest Manetho likewise wrote a summary of his country's history, and again, of course, he used Greek. Both writers exploited an opportunity that Greek thinkers themselves had made available when they admitted the existence of far older cultures that could legitimately claim to be the true cradles of civilization. Egypt and Babylonia both now staked their claims to that position.[16]

This is the context in which we should see the Jewish interaction with Greek thought, as Jews framed their beliefs according to cosmopolitan standards. (That word "cosmopolitan" was coined in the fourth century BCE, and it was a defining characteristic of the Hellenistic era.) Many educated Jews thought in Greek. One Jewish author from this time whose name we know is Eupolemus, who was probably the ambassador that Judah the Maccabee sent on a diplomatic mission to Rome around 160. Eupolemus wrote a now-lost history of the Jewish kings and people and was the first to integrate biblical sources with Greek historical materials, drawing from Egypt and Phoenicia as well as Greece itself. Besides this work, other texts purporting to come from his hand make striking claims about the Jewish contributions to the founding of civilization. Whether genuinely Eupolemus's work or not, these other fragments assert that Abraham taught cosmology and astrology to neighboring Near Eastern cultures.[17]

Most such writers tried to show how closely Jews conformed to Greek standards, but a few subversive voices were also heard. A few years after Eupolemus, an anonymous Egyptian Jew surveyed the contemporary Greek world through a pseudoprophecy collected in the Sibylline Oracles. Not only did the "oracle" make Jews an integral part of world history, but it did so through proud assertions of Jewish strength and dignity. Jews were "a holy race of godly men . . . keeping to the counsels and mind of the Most High. . . . For to them alone the mighty God his gracious counsel gave and faith and noblest thought within their hearts." Jews demonstrated their superiority to vulgar pagan idolatry and abstained from the pederasty that was the standard practice of most other nations. In the context of the time, the author verged on blasphemy by denouncing the works of Homer, whom he saw as a liar, plagiarist, and fabulist, with his ludicrous portrayals of bogus pagan gods. But for all the carping, even this text shows how carefully Jews had to think through their relations with the larger Greek world.[18]

JEWS TRAVELED AND settled across the Hellenistic world, so that a very wide-ranging Diaspora was in existence by the end of the third century BCE. The Diaspora experience was anything but new in this era. Jews had been forcibly transported to Babylon in the sixth century, but plenty of other examples point to voluntary migration in the intervening years. Much of Jewish history in the Crucible years took place in Egypt or was profoundly affected by developments in that country, while Samaritans also began their own wide Diaspora. Egypt had its own Jewish temples, counterparts of the great edifice in Jerusalem. In the sixth century, a temple was built to serve a Jewish community at Elephantine in upper Egypt, where YHWH was associated with other deities. Diaspora Jews were the first to create synagogues, local houses of assembly, prayer, and worship that made no attempt to compete with the great sacrificial rituals of the temples. The institution of the synagogue developed in Egypt in the third century BCE before spreading to Palestine itself.[19]

The greatest Diaspora center was Alexandria itself, the pinnacle of the Greek civilizing and Hellenizing mission. The city attracted a large Jewish population, and by the second century it was a key Jewish center, exceeded in importance only by Jerusalem itself. By the first century CE, the city had five sections or quarters, two of which were mainly Jewish. The city's importance for Jewish culture can hardly be exaggerated. This was above all the home of the philosopher and scholar Philo (20 BCE–50 CE), to whom we will often have cause to return.[20]

Later Jews looked back fondly on the Ptolemies and their experiences in Egypt. Ptolemy I in particular left a golden reputation, and he reportedly made strong efforts to encourage Jews and Samaritans to settle in the land. But political factors also favored such glorification of early Gentile rulers, who were retroactively contrasted with their evil successors. Writing in hindsight, Jews wrote up the

Ptolemaic dynasty in opposition to the rival dynasty of the Seleucids, with whom they had had such disastrous experiences.

The earlier Ptolemies also looked very benevolent when compared with their later successors, and that fact encouraged a degree
of romanticization. By the first century CE, Alexandria's Jewish community repeatedly struggled with non-Jews, and some of these battles approached the status of civil wars. Writers of the time idealized
relations in bygone times in order to stress the positive role that Jews
had played in founding the city. The later text 3 Maccabees actually
claims that in the late third century, Ptolemy IV persecuted and tried
to destroy Egyptian Jews, but this assertion has no basis in reality.
This work includes the unforgettable image of the king attempting to
annihilate the Jews by having them trampled by enraged elephants.[21]

Just how centrally the Ptolemies loomed in Jewish memory is
indicated by Josephus's history of the Jewish people. Much of his
account of the third century was focused on Egyptian events and
conditions, and he especially praises Ptolemy Philadelphus for his
excellent relations with Jews. Ptolemy generously frees many thousands of Jews whom the Persians had taken into captivity in Egypt
and sends rich presents to the Jerusalem Temple. Another story
recorded by Josephus shows just how thoroughly at home Jews felt
in Ptolemaic Egypt. During the lethal factional feuds in Jerusalem in
the 170s, Onias, son of the high priest, sought refuge in Egypt. The
then king, Ptolemy VI Philometor, received him warmly, granting
him permission to build at Leontopolis a new Jewish temple, supposedly an imitation of the main Jerusalem sanctuary. Like Jerusalem, it was staffed by priests of the proper lineage and maintained
all the forms of the sacrificial cult. As it would have had the requisite complement of scribes, Leontopolis might well have been yet
another center of Jewish literary activity, over and above Jerusalem
and Alexandria. This alternative Egyptian temple remained in operation for 240 years. Around 150 BCE, the same Ptolemy again ven-
tured into Jewish affairs when he agreed to decide a dispute about
the rival historical claims of Jews and Samaritans. One Andronicus

championed the cause of the Jewish Temple, and the king deemed him the winner. He then executed the rival Samaritan debaters.[22]

Josephus tells the famous story of the first Ptolemy building up the library of Alexandria, as his librarian sought out the books of the Jews for collection and translation. This resulted in the translation of the Bible into Greek, the Septuagint, so called because it was supposedly the work of seventy-two scholars. (This story is also found in the Letter of Aristeas, written in the second century BCE.) Reputedly, when the translation work was completed, the joyous community that heard it read found the work nothing less than perfect. The priests and the elders of the translators, the Jewish community, and the leaders of the people stood up and said that "since so excellent and sacred and accurate a translation had been made, it was only right that it should remain as it was and no alteration should be made in it." The translation work owed something to a desire to inform Gentiles about the Jewish religion, but by far the most important audience was Jews themselves, who increasingly found it difficult to read in Hebrew or Aramaic. Already by 160, this Greek translation was the main biblical source used by Eupolemus. For centuries to come, the Septuagint was the primary means by which Jews read the Bible, and that translation was the foundational text of early Christianity. (Other Greek translations circulated in various parts of the Jewish world, but the Septuagint was the most significant.) The New Testament is incomprehensible without grasping its very frequent references to the Old Testament, whether through direct quotations or by more subtle recollections and reminiscences. But throughout, the Old Testament is quoted through the Septuagint, that is, through an Egyptian Greek translation.[23]

Alexandria is the likely source of origin of many Jewish writings in the Crucible years. Repeatedly, such works use Egyptian locations or characters or deal with issues particularly relevant to Egyptian Jews. Several Jewish writers flourished in second-century Alexandria. Although most of their works are now lost, we at least know the names of Demetrius the Chronographer and the epic poets

Philo and Theodotus. One surprising text is the Exagoge of Ezekiel the Tragedian, a Jewish dramatist living in Alexandria in the second century BCE. At first sight, the Exagoge is a standard Greek tragedy in five acts, in iambic pentameter. Its theme, though, is the story of the Exodus, with extensive speaking parts by the character of Moses himself. Jewish history has been transmuted into a format that we are more accustomed to seeing as a vehicle for the tales of Greek mythology.[24]

Rarely do we know the precise circumstances in which biblical books were written, but one exception is Sirach, or the Wisdom of Jesus ben Sira. It was originally written by the scribe of that name—actually, Yeshua ben Eleazar ben Sira—in Jerusalem, in Hebrew, around 190 BCE. His grandson then translated it into Greek, "when I came to Egypt in the thirty-eighth year of the reign of [Ptolemy VIII Physkon] Euergetes and stayed for some time" (prologue). That dates the grandson's move precisely to 132 BCE. This is a specific reference to a Jew traveling to Egypt and making a text available to his Greek-speaking contemporaries. The story represents in microcosm a whole world of intercultural contact and exchange.[25]

Besides Ptolemaic Alexandria, the emerging Jewish Diaspora had a center in the Seleucid realm, at Babylon and its nearby successor capitals. Babylon has always played an ambiguous role in Jewish history, both as a symbol of oppression and as an idealized cultural homeland. Jews had been settled in Mesopotamia/Iraq during the exile of the sixth century, and a community had always remained. Jews flourished during the Seleucid Empire that ruled the land from the fourth century through the second and then under the Parthian Empire that conquered Seleucia in 141 BCE. For some centuries, that city was an eastern mirror image of Alexandria. The Jewish presence in Mesopotamia grew ever stronger as successive generations of Jewish rebels and dissidents took refuge from the power of Rome. In the early centuries of the Common Era, Babylonia became the intellectual heartland of Judaism worldwide.[26]

JEWS DID NOT even have to look to the Diaspora to see Greek influences, as so many Greek and Gentile settlers were to be found in the land of Palestine itself and on its immediate borders. Palestine had always been an ethnically mixed region, and ancient stories of conquest and conflict record relations with neighboring tribes and peoples, notably the Philistines, who feature in the history of the early monarchy. Palestine was never homogeneous or uniformly Hebrew. But the situation became still more diverse during the era of Greek supremacy.[27]

We observe this from a disaster suffered by the ruling Hasmonean dynasty in 143 BCE. The Hasmonean leader, high priest Jonathan Apphus, fell into a trap set by his enemy, the Seleucid general Trypho. Under the pretense of arranging a peace settlement, Trypho captured Jonathan and eventually killed him. The story in itself was a familiar-enough example of the backstabbing politics that prevailed in this era. For present purposes, what matters is the setting of the crime at Scythopolis, in what is now Beit Shean, in northern Israel. Scythopolis is literally the city of the Scythians, a warrior people who originated in the Pontic-Caspian steppe region of eastern Europe, north of the Black Sea, and supplied mercenary forces to Hellenistic rulers. In this instance, an ancient city settlement had been refounded no later than the third century as the home of a body of discharged pagan soldiers, who gave it its name.[28]

Under a policy dating back to Alexander the Great, successive Hellenistic regimes settled veterans like the Scythians in new lands as a means of rewarding followers, with the added bonus of establishing loyal bastions among restive alien populations. Greek kings deliberately settled new populations to spread Hellenization and to serve as cultural magnets for native peoples. Greek cities were concentrated along the coasts and also in the northeastern corner of Palestine, across the Jordan River in the region known as the Decapolis. These Ten Cities include Philadelphia (modern Amman), Gadara, Pella, and Gerasa, while Damascus was loosely affiliated. Adding to their impact, such communities were located physically very close to the better-known Jewish areas, in what to American eyes looks like a tiny area. Palestine, in its historic sense, covers a mere 11,000 square miles. As the crow flies (and ignoring modern borders and security walls), traveling from Jerusalem to Damascus in Syria is a mere 160 miles, while Jerusalem to Nazareth is around 70 miles. Only a few days' walking allowed people to travel between multiple regions of culture, language, and faith.[29]

These multicultural settlements, this reverse Diaspora, encouraged intermarriage and a degree of hybridization. Palestinian Jews were thus regularly exposed to interactions with Greek thought and culture, much like their counterparts in Alexandria or the wider Greek world. Less happily, Jews also learned Greek and Gentile ways during their time as prisoners or slaves to Gentile masters, from which at least some were ransomed. Such diversity contributed to religious creativity and innovation, and also to heterodoxy.

FOREIGN TRADITIONS FLOWED easily into Jewish culture, enhancing and strengthening it. At the same time, those influences created a reaction and a call to return to older and purer standards. The tension between those two impulses, of accommodation and restriction, is a major part of the history of the Jewish people in this period, as it would be in so many later eras, especially in the post-Enlightenment world.[30]

Jewish elites vigorously debated what aspects of traditional faith and practice might be adjusted or even abandoned in order to promote accommodation, without betraying their fundamental ways. Critically for later concepts of the divine, Jews also discovered Greek philosophy during this period, causing an enduring dilemma. (I will discuss this at greater length in Chapter 9.) Yes, they wanted to absorb the latest forms of cutting-edge sophistication, yet at the same time, Jews resented the loss or contamination of older values. They knew that they must confront and absorb Greek philosophical ideas if they hoped to engage in communication with the educated world, but even so, they had to avoid any connection to pagan deities or anything hinting at polytheism.

Two features of Greek culture made the new empires potentially very dangerous to Judaic traditions. One was cultural inclusiveness. The Greeks, generally, were very open-minded about the cults and religions of the regions in which they settled, and Hellenistic cultures often reimagined local deities in forms more congenial to them. In Egypt the first Ptolemy deliberately created the new Greek-styled cult of Serapis in order to unify the empire's old and new populations. This new god merged the ancient native cults of Osiris and Apis into a composite figure in the best Greek mode, and he attracted a widespread following. (We have already seen the royal adoption of Egyptian styles on the Rosetta stone.) The goddess Isis, meanwhile, was combined with multiple female Greek deities to construct an all-powerful Queen of Heaven. Sometimes such a foreign-derived figure became the centerpiece of one of the Greek mystery religions that were in vogue from the third century onward. Such movements took believers through successive levels of initiation and ritual performance in a process that granted them the promise of eternal life and happiness.

Beyond their natural syncretism, Greeks also possessed superlative skills of visual representation in sculpture and painting, allowing them to visualize deities according to the extraordinarily high aesthetic standards prevailing at this time. They were superb at making ethnic and regional gods look wholly Greek, as they did with Serapis himself. In central Asia and on the Indian frontiers, local gods and kings were portrayed in Greek form in statuary and carvings. For several centuries, the emerging faith of Mahayana Buddhism represented its bodhisattvas in pure Hellenistic style; today, scholars study the phenomenon of "Greco-Buddhism." One famous Buddhist scripture features a noble patron of the faith called King Milinda, who was actually a Bactrian Greek sovereign called Menander Soter, the Savior. He ruled from ca. 160 to 130 BCE, making him a close contemporary of the Maccabean brothers who led the Jewish nationalist revolt. Menander, incidentally, had his capital at yet another city called Alexandria, which we know today as Kandahar, in Afghanistan.[31]

If those cultural pressures were so powerful as far afield as Kandahar and northern India, how much stronger were they for a Mediterranean community living amid Greek and pagan neighbors? In such a world, there was a natural temptation to assimilate the Jewish deity to Greek normality and ultimately to portray YHWH himself with an iconography close to that of Zeus. When pagans actually did penetrate the Holy of Holies—as did the forces of Antiochus IV in the 160s and the Romans a century later—they were stunned and baffled to find no actual figure of the deity, an absence quite contrary to the religious thought of the day. As far as we know, nobody actually dared take the step of commemorating YHWH in concrete form, but some such move was the logical next step in the Hellenization pushed so hard by Jewish enthusiasts. Perhaps a future statue in the Temple precincts might combine YHWH with one of the gods beloved by the Seleucid kings, such as Apollo or Zeus-Olympios (and as we will see something like that did happen in the 160s). Why should YHWH not merge into some new composite divinity who could generate the same broad multiethnic appeal as Serapis? The question was not whether there would be a Greco-Judaism, but rather how syncretistic it would become.

Politically, too, Greek assumptions posed serious difficulties for faithful Jews. Hellenistic kings made exalted claims for themselves, with their godlike rhetoric and their divine titles. When Alexander invaded the Persian realm in 334 BCE, Greek kingship still retained a good deal of popular approval and consultation, so that at least initially Macedonians did not claim a divine right to rule in anything like the Persian sense. Rapidly, though, Alexander's successors adopted Persian and Egyptian concepts of divine kingship. Over the next three centuries, Seleucid and Ptolemaic kings regularly bore such titles as Soter (Savior), Epiphanes ("Made Manifest," as in the

Christian word "epiphany"), and even Theos (God). Initially, a title like Soter might reflect praise for a military victory, but over time the religious components became more explicit: they were considered true cosmic saviors.

As we have seen, it was in the early second century that the Ptolemies made the transition into divine Egyptian pharaohs. Court ceremonial developed apace in all the Hellenistic realms, mimicking Persian court customs, as did titles and court formulas. By the Crucible era, kings wore elaborate solar crowns and diadems. They were gods on earth and expected to be treated as such. The king was no mere first among equals but a lord, a *despotes* (the source of our word "despotism"). While such developments were most immediately apparent in the courts themselves, they soon had their impact on every corner of the empire and beyond, wherever might be found coins proclaiming all the new royal pretensions.[32]

Those divine pretensions were integral to the ideology of power. By this time, many older Greek deities had fallen out of fashion, to be replaced by either local gods and mystery cults or else the popular cult of Tyche, that is, Fate or Fortune. The other main religious expression of the time was the cult of the kings themselves, with their exalted titles that proved they were the ultimate beneficiaries of Tyche.[33] That glorious achievement was celebrated in images, whether sculpted or painted, that demanded the homage and respect of subjects. For Jews, such figurative representation aroused concerns about idol worship and violating the commandment against graven images.

Kings demonstrated their wealth and power by ostentatious displays, through mighty building activities, and by organizing public shows and games, all of which featured ritual acts and consecrations. Pagan sacrifices were an integral part of all public life and communal action. Kings proved their Greekness by building cities with the requisite manifestations of culture, including gymnasia and baths. But even those seemingly harmless institutions posed new difficulties, in that games and gymnasia required nudity (*gymnos* signifies "naked"). Jewish participants could not participate naked without revealing the fact of circumcision, which Greeks considered an embarrassing form of mutilation. The only solution was to undergo a procedure to conceal that circumcision.[34]

Among both Jews and Gentiles, elites found these new ideologies attractive and tempting, encouraging lords and aristocrats of various kinds to adopt Greek styles. It was good to be a despot and still better to be a god-king. Jewish kings were not immune to these temptations, and that included the Hasmonean rulers who owed their power to the nationalist revolt against the Seleucids in the 160s. Ironically, by the end of the second century BCE, Hasmonean dynasts all adopted Greek royal names; it was an Aristoboulos who officially took the kingship in 104. Names as such were not necessarily ideological, and even faithful Jewish sages and rabbis might bear surprisingly Greek names (one famous scholar was Antigonus of Sokho). But the Hasmonean commitment ran still deeper. Archaeologists have recovered parts of the Hasmonean palace in Jerusalem, which was built according to the finest standards of contemporary Greek architecture. No less suited for the new Greek world was their winter palace near Jericho, with its very modern pools, baths, and gardens.[35]

But could faithful Jews acknowledge worldly rulers as gods on earth? If some Jewish elites envied and copied those styles, they were anathema to most religious believers, who denounced and parodied them in ways that echo through later scriptures. Over time, smoldering resentment developed into active political opposition and even (by the start of the Common Era) into militant religious nationalism. The more the Jews confronted what they saw as ruthless, blasphemous power, the grimmer and more threatening became their vision of cosmic warfare. Hellenistic theories of power in turn shaped Roman imperial ideologies, which are rejected so starkly in the New Testament and especially the book of Revelation. Jesus himself mocked the Gentile kings who loved to take such immodest titles as Benefactor (Luke 22:25). He also fielded thorny questions about how to handle coins that featured pagan images.

The anti-Greek reaction had its impact on concepts of the heavenly realms, as the large and very hierarchical Hellenistic courts contributed to emerging Jewish concepts of the ranks of angels serving and hymning God. But darker visions also prevailed. Some scholars see the evil fallen angels in 1 Enoch as veiled attacks on the Hellenistic rulers, with their divine claims and titles. This text, like many others from this period, might be a caricature of Hellenistic kings and magnates, the godling princes and proud courtiers whose supernatural counterparts likewise served an anti-God.[36]

BY THE START of the second century, Jewish society was drifting ever closer to absorption into the transcontinental Greek political and cultural realm, the *oikou mene*. In such circumstances, it hardly seemed possible for either people or religion to retain its traditional identity, and far from resisting such a synthesis, Jewish elites themselves were actively promoting it. The most intense debates, and the most violent confrontations, occurred not in far-flung Diaspora territories but in Jerusalem itself.

Chapter 3

ANTIOCH IN JERUSALEM

The Limits of the Law

In those days went there out of Israel wicked men, who persuaded many, saying, "Let us go and make a covenant with the heathen that are round about us: for since we departed from them we have had much sorrow."

1 MACCABEES 1:11, KJV

IN 175 BCE, the high priest Onias was succeeded by his brother, Jason, who won the office by means of a sizable gift to the king Antiochus IV. Jason offered to advance the cause of Hellenization, to bring his people over to the Greek way of life, *Hellenikon charaktera*. Before adopting his Greek name, "Jason" was originally Yeshua or Joshua, and he also proposed to rename his city in proper Greek form, as Antioch-in-Jerusalem. That would imply all the trappings of such a city, including a temple to serve as a center for the royal cult, while schools would offer Greek education, *paideia*. Jewish historians remember this as the height, literally the *acme*, of Hellenization. In 172 the high priesthood passed to one Menelaus (formerly Honi), who won the office by giving the king an even larger bribe. Although Menelaus was also a vigorous Hellenizer, Jason attacked him as insufficiently Greek oriented and not truly loyal to the king. Each faction accordingly escalated its cultural bids. Jason, incidentally, was the son of the long-reigning high priest Simon, whom we have already encountered (2 Macc. 4).

In retrospect, such extreme policies of Hellenization look like acts of profound betrayal. The book of 1 Maccabees even calls the Hellenizers "lawless men" who "joined with the Gentiles and sold themselves to do evil" (1:11–15). The word "lawless"—or, better, Law-less—was much used in these years to condemn the Hellenizers, suggesting as it did a rejection of God, Covenant, culture, and nation.

Today, that whole controversy is recalled, if at all, through the Hanukah story, as a struggle for Jewish identity and freedom against persecution and tyranny. At the time, the dividing lines were far less clear, and conflict on that scale was anything but inevitable. Far from being alien intruders, the Hellenizers were an authentic and well-established faction within Judaism, with a lengthy history dating back generations before the immediate crisis of Jason's time. They asked critical questions about the place of Jewish identity and belief in a complex world. As both modernizers and progressives, they spoke for educated city dwellers, while the nationalists found their following in the countryside. The resulting conflicts ushered in a century of chaos within the Jewish world. Over time, pro-Greek views would be so heavily defeated that their adherents were utterly discredited.[1]

THE RELIGIOUS REVOLUTION coincided with an era of acute political tensions and struggles within the Jewish nation. Our sources for that era are, however, slim and inconsistent, amazingly so in contrast with most periods of Jewish history. In stressing that relative silence, I am not merely making a professional complaint about the poor resources available to historians for a particular period; rather, I am drawing attention to a vital cultural transformation that occurred in Jewish cultural and religious life. The fact that our resources improve so enormously in the later third century indicates the rapid progress of several critical developments. Together, these developments contributed not just to creating bold new ideas but also to recording them and presenting them to a diverse public. This era marked a real watershed, and it was intimately connected to Hellenization.

Historians face real difficulties in approaching Jewish history in these years. Specifically, Jewish sources are virtually nonexistent for the years between roughly 310 and 260, which we know to have been a period of constant strife between the great Hellenistic empires, and these conflicts surely must have impinged on Palestinian realities. Certainly, some writings do survive for the larger period between 350 and 250, including several books now found in most Bibles—Chronicles and Proverbs as well as (possibly) Job and Jonah (see Table 1). What we are missing are sources that unquestionably tell us about the political and social conditions in Palestine at the time.

Just why those sources are so sparse demands explanation, and the problem is not just a matter of the chances of survival. If such sources ever existed, as at least some must have, they disappeared at a very early stage. Writing about 90 CE, historian Josephus struggled to say anything worthwhile about Jewish events in the long third century. His silence is all the more telling because his social standing would have given him excellent access to any materials that were available. The twelfth book of his *Jewish Antiquities* notionally covers the period from the death of Alexander the Great to the death of Judah the Maccabee, that is, from 323 through 160 BCE. About half of it, though, focuses on the very late years in that period, from the 180s onward. Even allowing for the fact that he was using legendary material or dubious documents, much of what he has to say about the third century concerns developments in Egypt or Asia Minor. The material on Palestine itself is painfully thin.[2]

Jewish religious sources present a similar picture. Anxious to claim continuity from Mosaic times, much later rabbinic authors described a learned tradition through the prophets and the Great Assembly (*Knesset HaGedolah*) that supposedly operated from the sixth century onward, and they credited to this assembly many vital decisions about Jewish law, liturgy, and biblical canon. Scant evidence exists for the historical existence of such an assembly. The real sequence of known scholars whose work is preserved dates only from the late third century, beginning with Simon the Just and his intriguingly Greek-named pupil Antigonus of Sokho. From Simon onward, we have an important series of legal decisions and wise sayings or apothegms, although we are less confident about the biographical details that later rabbis supplied for these venerated forefathers. Before 250 or so, then, sources are lacking, but matters changed fundamentally at the end of the century.

While the element of chance goes some way toward explaining the lack of documents (whether religious or secular) before 250, the volume of relevant material being produced in those years was almost certainly much more limited than in later eras. That lack of writing is all the more striking when compared with the phenomenal creativity that is evident from the end of the century (see especially the impressive list of dated works in Table 1). In order to explain this contrast, we need only look at the new forces coming into play in the later period that so stimulated cultural life but which had evidently played a smaller role in earlier times. Among those emerging themes, we can identify a vigorous tradition of competing schools and factions of religious thought, abundant opportunities for writing, diverse sources of patronage, and the greatly enhanced role of Diaspora communities. Through all these developments, moreover, we see the multifaceted role of Hellenization.

FROM THE LATER third century, when we begin to see more writing, thought, and debate, Jewish culture was characterized by what we might call creative fragmentation. Rabbinic tradition recalls this as the age of scholars and jurists who coexisted in learned duos or pairs, *zugot*, and a few of whose opinions were preserved in the Talmud. The proliferation of new theological currents spawned a range of schools of thought, some of which evolved into sects. Later rabbinic tradition plausibly dates the origins of the Pharisees and Sadducees to the start of the second century—indeed, to disputes among the pupils of Antigonus of Sokho. The Essenes emerged around the same time. Each movement explored its ideas through a variety of innovative forms and genres and presented its views in competition with its rivals. This suggests a real diversity not just of ideas but of centers producing and preserving writing. That in turn implies different kinds of patronage and support for intellectual endeavor beyond the older monopoly of the Temple and its elites.

Throughout these changes, too, Greek influences played a critical role. They supplied a massive incentive for work in that language, including new kinds of history and religious polemic. If you wanted to reach a wide and educated audience, you had to write in Greek. Even among the religious elite, the legal council dominated by the *zugot* was the Sanhedrin, which takes its name directly from the Greek original *synedrion*. At the same time, the ubiquitous Greek presence stirred a reaction and demanded intense debate about the proper limits of cultural accommodation. Jewish communities outside Palestine, especially in Egypt and Mesopotamia, were deeply involved in all these debates. One of the few later biblical books we can reliably attribute to a particular author is 2 Maccabees, which recounts the story of the Maccabean revolt. The book as we have it is an abridgement of a now lost multivolume work written by one Jason of Cyrene, in modern Libya; the authorship indicates its Diaspora context. For multiple reasons, then, the resulting era was incredibly fertile in producing pathbreaking scriptures, new religious insights, and also historical sources for political developments.

To understand the earlier, less fruitful, era, let us transform those later positives into negatives. Imagine a world without that spiritual ferment, without those rivalries, and without the same means of expressing ideas. Extending that contrast would lead us to expect a much more limited intellectual world between, say, 350 and 250 BCE, with fewer centers supporting the work of scholars and thinkers. At that time, there simply did not exist the kind of divisive movements and sects that we know from later years and presumably not the same kind of innovation and debate. Nor, in that earlier era, were external cultural pressures anything like as immediate or acute, whether the influences we are looking at were Persian or Hellenistic. Given the number of later works that critique imperial rule, albeit in coded guise, we must be struck by the lack of any such literature directed against the long era of Persian rule. In those earlier times, moreover, Diaspora communities were not as culturally active or vigorous. Fewer resentments and disputes existed to stir literary activity, and even then there were fewer opportunities to engage in such work.

Only in the midyears of the third century was a real change marked by the rise of the daring thinkers and activists who developed the explosive Enochian literature to be described in the next chapter. As we will see, some of that literature was highly critical of the Temple, implying that it must have originated from centers outside the older clerical world of Jerusalem. It was also suffused with diverse cultural influences, including strands from the Greek, Egyptian, and Babylonian worlds.

The hazards of arguing from silence are obvious enough, but in this case understanding the reasons for that historical obscurity points to momentous developments in cultural life from about 250 onward. Something very significant changed at that historical moment.

DESPITE THE GAPS in our knowledge, we can still say some things about Jewish history within the Greek imperial order. In terms of Palestine itself, Hellenistic rule differed substantially from the Persian precedent. For one thing, the new empires were physically much closer at hand, so that Palestine was much more directly affected by the doings in such great imperial cities as Antioch and Alexandria. In the latter days of the Seleucid Empire, its capital was very close by, at Antioch or even Damascus. Palestine was deeply and perilously involved in imperial rivalries, as factions within the Jewish polity defined themselves in terms of loyalty to one or another empire or dynasty.[3]

Third-century Palestine was part of the Ptolemaic Empire and was governed from the city of Ptolemais, the later Akko or Acre. But despite knowing so much about the dynasty and its Egyptian territories, we can say remarkably little about what was actually happening in Palestine in that era. Some evidence indicates a period of surprising peace and prosperity, barring sporadic raids from eastern nomads. When the Ptolemaic bureaucrat Zenon toured Palestine in 259–258 BCE, the record he left offers a picture of peace and order, with no reference to battles or civil unrest. The best literary monument of these Ptolemaic years is the book of Ecclesiastes, which depicts a stable and peaceful (if very unequal) society. All is futility, says the writer, even though he personally had gathered vast treasure, spent lavishly on building projects, accumulated legions of slaves, and acquired a harem (2:1–8). Although it survives in Hebrew, Ecclesiastes is richly laden with Greek concepts and philosophical terms, and it suggests the influence of Stoic, Epicurean, and rationalist perspectives. By the end of the third century, the Judean aristocracy moved from the countryside and the small towns to base itself in Jerusalem so as to participate fully in both the politics and the cosmopolitan cultural offerings of the growing metropolitan center.[4]

Ancient empires of necessity granted a lot of autonomy and recognized the power of local elites. That was not a question of enlightened liberalism, but rather a recognition of the weakness of effective government outside a regime's core areas. In the Jewish case, political power was and had been for many centuries—concentrated in the Temple and the high priesthood. Both institutions became strongly partisan and dynastic.[5]

The Jerusalem Temple was a place of special holiness, and the high priesthood was an enormously prestigious office, with strong theocratic and even messianic elements. Around 300, Hecataeus of Abdera described Jerusalem as a temple-state ruled firmly by a high priest who was "a messenger [*angelos*] of God's commandments." As such, the high priest expounded the commandments and "announce[d] what [was] ordained in assemblies." There was even a theory that the high-priestly office carried with it a kind of prophetic or charismatic status. Of later king and high priest John Hyrcanus (134–104 BCE), Josephus records that God had given him three great privileges, namely, "the government of his nation, the dignity of the high priesthood, and prophecy; for God was with him, and enabled him to know futurities." That power took material form in the legendary Urim and Thummim that formed part of the priest's regalia and were used to foretell the future through a kind of sacralized coin toss. Some theorists claimed that the Urim and Thummim responded to questions by producing tongues of supernatural fire.[6]

Contemporary writers lauded the high priesthood in terms that went far beyond the conventional praise of powerful benefactors. Around 190 BCE, Sirach extolled the office to an amazing extent, raising the tradition of Aaron, founder of the priesthood, even over that of his brother, Moses. The work ends with extravagant praise of the current incumbent, Simon the Just. According to this panegyric, Simon was not merely a member of the long sequence of Israel's glorious heroes and prophets, but almost their culmination and conclusion.[7]

In theory, the high priesthood and the Temple establishment should have proved a mighty bulwark for traditional values amid all the cultural change swirling from the mid-third century onward. Yet for all the priestly prestige, we also see signs of division, with recurring conflicts between the high priests and the *gerousia*, the aristocratic council, with its much intermarried local aristocrats and warlords. Those schisms were reflected in religious texts and scriptures, in which we trace a potent anti-Temple critique. Those internal divisions opened the way to accepting cultural innovations pressing in from the outside world.[8]

For much of the biblical period, the First Temple had enjoyed special sanctity among writers who exalted it and gave it a special role in their visions of God's actions on earth, present and future. That is a common trait among religious traditions throughout the world. As religions become literate and hierarchical, great ritual sites become centers of scholarship and learning, where priests and scribes write ever more ambitious hymns to the role and function of their mighty temples and the cities in which they stand. The city becomes a microcosm of the universe; as time goes on, the city itself is seen as the center of the universe or a metaphor for the whole of Creation. Jerusalem was the sacred space in which human history would be performed. When fifth-century reformers restored the Temple, they hoped that the restored structure would inherit that older sanctity. Our major source for the restored institution is the highly partisan books of Ezra and Nehemiah, which present a story of the triumph of rigid monotheism. The Temple is restored, and so are the people of Israel, once they have been forced to renounce their foreign wives and families. They all lived piously ever after.[9]

But referring to the "Second Temple" can give a false sense of unbroken continuity, as the new institution never regained the awe that had been attached to the predecessor built by Solomon. However splendid the structure, and despite the pageantry associated with its priests, the new Temple enjoyed far less prestige and evident sanctity than the first. It was multiply tainted, both by its association with successive Gentile rulers and with a rapacious and often unpopular high priestly caste. Around 200 BCE, a pseudoprophecy recorded in the book of Tobit promised the return from Babylonian Exile and the restoration of the Temple, implying that the current Temple was grossly lacking. Even so, this new institution would "not be like the former one, until the times of the age are completed" (14:5).[10]

As the story of Ezra's ethnic and sexual cleansing suggests, the new Temple elite tried to enforce much greater orthodoxy and homogeneity than had previously existed, but Jerusalem's leaders enjoyed very mixed success. Issues of assimilation proved contentious and durable. In fact, between the fifth and the third centuries BCE, a series of literary works expressed views on segregation and intermarriage quite antithetical to those of the priestly rigorists. This includes such biblical works as Jonah, Ruth, Tobit, and Esther, all of which offer favorable accounts of neighboring peoples, while Ruth and Esther both praise mixed marriages. The Song of Solomon idealizes sexual love between an Israelite and a foreign woman. Each text, in its way, was guaranteed to offend, and each would have had a special appeal for assimilationist enemies of the tradition of Ezra and Nehemiah.[11]

Meanwhile, the priestly class itself was riven by bitter conflicts. Splits were partly a matter of class and prestige, with lesser orders or families pitted against the elite. Those exalted clerics claimed the title of Zadokite, the descendants of Zadok, who had served as high priest under King David himself, and increasingly, they also boasted of their inheritance from Aaron. The Babylonian Exile destabilized older assumptions, allowing once inferior groups to gain confidence and independence. By the third and second centuries, some factions were openly rejecting the Temple and its hierarchy, urging a thorough purging and reformation. When postbiblical religious writings addressed the Temple, as they often did, it was in a different and more critical context than in earlier centuries. Yet even when they rejected the earthly Temple, as did some sectarians, it was because the Temple that did exist fell so badly short of the desired purity and perfection.[12] The restored Temple divided as much as it united.

ALTHOUGH JOSEPHUS KNEW little about third-century conditions, he does sketch the history of the great families who dominated Palestine in this era. His major source is a novelistic family saga that is anything but an objective history and is usually called the Tobiad Romance. (It probably dates from the 170s BCE.) Through these stories, we see how family and clan loyalties shaped political divisions, which were intimately linked to issues of patronage and to access to the imperial court. Ultimately, too, they were conditioned by dynastic rivalries, which reached a new plateau in the mid-third century.[13]

Josephus discusses the interplay of two key aristocratic families, whose stories highlight the influence of the Ptolemaic and Seleucid dynasties on Palestinian elites. One clan, the Oniads, exercised total control of the high priesthood. One Onias held office

between about 320 and 280, and thereafter, we trace a sequence of
Oniads through the next century, as son followed father or brother
succeeded brother. The Simon who is so extravagantly praised in
Sirach was one of their line (see Table 3.1). Their rivals were the
Tobiads, who formed the subject of the romance. That family traced
its ancestry to a Tobiah/Tobias who was already an enemy of the
emerging Second Temple establishment as far back as the time of
Nehemiah, in the late fifth century. That particular Tobiah was thoroughly intermarried with the other great families of the time and
boasted a daunting network of aristocratic friends and oath-bound
followers. By the mid-third century, another Tobias was a great feu-
dal lord with estates across the Jordan (and whom the bureaucrat
Zenon met on his visit). At his fortress of Ammanitis, Tobias commanded an army of mixed Jewish and Greek soldiers.[14]

Josephus records some episodes in domestic political history,
although problems of chronology mean that we must read his words
with some caution. He describes an incident in the 240s, when the
high priest Onias II withheld twenty talents in taxes due to the king,
Ptolemy the Benefactor. Josephus tells the story as if it resulted
from Onias's simpleminded meanness. In the context of the time,
however, such nonpayment was an overt act of rebellion, which
local elites undertook at the risk of their heads. Such a gambit would
make sense only if Onias was plotting a defection from the Ptolemaic Empire to the Seleucids, perhaps during a period of war or
diplomatic crisis.

Ptolemaic forces prepared to invade and threatened to dispos-
sess the Jews altogether. The crisis resulted in a shift of power to
Tobias, who was married to Onias's sister, and their son Joseph now
claimed the high priesthood. Joseph undertook a diplomatic mission
to Ptolemy, where he made an excellent impression and was given
the position of tax farmer or collector. Such a collector contracted
to deliver a particular sum to the government, but he kept what he
could extract over and above that sum, making it a vastly profitable venture. So ruthless were his exactions that the Ptolemaic court

TABLE 3.1. HIGH PRIESTS, 320–37 BCE

Onias I, ca. 320–280
Simon I, son of Onias, ca. 280–260
Eleazar, son of Onias, ca. 260–245
Manasseh, ca. 245–240
Onias II, son of Simon, ca. 240–218
Simon II, son of Onias, 218–185
Onias III, son of Simon, 185–175, murdered 170
Jason, son of Simon, 175–172
Menelaus, 172–162
[Onias IV, son of Onias III, fled to Egypt]
Alcimus, 162–159
[No known high priest—possibly name or names lost, 159–153]
Jonathan Apphus, 153–143
Simon Thassi, 142–134
John Hyrcanus I, 134–104
Aristoboulus I, 104–103
Alexander Jannaeus, 103–76
John Hyrcanus II, 76–66
Aristoboulus II, 66–63
John Hyrcanus II (again), 63–40
Antigonus, 40–37

openly joked that he had stripped his province to the bone. The empire also entrusted his family with devolved military powers.[15]

Joseph now became *prostates*, effectively the Jewish liaison in dealings with the Ptolemaic regime and a secular counterpart to the high priesthood. He cultivated excellent relations with the imperial family and operated as much in Alexandria as in Palestine. Around 240 Ptolemy III himself might have visited Jerusalem and offered sacrifice in the Temple, a glorious example of the biblical theme of Gentile rulers acknowledging the God of Israel. For twenty years, Joseph the Tobiad combined the sophistication of a courtier with his role as a border baron. He was as much at home in Greek language and culture as in the Jewish world or indeed the border societies of the East. (Reflecting the habits of the Greco-Egyptian court, he married his own niece, in flat violation of Jewish codes.) Like any dynast, Joseph sought to pass on his power to his heirs, and his son Hyrcanus inherited his military command on the eastern shores of the Jordan.[16]

Joseph's descendants were central to the conflicts over Hellenization in second-century Judea. With Greek influence so strong in Jerusalem, we cannot speak of a simple schism between pro- and anti-Hellenizers. However, the Tobiads were normally the party opposed to the Temple establishment and also most sympathetic to sweeping Hellenization. As we will see, the Tobiads were probably the sponsors or patrons of the book of Tobit, which spoke disparagingly of the existing Temple.

Even the name Hyrcanus is suggestive in this context, as the term "Hyrcania" normally refers to a region on the Caspian Sea, with its Iranian peoples. Possibly the Tobiad name reflects a different derivation, but it might well represent some kind of otherwise unknown family linkage by this cosmopolitan house. As we have seen, foreign peoples like the Scythians were also present in Palestine itself. Whatever its origin, the name "Hyrcanus" would reappear in the Jewish context, including in the Hasmonean dynasty. A son of the historian Josephus bore the name Flavius Hyrcanus.

THE APPARENT HISTORY of internal tranquillity ended at the close of the third century, when foreign invasion was accompanied by fratricidal civil war. Seleucid emperor Antiochus III warred against Ptolemy IV Philopator and his successors. Antiochus invaded Palestine in 219 and won repeated victories until he was defeated at Raphia. In 200 Antiochus III in turn defeated the Egyptians at Panias, decisively winning Palestine for the Seleucid Empire.[17]

When territory shifted hands following the victory of one or another empire, each empire rewarded its partisans and proxies and severely punished those who had betrayed or abandoned it. Mass executions were a likely prospect for those who chose the wrong side. Hyrcanus the Tobiad was faithfully pro-Ptolemaic, but the high priests and most of his family were pro-Seleucid. The political crisis was disastrous for the Tobiads, as the elders and other members of the elite families turned against Hyrcanus and made war on him. The resulting struggle deeply divided what Josephus calls "the people" or "the multitude," but a majority sided with the elders against Hyrcanus, as did his kinsman Simon, the high priest. This was a rare instance of popular politics being drawn into the elite world of family factions and dynastic feuds. Hyrcanus fled to his mighty fortress on the Arabian border, his so-called Tyre, which we know as the spectacular Hellenistic palace site of Qasr al-'Abd, in modern Jordan. (Accounts of Hyrcanus's vast building activities make him sound as prodigious as that other later Transjordanian Herod the Great.) From this base, he remained in "perpetual war" with the local peoples. He remained there for seven years, until the accession of a new Seleucid ruler, Antiochus IV, in 175, which drove him to suicide.[18]

Other tremors shook the high priesthood through the 170s. A different official named Simon, the Temple captain, alerted Seleucid authorities to the presence of treasures in the Temple, including money deposited by Hyrcanus (2 Macc. 3:11). This was a sizable sum, four hundred talents of silver and two hundred of gold—a signal demonstration of just how profitable a couple of generations of tax farming could be. In 178 Seleucus IV duly attempted to seize the precious goods, provoking yet another conflict between priestly factions and an open battle for the high priesthood. The tale is convoluted, but it demands some discussion because both the events and the characters will appear later in this story. Moreover, it is an excellent example of the kind of constant backstabbing and conflict that wracked Palestine during this period.

On one side was the Simon who had been responsible for inviting royal forces to appropriate the treasures and who plotted against high priest Onias III. (Reputedly, the agents of this Simon advanced their cause by assassination.) Both parties now appealed to the Seleucid court to vindicate their claim. Onias was succeeded as high priest by his brother, Jason, and he in turn was followed by Menelaus, brother of the conspirator Simon. Menelaus had the support of the Tobiads in their long-running feud with the Oniad Temple elite. Between them, Jason and Menelaus now engaged in the dueling Hellenisms that we witnessed at the start of this chapter. Jason built a gymnasium, and the Jewish elite went further than ever before in adopting Greek clothes and fashions. Priests neglected their services in order to become spectators at contests in wrestling and discus throwing. Jason's enthusiasm for things Greek seemed to know no bounds, and when the king held games at Tyre, the high priest sent money for sacrifices to Herakles (2 Macc. 4). Although his effort was thwarted, that would have meant a Jewish high priest directly, and unthinkably, sponsoring sacrifices to pagan gods.[19]

The family vendetta escalated when Onias exposed Menelaus's theft of some Temple treasures, and in 170 Menelaus provoked his murder. Hearing a false rumor that the king Antiochus IV had died, Jason the Oniad hurriedly gathered a thousand men and launched an unsuccessful coup in Jerusalem, forcing Menelaus to take refuge with the Seleucid garrison. Antiochus saw such a blow against his authority and prestige as a deadly insult, if not a direct revolt against Seleucid rule. This was the detonator that led the king to attack Jerusalem himself.

THE LATE THIRD and early second centuries were marked by endemic turbulence and civil war. Even times of notional peace were marked by factional feuds, conspiracies, and murders, and high-priestly office played a pivotal role in all of them. Analogies with the Renaissance era, the age of papal Rome and the Borgias, are tempting. As the second century progressed, moreover, wars escalated into open revolution against the Seleucids. So extreme and persistent was the violence in this era that it must make us question the apparent stability we think we see in earlier times. We have no record of such domestic feuds in the early third century, but does that mean they were not occurring? Were the earlier decades in fact so tranquil? We know that Alexander's various "successors" were rampaging through the Near East in the first quarter of the third century, while the Ptolemies and Seleucids were at war from 274 to 271, 260 to 253, and again from 246 to 241. Periods of warfare, in fact, were almost as frequent as those of peace, and it seems curious that they are so absent from the Jewish historical record. If fuller records were available for, say, the era 300–250, we might know more examples of border warlords like Hyrcanus, battling against or alongside successive high priests. We should be alert to the possibility of earlier crises and struggles that have simply dropped from the historical record.[20]

I have already mentioned several texts that shed some light on divisions and concerns in the post-250 era, including Sirach and Tobit. Other texts derive from this era, but their exact historical context is open to debate. One of the most cryptic, and influential, Old Testament texts is the final six chapters of the prophetic book of Zechariah, a section that is commonly labeled Deutero-(Second) Zechariah.

First Zechariah was a landmark text, but its later counterpart was arguably even more significant. First Zechariah belonged to the end of the sixth century BCE, and it was a kind of protoapocalyptic text, so it is not surprising that a later author would choose to expand on those elements. Virtually all scholars agree that this second portion was indeed written later, but there is wide disagreement about what the exact time interval might be. That question matters so much because Deutero-Zechariah exercised such an enormous influence on later religious thought. The story, which to us reads very cryptically, tells of a holy man who adopts the role of a false prophet, a wicked shepherd, who serves as a kind of provocateur. Ultimately, his misdeeds lead to his violent death. That in turn forces the people to realize their sinful state, and this initiates an apocalypse, in which Jerusalem is at the heart of a cosmic war against invading nations.[21]

Most surprising for modern readers are what look like numerous Christian references, or foretastes. Within a very short space, we find perhaps a half-dozen lines that would be quoted or referenced in the gospel accounts of Jesus's final days. One verse describes a messianic king entering the city mounted on an ass; another speaks of selling a person for thirty pieces of silver. Still other phrases are quoted or included in the Christian Passion narrative, namely, "They will look on one they have pierced" and "Strike the shepherd, and the sheep shall be scattered." Zechariah's closing verse even imagines a Temple in which there are no traders, suggesting Jesus's expulsion of the money changers. That is a potent list. Taken together, Deutero-Zechariah looks like a Passion Play in miniature. At the very least, the authors of the gospels were drawing heavily from this text in forming their view of Jesus and his messianic role. Conceivably, Jesus himself was deliberately modeling his actions upon these passages.[22]

Deutero-Zechariah must date from some point between 500 BCE and 170 BCE, but a more exact dating is difficult because so much of the text is hopelessly obscure to modern eyes. We cannot with any confidence say which kings, prophets, or priests are symbolically represented in the story of the wicked shepherd. The most likely context falls within the long third century, at either the start or the end of that period and referencing the imperial wars in the region. References to *Yavan*, Greece, point to a time when Israel was abundantly aware of Greek power and influence (Zech. 9:13). Apparent prophetic citations to Egypt and Assyria work well as metaphors for the Ptolemaic and Seleucid Empires rather than as literal characterizations of those historic states.[23]

If we are looking for a tumultuous period of intense crisis that fits the general description, the best candidate would be the years between about 205 and 175. Foreign invasion coincided with a multisided civil war in which the high priesthood was deeply implicated. Throughout, the wars involved the two empires of "Egypt and

Assyria" as well as "the Greeks." Intriguingly, the Zechariah narrative prominently mentions the stronghold of Tyre, which was a famous Mediterranean city—but it was also the name that Hyrcanus had given to his desert fastness.

THIS EXTRAORDINARILY SIGNIFICANT text likely emerged as a direct response to this specific era in Jewish history, from 205 to 175. If that dating is correct, then this pioneering manifesto of apocalyptic and messianic ideas grew directly out of these specific historical and political events. Not for the first time, apocalyptic crisis generated apocalyptic literature. And the first half of the second century would be profligate in creating visions of the End Times.

Chapter 4

ENOCH THE PROPHET

Startling New Scriptures Remap
the Spiritual Universe

———————

The words of the blessing of Enoch, wherewith he blessed
the elect and righteous, who will be living in the Day of Tribulation, when all the wicked and godless are to be removed.
And he took up his parable and said—Enoch a righteous man,
whose eyes were opened by God, saw the vision of the Holy
One in the heavens, which the angels showed me, and from
them I heard everything, and from them I understood as I saw,
but not for this generation, but for a remote one which is for
to come.

1 ENOCH 1:1–3

FOR SOME SEVENTEEN hundred years, the Ethiopian church has
included in its Old Testament canon the book of the prophet
Enoch, which dates from the heart of the Crucible era. Little in
that text offends readers' sensibilities, as so much of it fits perfectly
into the Christian tradition, not least the searing vision of Judgment
Day with which the work opens. The book depicts mighty archangels and angels, such old friends of ours as Gabriel and Michael,
alongside their diabolical counterparts. Enoch ranges through glorious heavens and burning hells. That is, we may think, precisely
what might be expected of ancient religious writings, whether from
Judaism, Christianity, or Islam. Surely, Enoch is no more than standard religious fare.[1]

In fact, this book (now properly described as 1 Enoch) was anything but conventional or familiar in its time, the late third and early second centuries BCE, and it represented a breathtaking departure from the Old Testament worldview. With its focus on eschatology and heavenly visions, its angels and devils, the book powerfully prefigures so many later texts, including the New Testament itself, as well as a broad sweep of apocryphal writings. Beyond foreshadowing them, 1 Enoch actually shapes many of those later works, and without the Enochic writings, early Christianity would have been unthinkable. More striking than any single statement in the Enochic corpus is the lack of suggestion that this was anything terribly new or surprising in its time.

Such texts did not spring into existence from a vacuum. However brilliant these works' insights, their ideas would never have achieved the impact they did unless there was already an audience willing to hear them. As I have remarked, the Jewish world in these years was passing through a cultural revolution, marked by an influx of troubling new influences and new questions from the transcontinental Hellenistic realm. Meanwhile, thinkers had an unprecedented range of opportunities to present and develop their responses to these pressing challenges, at centers both within Palestine and beyond. Although 1 Enoch is by far the most significant monument to the new world of spiritual inquiry, this transformation was also reflected in several works that were more or less closely related to it. These included the now lost book of Noah that is partly preserved in the Enochic text, as well as the book of the Giants, the book of Jubilees, and more conventional biblical books like Tobit and Sirach. Although they varied greatly in their interests and emphases, these books drew on a common treasury of images and beliefs and shared a similar cast of supernatural characters. Each in its way was concerned with the quest for authentic wisdom, and they all indicated tempting new avenues of spiritual inquiry.

Taken together, this literature reveals the multiple debates and tensions that were growing within the Jewish world, as we witness the revolution in progress. It is in these texts that we most clearly find the key issues and ideas that would divide Jewish factions and parties up to the fall of the Second Temple in 70 CE and drive the vicious struggles among Pharisees, Sadducees, and Essenes. Beyond that, the texts supplied the materials for interminable debates between Jews and Christians. These remarkable scriptures proclaimed the agendas for religious controversy for centuries to come.[2]

ENOCH'S SCRIPTURES HAVE passed through phases of extreme popularity and near-total oblivion. Once hugely influential, 1 Enoch was forgotten for centuries until its rediscovery in modern times. As they rediscovered the work, scholars have become ever more conscious of its significance.

Enoch himself is mentioned briefly, cryptically, in Genesis, where his main achievement is disappearing to be with God, seemingly without dying. As the text tells us, "Enoch walked with God and then he was gone, for God took him," potentially giving him a role as an intermediary between human and divine worlds (5:22–29). As the word for God is *ha-elohim*, that vestige of a plural concept of deity, later writers were encouraged to place him in the company of angels and semidivine beings. Moreover, Enoch's age of 365 years opened the way to astronomical and astrological speculations. Already in the third century BCE, Enoch was regarded as an exemplar of wisdom and science; in the second, he was cited as the discoverer of astrology. A great many books were credited to him, several of which have come to light only in our own time.[3]

In the early Christian church, Enoch was a highly regarded prophet, and the New Testament Epistle of Jude cites 1 Enoch as scripture. Over time, though, both Christians and Jews rejected the work, which largely vanished from the West. Still, it remained fully canonical in Ethiopia, and in 1773 a Scottish traveler brought the Ethiopian text back to Europe. When it was translated, scholars recognized the book's influence on early Christianity. Later archaeologists recovered other portions of the work from Egypt.[4]

A new breakthrough occurred in the 1970s, when scholars studied Aramaic fragments of 1 Enoch found among the Dead Sea Scrolls. Paleography—handwriting evidence—showed that parts of the surviving text dated back to perhaps 200 BCE, suggesting that portions of Enoch were much older than had been assumed. Some, it now appeared, predated the great outpouring of apocryphal and apocalyptic literature in the second and first centuries BCE and were in fact a major influence on it. Over the past forty years, Enoch Studies has come to occupy a central role in scholarship on Second Temple Judaism, Christian origins, and apocalyptic and messianic thought as well as rabbinic history and Islamic origins. Scholars now speak of Enochic Judaism, and today the term "Enochic" is commonplace in the academic literature of all these fields.[5]

THE BOOK OF 1 Enoch is a substantial work, running to some thirty-eight thousand words in English translation (for comparison, the gospel of Matthew is about twenty-three thousand). It is anything but a tightly connected narrative. In fact, it is not so much a self-contained book as an anthology or compendium of writings that were authored at various times and places and originally circulated separately. Those sections are usually identified as follows:

> **The Book of the Watchers—chapters 1–36:** the fall of the angels and their seduction of humanity, the Flood, and predictions of the messianic age; Enoch's vision of the world and of the underworld where the fallen angels are consigned

> **The Parables (or Similitudes) of Enoch—chapters 37–71:** visions of the blessed and of judgment; the Messiah and the Son of Man

> **The Astronomical Book—chapters 72–82:** visions of the cosmos; astronomy and astrology—the sun, the moon, and the wind

The Book of Dream Visions—chapters 83–90: a history of the world up to the coming of the Messiah, told in the form of prophetic predictions granted to Enoch

The Epistle of Enoch—chapters 91–108: more prophecies and exhortations; the fate of the righteous and sinners in the End Times

These divisions have an arbitrary quality, and it is not difficult to find in one section discussions of a topic that is described at greater length in another portion. Also, other now freestanding works like the book of the Giants historically had some kind of relationship to this literature, but for whatever reasons of conviction or convenience, they were not included in the final compendium. For present purposes, let us accept this five-part division, which gives us "Enoch's Pentateuch."[6]

It would be invaluable if we could say for certain that 1 Enoch was written and collected at a particular moment in history, in one decade or even one century. There is no such consensus on this point, however. After long controversy, scholars now place different segments at the very early end of the range of proposed dates, largely the period before 150 BCE.

Dating works that use symbolic names or figures to comment on present-day events is difficult and subjective. Sometimes the references are fairly explicit, but often they are not, and scholars vary widely as to which particular king or priest might be the subject of an apocalyptic or pseudoprophetic text. One much-discussed section of 1 Enoch is the Animal Apocalypse in chapters 83–90, which uses ornate visions of the struggles of various animals and birds in order to tell a symbolic story of real events. In theory, it should be possible to decode any and all of the veiled references to specific conflicts of Ptolemaic and Seleucid rulers and their Jewish allies, but none of the explanations offered so far is wholly satisfying.[7]

With those caveats, some portions of the work can be dated with fair confidence. One valuable piece of evidence is the library of Qumran, the Dead Sea Scrolls, which mainly date from between 200 BCE and 70 CE. The Qumran community held the Enochic writings in high regard. Fragments of four of the book's five sections were found among the Scrolls, and these portions belonged to no fewer than eleven separate manuscripts, not counting materials from the book of the Giants. That means that most of 1 Enoch was certainly written before the first century CE and likely in or before the second century BCE. Its original tongue was Aramaic or possibly Hebrew. The oldest work in the collection is the Book of the Watchers, which took its current form by the end of the third century BCE. Not much later is the Astronomical Book, which should be dated before 200.[8]

The exception is the lengthy Parables, and in this instance, the issue of dating has a significance that goes far beyond technical scholarly debates. In fact, finding an exact date raises significant questions about Christian origins. Reading the Parables, we find so much that sounds akin to early Christianity, with substantial passages about Hell, the Messiah, and even the resurrection of the dead. But the fact that the section was not found at Qumran has led some scholars to date it very late, perhaps from the start of the Common Era. If in fact the Parables were written so late, then the work reflected the common currencies of only that era, with potential borrowings from early Jewish Christianity. But if it is significantly older, then potentially explosive conclusions can be drawn about the work's influence on that same early Christianity. Over the past forty years, opinions about dating the Parables have fluctuated, but recent scholars have tended to agree on an early date. This decision has been made through interpreting what seem to be contemporary allusions to political events, as well as the total absence of any material specifically referencing Jesus or early Christianity. The modern consensus overwhelmingly assigns the Parables to the earlier era, the second or first centuries BCE. If that is correct, it revolutionizes our understanding of the origins of the various trends of the Crucible years and of Christianity itself.[9]

The book of 1 Enoch, then, is the oldest monument to the new concepts of the spiritual universe. It drew a new road map of the heavens, and it largely did so between about 250 and 100 BCE.

WHY WOULD SUCH innovative writings appear at this particular time? We can at least offer plausible speculation. The whole oeuvre fits very well into the pattern of cultural and theological change that I outlined in the first chapter. We might imagine one or more farsighted Jewish thinkers working in the late third century, perhaps in the time of Joseph the Tobiad. They observed the evils and injustices of the world, which were acute in this era, but they did not know how these issues might be reconciled with their understanding of divine justice and goodness. Living in an age of intense cultural encounters and rapid social change, they knew that the greatest power and wealth belonged to regimes that were not just pagan but brutal and exploitative. After a full century, moreover, Greek power was no passing phenomenon. What did that say about the Hebrew God? Must Jews too resort to the solutions of their Greek neighbors and rulers? Should they erect statues of Tyche (Fortune) and ascribe all unexplained boons and curses to this capricious goddess? Were the Greeks alone able to interpret the heavens and their influence on human actions?

But the Jewish tradition had its own resources to answer such questions. In an age when Babylonian and Egyptian scholars were advancing their respective claims to be the oldest civilization, Jewish writers could cite their own records of the pre-Flood world and its sages and patriarchs. They also had their own fast-evolving theories to account for natural and human evil in a world ruled by one absolute God. As we have seen, these issues were touched on in several post-Exilic works, although the ideas introduced there were not fully developed or integrated into a larger whole. The transition to mono-theism involved a proliferation of intermediary subdivine beings and also raised the prospect of a Day of Judgment that would condemn an evil world. Angelic revelations appeared in First Zechariah, while Joel imagined something like the Day of Judgment. Job, meanwhile, addressed concerns about God's ultimate justice. Those themes and concerns together—theodicy, eschatology, and a belief in angelic beings—already constitute many of the key elements of the Enochic writings, at least in embryo. Other trends of the previous two centuries supplied the means by which such ideas could be explored and published, namely, through writing pseudoancient texts containing truths theoretically revealed by angels. Like many societies facing extreme stress, these writers constructed a mythology to account for their situation and to offer hope for survival and ultimate victory.

I will discuss the angelic dimensions in a later chapter, but here let me stress some of the book's other innovations, namely, in eschatology, the understanding of the End Times.

THE BOOK OF 1 Enoch is centrally concerned with judgment and the Last Day and opens with a scene from the Day of Tribulation. The first chapter continues with a description of the earth being rent asunder, the mountains shaking, and a universal judgment of good and evil. God would intervene to save the righteous: "And behold! He cometh with ten thousands of His holy ones to execute judgment upon all, and to destroy all the ungodly."[10]

Apart from speaking generally of judgment, 1 Enoch pioneers new visions of apocalyptic. In the Epistle, Enoch warns Methuselah and his family of events in the far future. In successive ages ("weeks"), he says, the world would become ever more sinful and violent, as pagan nations exalted themselves. But that would only serve as a prelude to a divine intervention that would sweep away the evil world:

And all the idols of the heathen shall be abandoned,
And the temples burned with fire,
And they shall remove them from the whole earth,
And they [that is, the heathen] shall be cast into the judgment of fire,
And shall perish in wrath and in grievous judgment for ever.[11]

Although there are echoes of earlier works like First Zechariah, this section is in fact the first surviving apocalypse in Jewish literature. The words feel so familiar because they have supplied the matrix for a whole genre that would produce countless examples over the coming centuries. Like so many later writers, Enoch promised a time when "all the works of the godless shall vanish from all the earth, and the world shall be written down for destruction. . . . There shall be the great eternal judgment, in which He will execute vengeance amongst the angels. And the first heaven shall depart and pass away, and a new heaven shall appear."[12] The New Testament book of Revelation famously offers the vision of "a new heaven and a new earth."

Judgment has eternal consequences, and portraits of the afterlife are another core theme of 1 Enoch. Hellfire, in fact, was now invented. The Book of the Watchers envisions a fiery place of ultimate torment to which evil angels are consigned for transgressing the divine will. Enoch sees "a great fire there which burnt and blazed, and the place was cleft as far as the abyss, being full of great descending columns of fire: neither its extent or magnitude could I see, nor could I conjecture." The archangel Uriel explains, "This place is the prison of the angels, and here they will be imprisoned for ever."[13]

But this fiery place, this first draft of Hell, is by no means intended for angels alone, as human sinners are likewise confined and tormented until the Day of Judgment. This dreadful place was "made for sinners when they die and are buried in the earth and judgment has not been executed on them in their lifetime. Here their spirits shall be set apart in this great pain till the great day of judgment and punishment and torment of those who curse for ever, and retribution for their spirits. There He shall bind them for ever. . . . Such has been made for the spirits of men who were not righteous but sinners, who were complete in transgression, and of the transgressors."[14]

Adding to the foretastes of Christian medieval art, it is the angels who lead the damned to their fate. Hellish visions became more common, and more detailed, in the (later) Parables. These sections tell how "the kings and the mighty" are cast into the deep valley of burning fire. Not only would the hosts of Azazel be cast into the furnace, but we are told the individual names of the angels who would undertake the task, namely, Michael, Gabriel, Raphael, and Phanuel.[15]

Beyond its vision of the afterlife, 1 Enoch offers the virtuous the promise of resurrection in terms of the restoration or revival of individuals. It is in these sections particularly that we find so many foretastes of later religious creeds. In words that perfectly foreshadow later Christian ideas, the Parables prophesy that "in those days shall the earth also give back that which has been entrusted to it, and Sheol also shall give back that which it has received, and Hell shall give back that which it owes." The same passage continues to link these events to the arising of a messianic "Elect One," who shall "choose the righteous and holy from among them, for the day has drawn nigh that they should be saved."[16]

ENOCH'S BOOK TELLS both of the end of the world and of its beginnings. Beyond portraying the End Times, some of the work's best-known sections describe the creation of the world and its sinful condition. Tracing the roots of that particular story helps us understand the book's origins and how Enochian themes spread through multiple related works. Those works—1 Enoch, Noah, Giants, and Jubilees—were anything but uniform in their approach, and opinions expressed in one might flatly contradict others. In their general approaches, though, and in their shared mythological framework, they offer a detailed picture of the new spiritual universe that was emerging in the century or so after 250 BCE. The appearance of multiple writings shows that an audience existed for such themes as the origin of evil, the nature and power of the heavenly host, the role of demonic forces in creating human civilization, and the continuing power of those forces in the material world. The world was a battleground of competing spiritual forces, good and evil, which were personified and named.

The core story involves the account of the Watchers in chapters 6–11, which hugely expands upon a strange passage in the sixth chapter of the biblical book of Genesis. (That text comes just a few verses after the description of Enoch.) According to Genesis, "The sons of God saw the daughters of men that they were fair; and they took them wives of all which they chose." The phrase *bene elohim* is here translated as "sons of God," but it might originally have been "sons of the gods." Breeding with human women, these supernatural beings begot giant offspring called the Nephilim, whom Genesis depicts as ancient heroes of the bygone past. Enoch's account is much more extensive and more sinister in its implications. According to Enoch, the evil angels give humanity all forms of knowledge, science and wisdom, the skills of earthly life, as well as astrology and magic:

And Azazel taught men to make swords, and knives, and shields, and breastplates, and made known to them the metals [of the earth] and the art of working them, and bracelets, and ornaments, and the use of antimony, and the beautifying of the eyelids, and all kinds of costly stones, and all coloring tinctures. . . . Semjaza taught enchantments, and root-cuttings, Armaros the resolving of enchantments, Baraquijal taught astrology, Kokabel the constellations, Ezeqeel the knowledge of the clouds, Araqiel the signs of the earth, Shamsiel the signs of the sun, and Sariel the course of the moon.

We hear of the potent demons Azazel and Shemihaza, while four good archangels intervene with God to protest that evil has come into the world. God responds with a worldwide Flood to destroy the Nephilim, and the evil angels are imprisoned and punished.[17]

If the Book of the Watchers cannot be later than 200 BCE, then any source materials it uses must be earlier. That includes the now lost book of Noah, which is the source of all the material relating to the Watchers and the spread of evil on earth as well as the subsequent Flood. That motif appealed to the Enochic writers or editors because the Flood was an ideal prototype or foretaste for the coming Judgment, which was so central to their vision. The book of Noah told the story of the generations beginning with Enoch and following through his descendants Methuselah, Lamech, and Noah, making Noah the great-grandson of Enoch himself. That Noah book, that "pre-Enoch," appeared in the mid- or late third century.[18]

Another text from the same era was the book of the Giants, which circulated widely in various versions through the Middle Ages but does not survive in complete form. The fact that Aramaic fragments were found at Qumran proves that this was an ancient and once popular work. The book of the Giants should, logically, have been integrated into the anthology of 1 Enoch. It looks like a lost sixth book of that (now) five-book collection.

The book of the Giants tells the standard Enochian story of the descent of the angels and the birth of the giants, but elaborates further and provides new details. In the version found at Qumran, the giants have dream visions of the coming Flood, and much of the work concerns dreams and their interpretation. The action involves writing tablets that are lost and recovered, including works by Enoch himself. Surely, the work must originally have concluded with the Flood and a titanic battle between the giants' leader and the archangel Raphael. It was an apocryphal enhancement of an already apocryphal work.[19]

The book of the Giants illustrates one powerful theme from this era, namely, the enormous expansion of existing lore through popular storytelling, scholarly exegesis, and imaginative speculation. Not only were writers developing stories, but they were doing so in florid form, creating whole new mythologies packed with abundant names and titles. This point emerges strongly in the Dead Sea Scrolls, where a single line or name might point to whole cycles of tales that are lost forever. Some authors were inventing the names of demons and giants afresh, while others were taking those names and adding their own contributions to the expanding mythos. They even appropriated names from other mythologies: the book of the Giants includes the name of the Akkadian epic hero Gilgamesh. Once that process of invention and appropriation began, it rapidly spread and expanded.[20]

ELEMENTS OF THE Enochic origin stories influenced another long-lost work to which we will often return in these pages. This is the book of Jubilees, also known as Little Genesis or the book of Divisions, which purports to reveal the message delivered to Moses by the Angel of the Presence. The text takes its name from the "Jubilee" units of forty-nine years into which the story is divided. Much like the Enochic writings, the book of Jubilees was once very influential for Jews and early Christians. Over time, Jews suppressed it within their own writings, and Christians largely lost contact with it, except in Ethiopia (the story of loss and rediscovery is itself reminiscent of 1 Enoch). Its full significance only came to light with the discovery of multiple copies among the Dead Sea Scrolls, indicating its profound importance for the Qumran sect. Among other things, these ancient manuscripts demonstrated just how faithfully the Ethiopian church had translated and preserved the Hebrew originals, which is encouraging for what it suggests about the accuracy of their translation of the original 1 Enoch.[21]

Jubilees is an extended commentary, or midrash, on the book of Genesis and the opening of Exodus, and, as commonly occurs when later writers develop a canonical story, they added a lot of frills and ornamentation. Although only a small part of the story concerns Enochic themes, the text draws on the Book of the Watchers and the Epistle, and it has much in common with the Book of Dream Visions. It also quotes extensively from the book of Noah. Jubilees lauds Enoch as a critical character in the divine plan and a vital transmitter of divine wisdom, especially through the medium of writing. He was

> the first among men that are born on earth who learnt writing and knowledge and wisdom and who wrote down the signs of heaven according to the order of their months in a book, that men might know the seasons of the years according to the order of their separate months. . . . And what was, and what will be, he saw in a vision of his sleep, as it will happen to the children of men throughout their generations until the day of judgment; he saw and understood everything, and wrote his testimony, and placed the testimony on earth for all the children of men and for their generations.[22]

As to its date of composition, the work's concern with circumcision and Sabbath observance indicates a relationship with the Maccabean era of the 160s BCE. Jubilees thus offers more evidence of the continuing interest in Enochian matters throughout the second century.

THE ARRAY OF interests and obsessions we find in the Enochian texts would often resurface in Jewish literature over the coming centuries. In the third-century context, though, these ideas were surprising, even shocking. Were these fantastic speculations really so popular in a world we otherwise know mainly through the mundane factional feuds of the Tobiad and Oniad clans? If so, we are missing a very large portion of the cultural life of that infuriatingly opaque period. If only the visiting Ptolemaic bureaucrat Zenon had taken the time to chat with his hosts about their religious ideas in the 250s. How shocked he might have been at the new ideas coming into existence, and how much stronger would be our sense of Jewish religious history at this pivotal moment.

Perhaps something can be deduced about the assumptions of that age. Although they are in no sense Enochic writings, two other writings from the very start of the second century BCE—Tobit and Sirach—tell us something about the interests of at least a part of the reading public in this age.

The first of those works tells the story of the noble and pious Tobit, supposedly in the eighth century BCE, and his heroic son Tobias. Based on both the names and the period, scholars have suggested that the work was composed under the patronage of the Tobiads, either Joseph or Hyrcanus, to honor men they claimed as ancestors. The book of Tobit is a romance that tells of two individuals under deadly threat. Tobit has been blinded, and Sarah, who lives in a distant land, is accursed by a demon, Asmodeus. Every time Sarah marries, the demon murders the bridegroom on the wedding night, with seven fatalities to date. This naturally concerns Tobias, as he journeys to become her next betrothed. He is, however, escorted by an angel disguised in human form, namely, the archangel Raphael, who defeats Asmodeus by means of a noxious fishy potion. Tobias and Sarah live happily ever after.[23]

Tobit is a wonderful story, not to mention funny, but historically it shows concerns highly reminiscent of those of Noah and the Watchers: the demonic threat on earth, and the role of guardian angels, strong and memorable characters who are given personal identifying names. Also recalling the Watchers, the demon Asmodeus is sexually interested in the human woman, Sarah. Another theme running through Tobit is that of wisdom, the importance of finding sound counsel by which to order one's life, and wisdom is likewise a primary concern of the Enochic writings. Readers who appreciated that story would have welcomed Noah and Enoch after it. Tobit was popular reading at the angel- and demon-obsessed settlement of Qumran.[24]

Also from these years is Sirach, which is above all a wisdom text and is in fact the most comprehensive example of its kind. The author, Ben Sira, writes at length about good conduct, sobriety, and sexual behavior. But he also praises God's work by means of a catalog of the heavenly bodies and their functions, sharing some of Enoch's characteristic interests. In one passage, Ben Sira warns readers against seeking to understanding matters beyond their grasp or indeed beyond all human understanding (3:21–24). Such wild speculations had often led men astray in the past and would do so again. Although there is no specific Enochic reference, such warnings would apply neatly to the vertiginous cosmic themes of that work. Perhaps Ben Sira was warning his pupils against the dangers of being carried away by the ideas that were in circulation in these years.[25]

OVER AND ABOVE any specific teaching, 1 Enoch carries broader lessons about the religious world of its time, with its emphasis on learning spiritual truths through writing and literary speculation. The Enochic writings are dominated throughout by visions of sacred books and heavenly writings, a vital new theme from this era that would so permeate the thought of the Abrahamic religions.

In this vision, truth came from scripture rather than direct charismatic or prophetic inspiration. Prophets are prophets only insofar as they faithfully transmit that wisdom inscribed above. To modern eyes, Enoch himself acts like a prophet, but the text actually calls him a "scribe of righteousness" or a "scribe of truth," and that exalted rank gave him special status in conveying divine truths. (Later Jewish tradition recalled him as the Great Scribe, *Safra Rabba*.) Throughout the Enochic writings, truths are passed on through writing, through books and tablets that might be heavenly as well as earthly. At the conclusion of the Astronomical Book, Uriel instructs the sage, "'Observe, Enoch, these heavenly tablets, and read what is written thereon, and mark every individual fact.' And I observed the heavenly tablets, and read everything which was written [thereon] and understood everything, and read the book of all the deeds of mankind, and of all the children of flesh that shall be upon the earth to the remotest generations."[26]

Enoch is so pivotal a figure because he transmits the true wisdom, which is in written form. He does so by taking truths from what is written on heavenly tablets, as disclosed to him by angelic intermediaries, and presenting those truths to humanity in the form of his own writings (92:3). He scrupulously transmits this information to his grandson Methuselah, writing down everything so that it might be carefully preserved: "So preserve, my son [*sic*] Methuselah, the books from thy father's hand, and [see] that thou deliver them to the generations of the world." Elsewhere, Enoch speaks "'according to that which appeared to me in the heavenly vision, and which I have known through the word of the holy angels, and have learnt from the heavenly tablets.' And Enoch began to recount from the books." That message of "Read and ye shall find" is what his disciples are meant to obey in later generations. Books and writings are a fundamental component of wisdom, which is here so often extolled.[27]

Jubilees, likewise, often mentions the discovery of mysterious writings and the truths they contain. In one example of many, Noah's grandson Kainam "found a writing which former [generations] had carved on the rock, and he read what was thereon, and he transcribed it and sinned owing to it; for it contained the teaching of the Watchers in accordance with which they used to observe the omens of the sun and moon and stars in all the signs of heaven." The ordinances to be followed by Israel, such as the round of feasts and holy days, are not merely written down in earthly scriptures, but "engraved and ordained on the heavenly tablets." Those tablets reflect a primitive and eternal reality that predates Moses's Covenant at Sinai and therefore takes precedence over it. As with any secular court or palace, decisions are meaningless until and unless they are inscribed in the official record and duly proclaimed.[28]

This vision of heavenly writings points to a common and vital theme in Second Temple thought, namely, the projection of earthly realities into a cosmic dimension. In a relativistic age when so many forms of authority were in flux, thinkers sought to establish absolute certainty by referring to such ideal heavenly originals. The Jerusalem Temple, for example, was a copy and image of God's Temple in heaven; the wisdom that human beings sought on earth was a shadow of the true supernatural Wisdom. Earthly writings thus had to reflect and restate heavenly writings. That idea would have a long afterlife in rabbinic Judaism, in the belief that the Torah known throughout Jewish history reflected a reality inscribed in Heaven, a Torah that existed before Creation. Jewish scholars long debated that concept. While some great thinkers rejected it—such as Maimonides in the twelfth century CE—the idea often reemerged in religious discourse. Meanwhile, the resort to heavenly texts also provided a solution to such lively political questions as the identity of true Jews and what was authentic faith and practice. Regardless of how contested the worldly debates over these questions were, participants knew that heavenly books preserved the names of the true faithful, the saints and the saved, which would be revealed on the last day.

Yet alongside such affirmations of the supremacy of the written word, a sketch of one of the evil angels offers a curious subversion of that whole trend. A section in the Parables tells us of Penemue, who "taught the children of men the bitter and the sweet, and he taught them all the secrets of their wisdom. And he instructed mankind in writing with ink and paper, and thereby many sinned from eternity to eternity and until this day. For men were not created for such a purpose, to give confirmation to their good faith with pen and ink" (69:8–11). That is anything but a ringing endorsement of writing or of the veneration of scriptures as such. What such a passage does convey is the fact that the use of writing in religion was under serious debate at this time, in a way it had never been in the era of the Old Testament proper. Such a passage only makes sense if some people were treating written materials as an authoritative source of spiritual truth, while others were advocating more traditional means, including charismatic experience.

1 ENOCH WAS a product of the cultural crisis of the third century—or, in the context of the time, a crisis of competing versions of wisdom. Multiple forms of wisdom were available, and it was crucially important to select the one that was truthful and godly: these were matters of eternal life and death. The theme of true and false knowledge runs throughout 1 Enoch, especially the Book of the Watchers. The angels granted humanity the many skills on which civilization was founded, but such treasures came at an enormous price. That story recalls the myth of the Garden of Eden, where humanity acquired the knowledge of good and evil, without which humans could not live in the everyday world, and as in Eden women play a critical part in the transition. Azazel is responsible not just for the technologies of war but also for the jewelry and cosmetics that give women their seductive powers. Worldly wisdom could be lethal or demonic. (For debates about Wisdom in this era, see Chapter 9 below.)

Great opportunities existed in a globalized age alongside powerful temptations. New forms of science, learning, and cosmic knowledge were pouring into the Jewish world, but all were associated with foreign cultures and traditions. Those new imports included the very idea of philosophy, the "love of wisdom." While the Enochic texts reflected developments within Judaism, they also mirrored the cosmopolitan world of the time, suggesting the vast repertoire of images and ideas that were available in these years. So abundant are these influences that it is rarely easy to tell whether the Enochic writers were drawing on sources that were Greek, Babylonian, or Egyptian.

The Enochic writings must first be read in their Hellenistic context. If in fact Noah dates from the late third century and parts of 1 Enoch not long afterward, then both belong to the Ptolemaic period. But classifying them as "Ptolemaic" also reminds us of the enduring Hellenistic (and indeed Egyptian) context and leads us to seek Enochian origins outside the familiar limits of Jewish thought, beyond Jerusalem and its Temple. Nothing in Noah (or Enoch) necessarily implies that it was written in response to any particular conflict or event. None of the demonic figures, such as Azazel and Shemihaza, need be read as a coded reference to any particular king or individual, any single Ptolemy or Antiochus or Seleucus. Still, we might legitimately understand the emphasis on the forces of evil as indicating real tensions at the time of writing.

Such conflicts help us understand the otherwise baffling Astronomical Book. At first glance, these chapters are utterly lacking in the scientific sophistication or observational precision that might be expected from the age of Hipparchus or his Babylonian counterparts. As astronomy or science, the Astronomical Book fails totally. Seen in the context of the time, though, it contributes to one of the bitterest intellectual controversies of the day, as different scientific establishments competed to determine the exact length of the year and the relative virtues of the solar and lunar calendars. Should the year be counted as 360 days, 364, or 365? Babylonians and Greeks had their views on the matter, while the Egyptians staked out an advanced position in the Canopus Decree of 238 BCE, with a year calculated quite accurately to 365 ¼ days. And even if that issue was resolved, how should these years be counted? In modern times, we appreciate the sensitivity of dating events by the Christian calendar, with terms such as "BC" and "AD." In the ancient world, calendrical issues were intimately linked to political claims, as the Seleucid dynasty had successfully persuaded much of the known world to count years by its own distinctive dynastic chronology, the Year of the Greeks. Instead of a space race, the Near East was locked in a Time Race, in which scientific achievements redounded to the glory of far-flung empires. In this ongoing contest, the Astronomical Book was the Jewish entrant. However symbolic or imperfect the science, the Enochian writings declared that these questions could be resolved only through the power and wisdom of the one true God, as revealed definitively through his messengers (1 Enoch 72ff). It is the godly angel Uriel ("God's Light") who gives Enoch the cosmological secrets that make up such a large portion of the Astronomical Book.[29]

Those competing Egyptian and Babylonian views remind us how far the Hellenistic cultural world was from being entirely Greek and how many multiple streams flowed through it. That transnational quality is also suggested by the central Enochic emphasis on ideas of judgment and the afterlife, which were so new to Jewish thought, and details such as the opening of heavenly books. The Persians were obvious candidates as a source for such ideas, and we know that Greek interest in the afterlife was surging in these years, as indicated by the widespread flourishing of mystery cults. The most significant protagonists, though, were the Egyptians. The Jewish people had been in close contact with Egyptian culture for centuries, and such interactions were all the easier under Ptolemaic rule. A vast number of surviving Egyptian writings indicate intense interest in personal immortality, in the fate of individuals after death, and in the stages of testing and judgment through which they would pass. Those texts depict gods sitting on thrones to pass judgment upon the soul that came before them, and they describe the concept of measuring sins and virtues in a balance. Postmortem trial scenes commonly use the idea of a judge or scribe opening the heavenly books in which these matters are recorded. That motif contributed to the idea of heavenly books or tablets that was already, separately, becoming so commonplace in Jewish spiritual writing. The prophet Daniel describes the heavenly court of the Ancient of Days, at the moment when "the books were opened." Later, an angel reveals "what is written in the Book of Truth" (10:21). In the Christian book of Revelation, God opens the Book of Life in order to judge everyone who has ever lived in order to assign their eternal rewards and punishments.[30]

ENOCH'S WORLD OWED even more to Mesopotamia, especially the ancient city of Babylon. Although Jewish links here were already strong, they were refreshed and invigorated when the Seleucid

Empire opened cultural channels between Mesopotamia and the Mediterranean world, including Palestine. Gaining access to such Babylonian wisdom meant tapping into ideas that were already ancient before the time of Enoch's book, indeed dating back to the earliest manifestations of human civilization. We have no idea where the various sections of 1 Enoch were written or collected, but the work was not necessarily done in Palestine, and a Mesopotamian location is quite conceivable.

Mesopotamia had a turbulent history marked by frequent invasions and dynastic changes, but successive civilizations retained scholarly and historical traditions dating back to the ancient Sumerian world of the third millennium. Among these were lists of kings, including those who had supposedly lived even before the ancient Flood, which was so central a part of Mesopotamian thought. (The biblical story of Noah finds its prototype in the Babylonian legend of Utnapishtim, who likewise survived a global inundation.) Whether those kings had any actual historical substance is not relevant here, but one notable ruler was Enmeduranki (or Enmenduranna), who has long been recognized as a model or prototype for Enoch. Enmeduranki was associated with divination and traveled to the heavens to read the mystic tablets of the gods. Like the Enoch recorded in Genesis, he thus walked with God, or the gods. The seventh and tenth names on this king list correspond to Enoch and Noah, who were, respectively, the seventh and tenth generations of the human race. That Mesopotamian link also accords well with the Enochic focus on astronomy and astrology. Enmeduranki was king of Sippar, a city dedicated to the sun, which supplies a context for Enoch's use of the solar calendar. Like Hipparchus himself, 1 Enoch teaches not just astronomy but specifically Babylonian astronomy.[31]

Even the genre of apocalyptic looked back to Mesopotamian precedent. The whole notion of a spiritual figure being carried to the heavens and receiving revelations is characteristically Mesopotamian. Older cultures in that region had written extensively about dream visions and also used retroactive prophecy as a framework for presenting history and interpreting current events. "Predicting the past" was not a Jewish innovation. Jewish apocalyptic pronouncements are "mantic" in form, using a format derived from the well-known Mesopotamian world of diviners, seers, and dream interpreters.[32]

Other Eastern cultures offer parallels to the Watchers, the fallen angels. Sumerian mythology had taught the existence of a group of deities called the Annunaki, and that idea carried on through subsequent civilizations in the area. These were the old gods, associated with the powers of the earth, fertility, and the underworld, and they were reckoned as inferior to the great gods, the Igigi. Many mythological tales feature the Annunaki, who often foreshadow Enochic portraits of fallen angels. In the tale of Gilgamesh, they are the judges of Hell. Another creation legend tells how the Annunaki raised a splendid city, in a passage that recalls the biblical tale of the building of the Tower of Babel. Some tantalizing hints of Enochic lore are preserved in the work of the second century BCE historian called Pseudo-Eupolemus. He is the source for the assertion that giants who had survived the Flood, Enoch's Nephilim, were responsible for building the Tower of Babel. That offers another close parallel to the Annunaki.[33]

The fact of living in a Greek-dominated global culture determined the particular stories and myths recounted in the Noah literature and in 1 Enoch afterward. From ancient times, Israel's prophets had spoken chiefly to their own people, however much they tried to incorporate the stories of neighboring nations, such as the Assyrians and Persians. Third-century writers were far more conscious of a universal dimension and the need to tell stories that applied to all humanity. Tales of Abraham or Moses were specific to the Jewish people, but by definition Noah was the ancestor of the whole of humankind. By biblical accounting, everyone alive in 200 BCE was descended from the survivors who had sailed in his Ark. Noah's story could thus be presented to Egyptians, Greeks, Indians, or Babylonians as an origin story applicable to their own culture. Enoch, equally, dated from that pre-Flood era, before the granting of a covenant to a particular race or people. Eupolemus helpfully tells his readers that Enoch was identical with the Greek hero Atlas.[34] A bold universalism shaped Jewish writings over the coming centuries, as writers so often turned to pre-Flood mythologies.

THIS RETURN TO primeval antiquity was inextricably bound up with the religious politics of the day. Although the exact alignments are obscure, the Enochic writings stemmed from a tradition that was deeply critical of many conventional Jewish assumptions and seems to have favored universalism over ethnic particularism. Those writings show just how fluid were the boundaries of Jewish thought in that era and illuminate the critical issues driving the formation of sects and new religious movements. The literary heritage suggests the diverse religious paths that might have been taken, depending on how political events developed. It also supplies tantalizing evidence as to which groups might actually have created the Enochic writings.

If 1 Enoch stood as an isolated literary monument, we might attribute it to an idiosyncratic genius creating his own mythical universe. Yet, as we have seen, the book's ideas were commonplace in the culture of the time. In fact, scholars have identified a whole alternate strand of Enochic Judaism that can be traced from its appearance in the century after 250 BCE and running at least up to the fall of the Temple and into early Christianity. This was a current of ideas, if not a fully defined movement or denomination, and it continued to produce other scriptures over a period of some centuries. Distinguishing marks of this tradition included an emphasis on the story of the Watchers and fallen angels as the source of sin and evil, the focus on the End of Days and the final Judgment, and a general interest in angelic lore and the afterlife. All those ideas are still found in the book of 2 Enoch, which was composed two or three centuries after the major portions of its better-known predecessor. That surely points to a continuing tradition.[35]

But if Enochic thought has common strands, it is no less marked by some truly surprising omissions, which include the institution of the Law, the Torah. A casual reader might conclude that 1 Enoch derived from a religious system that venerated Enoch as its primary prophet and inspiration rather than Moses. Nothing in the book relates to circumcision, the Sabbath, or dietary laws. (The Law of Moses is similarly absent from 2 Enoch.) Even the accounts of Judgment and Last Things draw little distinction between the fates of Jews and Gentiles or seem to recognize such categories. God's appearance on Mount Sinai features in the book's opening section, but that is in the context of the coming day of Judgment, rather than the Mosaic Covenant. That Covenant is not foretold in the book's apocalyptic sections, with their histories of Israel. Strictly speaking, we might not expect such references to events and people from long after Enoch's supposed time before the Flood. At his supposed time of writing, after all, neither Covenant nor Torah existed, nor were there even Jews or Gentiles. Yet it would have been an easy matter to have the prophet make retroactive predictions of future events and individuals, as was standard practice in pseudoscriptures of this sort. It is almost as if the authors deliberately ignored the larger trends in Hebrew religion over the previous three centuries, the whole Deuteronomistic movement and its central emphasis on the Sinai Covenant.[36]

Nor did 1 Enoch preach a high regard for the Temple. In the Book of Dream Visions, when the Jews returned from the Babylonian exile, they "reared up that tower [the Temple] and they began again to place a table before the tower, but all the bread on it was polluted and not pure." Related to that was a profound dispute with the Temple authorities over the correct calendar to be used in determining the correct dates for religious feasts and events. The author of Enoch favored the solar calendar, with a 364-day solar year, a scheme also advocated in Jubilees and followed by the Qumran community. The Temple followed instead a lunar tradition. By definition, then, the Temple's sacrifices must always be off schedule and, by their nature, improper and unworthy. Calendar-based debates proved deeply divisive throughout the Second Temple period.[37]

These views about the official religion of the Temple fit with other evidence about the factions and conflicts of the time. We have already seen the emergence of a new religious world from the fifth century onward in which the Temple was the subject of vigorous controversy. Besides stressing the Temple and its cult, the established priestly elite adhered strongly to ideas of the Covenant and Law. Alongside this school of thought, other rival critical attitudes to the faith can be traced in the third and second centuries BCE. One emphasized wisdom rather than the formal cult; from the Latin word for "Wisdom," this is termed "Sapiential." The Enochic tradition draws on this latter approach, but it stands much more sharply in opposition to the mainstream and to the Temple. Other critics were more rigorous in their attitudes to the Law, but still looked askance at the existing Temple.[38]

Some scholars have proposed the existence of a defined and distinct school of Enochic Judaism quite at odds with the official religion associated with the Temple elite, and, conceivably, this movement even rejected the Law. But such a view would be going beyond the evidence, and it is notoriously difficult to derive "sects from texts." The absence of particular themes of Law and the Covenant does not mean that the work's authors or compilers thought they were wrong or insignificant, and conceivably he, or they, simply felt that ideas like circumcision were too obvious to be mentioned. We might also relate the omissions to the book's universal aspirations and the desire to speak to a wider world instead of just to Jews, whether in Palestine or the Diaspora. But even if that is so, it is in marked contrast to many later writings, where such themes are so clearly placed in the foreground. Even a book directed at Gentiles might be expected to state more explicitly the special role of the Jewish people and their covenants.[39]

What we can legitimately say about the Enochic writings, therefore, is that they suggest an active critique of the Temple, but they do not overtly attack or reject the Law as such. The attitude to the Law is one of omission rather than commission, in other words. That distinction is important in approaching the theories that have been proposed to contextualize the writings and to associate them with known historical movements.

Scholars have long recognized a linkage between the Enochian literature and the distinctive ideas of the Essene sect and after them of the Qumran settlement. The economical explanation is that the Essenes (or a group very like them) produced the Enochic literature from the late third century onward, and the Dead Sea community, the *yahad*, then spun off from that Essene mainstream. Such a lineage would explain why that library was so rich in Enochic writings. Nor would it be surprising to find the Qumran believers fixated on such core Enochic themes as the End of Days, the hierarchies of angels, and the solar calendar. The Qumran community also rejected the Temple and its worship, at least as it was presently constituted. Essene origins are controversial, but some scholars believe that the group actually originated in Mesopotamia itself before migrating to Palestine. If that view is correct, and it is a minority opinion, it would explain the strongly Mesopotamian elements within Enoch.[40]

Before speaking of an "Enochic/Essene" continuity, though, a serious objection must be resolved. Enochic writings seemingly ignored the Law and Covenant, but in stark night-and-day contrast, the Essenes had a rigid and expansive view of these matters, to the point of executing anyone who blasphemed the name of Moses. No less dedicated to the Law was the Qumran sect. Those believers preached a still more rigorous new covenant, grounded in the seeming failure of Israel to fulfill its Mosaic obligations. The group's writings had little use for Gentiles, who were dangerous outsiders threatening ritual purity. Universalism in any sense was absolutely not on their agenda.[41]

Surely, we might think, a movement or sect could not really move from rejecting Law and Covenant to making those ideas a core and indispensable component of its belief system. Yet this paradox can be resolved if we look at other texts that neglect to mention overtly doctrines that they actually held quite fiercely. Specifically, we might look at the book of Jubilees.

In many ways, Jubilees relates to the Enochic tradition and draws on the book of Noah. At the same time, it is militantly legalistic, stressing the significance of Law and Covenant just as flatly and conspicuously as 1 Enoch ignores them. So much of the work assumes a rigorous and even rigid adherence to the Law, to the point of denying salvation to the uncircumcised. Circumcision was what separated the "children of the covenant" from "the children of destruction," who were "destined to be destroyed and slain from the earth." Gentiles were damned without hope. The work thus deploys the Enochic mythology, but it applies it to diametrically opposed ideological conclusions. At first, that seems like a glaring contradiction.[42]

Despite all its materials about Moses, Jubilees also has oddly little to say about the Sinai Covenant. The author can do this not because he undervalues the Law, but rather because he magnifies it so mightily and literally praises it to Heaven. In Jubilees God's choice of Israel occurred at the Creation, on the first Sabbath on which God rested. All subsequent accounts of covenants between God and Israel proclaimed on earth just reasserted that primal event, which was recorded on heavenly tablets. "This Law is for all the generations for ever . . . for it is an eternal ordinance, ordained and written on the heavenly tablets." Jubilees also cites Moses as a primary conduit for heavenly authority. Hebrew was the language of Creation, and all the feasts and ceremonies were decreed and warranted by eternal tablets written in Heaven. Indeed, Adam was the first in the successive line of priests. In Jubilees, then, the lack of attention to events like the Sinai Covenant does not mean that the author did not believe them, but rather that he contextualized them in a much vaster metahistorical reality—the Covenant predated Sinai.[43]

Whatever the intentions of the original Enochic writers, a similar approach might explain why strong legalists found their approach so congenial. Very probably, Enochic ideas were formulated in opposition to the Temple and its ideologies, or at least the Temple as it was constituted at the time rather than its idealized state. Under the extreme stress of the cultural and political crisis of the mid-second century, some groups brought those themes much closer to the orthodoxy of Law and Covenant. Such an interpretation would explain why those general themes came to be associated with the stringent views of Covenant that we find in Jubilees. Groups like the Qumran sect read Enoch enthusiastically for the themes in it that they approved of and ignored the mysterious absences. They likely resolved the problem by reading their own distinctive views into the text.

Some kind of historical sequence must unite the three major strands of Enoch—Essenes—Qumran, though the details are anything but clear.

SUCH A PROPOSED history is hypothetical, and at every stage it involves logical leaps of varying degrees of probability. But we can say confidently that the Enochic tradition did exist and that it reflected enormous changes coming to prominence within Jewish thought during the century or so after 250 BCE. Whether we are looking at religious themes as fundamental as the beginning of the world and its end, the nature of heaven and hell, or the understanding of good and evil, all these ideas first found clear expression in the Enochian writings. Soon they would become mainstream and commonplace. That transformation was made possible by the collapse of the old political order amid the furor of nationalist religious revolution.

Chapter 5

TYRANTS FOLLOW TYRANTS

A Century of National Agony

——————

And in the latter time of their kingdom, when the transgressors are come to the full, a king of fierce countenance, and understanding dark sentences, shall stand up. And his power shall be mighty, but not by his own power: and he shall destroy wonderfully, and shall prosper, and practise, and shall destroy the mighty and the holy people. And through his policy also he shall cause craft to prosper in his hand; and he shall magnify himself in his heart, and by peace shall destroy many: he shall also stand up against the Prince of Princes; but he shall be broken without hand.

DANIEL 8:23–25, KJV

THE REVOLUTION IN religious belief was a direct outcome of war and insurrection—not just the extraordinarily bloody events of the Maccabean revolt of the 160s, but also the cumulative violence of the following decades, when Jews fought each other. As we will see in the next two chapters, chaos and internecine conflict sprawled over more than a century, and that political agony had its direct impact on religious thought. These revolutions and wars provide the essential context for understanding the spread of radical new ideas and above all the Enochic visions of cosmic conflict and the struggle against supernatural evil.

To borrow a phrase from the famous story of Daniel, the whole Jewish nation now "fell down bound into the midst of the burning fiery furnace" (3:23). Like the young Hebrews who were the victims of that attempted execution, that nation also miraculously survived, albeit in a radically transformed way. They passed through the crucible.

THE FALL OF empires is usually followed by a chaotic period in which ambitious leaders and states struggle for a place in a new political order. The second century BCE was such a time of withdrawal and near collapse for the old Hellenistic powers that had dominated the Middle East, leaving a power vacuum.

The last great Seleucid ruler was the conqueror Antiochus III (241–187 BCE). Unfortunately for him, he faced a new rising power in the West in the form of Rome, which in a desperate series of wars had recently defeated its North African rival, Carthage. By 200 BCE, the Romans were deeply interested in affairs in Greece and Asia Minor, partly through natural aggressiveness, but also because they feared the rise of another enemy as fearsome as Carthage. (Rome's deadly Carthaginian enemy Hannibal actually took refuge at Antiochus's court.) The Romans resoundingly defeated Antiochus, culminating in the pivotal battle of Magnesia (190). In the ensuing peace treaty, the Romans imposed strict limitations on Seleucid military power. The Roman victory partly resulted from the tight organization and shrewd leadership of that rising state, but it also reflected an ongoing revolution in military affairs. Disciplined and flexible Roman legions easily defeated the unwieldy phalanxes of massed spearmen that had formed the mainstay of Greek military power for centuries. Magnesia was no chance victory, and it showed that the Romans were likely to win most conflicts with Eastern empires.[1]

The Romans expelled the Seleucids from western Asia Minor. They also imposed a vast war indemnity of fifteen thousand talents of silver, a fact that would have far-reaching consequences for later Jewish history. Severely weakened, Antiochus III struggled both to pay the indemnity and to reassert family prestige. Both strategies demanded finding easy and profitable wars to win, which was increasingly difficult in a Roman-dominated world. That was the situation inherited by his son Antiochus IV. The younger Antiochus won great victories in Egypt, coming close to annexing the whole land, but his attempt at a second campaign in 168 gave him a potent object lesson in the new realities of power. An elderly Roman ambassador confronted Antiochus IV and demanded his immediate withdrawal, or else he would face a new war with Rome. Nor did the ambassador even offer a diplomatic face-saving solution. Rather, he chose a crude assertion of Roman power, as he drew a circle in the sand around the god king and ordered him to make his decision before he stepped beyond it. Antiochus capitulated.[2]

That imperial weakness supplies the essential background to the Maccabean revolt. Josephus reports that different factions were hungry for power, and "those that were of dignity could not endure to be subject to their equals." We have traced the bloody series of coups and plots as the Oniads tried to regain power from the high priest Menelaus, who was supported by the Tobiads. Both sides tried to appeal to the Seleucid imperial court by presenting themselves as the purest exponent of Hellenism, until Jason finally used his private army to launch a coup in Jerusalem. Antiochus IV was returning from his latest humiliation at the hands of the Romans when he heard about this grab for power, which he viewed as yet another blow against his own authority and prestige. He stormed the city, raided the Temple, and suspended the sacrificial cult. Reputedly, he did so with the consent of Menelaus, who thereby earned the reputation of a national traitor. The king welcomed the opportunity to seize the Temple treasures, a predictable move in his desperate efforts to pay the Roman indemnity, and he grabbed a lucrative eighteen hundred talents. Meanwhile, the legitimate Oniad heir, Onias IV, fled to the protection of Ptolemy VI, and while in Egypt he built a facsimile of the Jerusalem Temple. After dabbling in numerous coups and conspiracies, Jason finally died in exile in the Greece he idolized, at Sparta.[3]

Antiochus IV did not wantonly decide to persecute or eliminate Judaism, out of either insanity or misplaced religious zeal; any such religiously motivated intervention would have been bizarre in the context of the age. Rather, he was imposing a specific punishment for insurrectionary actions. After facing repeated struggles and riots, his campaign moved to eliminate the distinctive traces of the Jewish religion and rededicated the Jerusalem Temple to Zeus Olympios (with the Samaritan Temple at Gerizim dedicated to Zeus Xenios, Friend of Strangers). Initially, the king won some successes. Gentile inhabitants had no difficulty sacrificing to particular deities, and many Jews agreed "to build altars and sacred precincts and shrines for idols, to sacrifice swine and unclean animals, and to leave their sons uncircumcised. They were to make themselves abominable by everything unclean and profane" (1 Macc. 1:47). Conceivably, they read the new Temple dedication as not to Zeus as an extraneous foreign deity, but rather to a syncretic form of YHWH, a new form of the old God. But others protested. Leading the fundamentalist reaction was Mattathias, a Jewish priest who attacked a Greek official who ordered the sacrifice to pagan gods. Mattathias had five sons, most famously Judah, whom the Christian Middle Ages remembered as Judas Maccabeus, the warlord leader of the ensuing revolt. Encouraging the Jewish dissidents were accounts of the Seleucid defeats in Asia Minor and of Roman strength. Rebellious subjects transformed the king's title, Epiphanes, "God Made Manifest," into Epimanes, "the Lunatic."[4]

WHAT FOLLOWED WAS in large measure a civil war among Jews, in which one faction invited Antiochus IV to come to its aid. The war pitted the militant traditionalists against Hellenized Jews, the "lawless and godless men" of the patriotic accounts (1 Macc. 7:5). Guerrilla forces attacked loyalist villages, forcibly circumcised boys, and destroyed pagan altars. Throughout the wars, the Seleucids could usually count on the support of at least some Jewish factions, whom surviving records denounce as simple traitors motivated by the cynical lust for gain. Menelaus retained the high priesthood, theoretically, until 162 BCE, when the Seleucids may have executed him for his role in sparking the rebellion. His successor was Alcimus, a descendant of Aaron, who was mortally opposed to the Maccabees. (He died in the Temple in 159, allegedly while undertaking the symbolically potent act of tearing down the wall that separated the court of the Gentiles from that of the Israelites.) Jewish Hellenists still appeared as a faction through the 140s. Besides these internal Jewish conflicts, Jewish rebels were at war with the Gentile inhabitants of the land as much as against royal forces. The war devastated the country, with frequent acts of massacre and ethnic cleansing.[5]

Despite these complexities, partisan texts like 1 Maccabees depict the struggle in heroic and religious terms, as a straightforward campaign of Jews against Gentile oppressors. Maccabean leaders regularly cited biblical precedent for their holy warfare, harking back to such ancient figures as Moses and Phinehas, the ancient hero lauded for his violent vigilantism against those who betrayed the Law (1 Macc. 2:54). Early in the insurrection, the brothers allied with the Hasideans, described as mighty warriors devoted to the Law and possibly the ancestors of the more famous later sects (see 1 Macc. 2:42–48, 7:5–25). That religious interpretation focused on the purging and restoration of the Jerusalem Temple in 164, which is celebrated in the feast of Hanukah. (The story of the lamps miraculously burning is found only centuries later, in Talmudic sources.) Reading such accounts, we have to recall the agendas of the writers and their patrons. Commonly, those patrons were Hasmonean princes and lords, descendants of the Maccabean founders, and they were often themselves locked in political and sometimes military battle with ultrareligious dissidents. It greatly behooved later writers to write the history of the revolt in pious terms, to show that those Maccabee ancestors had indeed been fighting a holy war rather than merely seizing power in a putsch.[6]

IN POPULAR MEMORY, the Hanukah legend distorts the nature of the Maccabean rising and its time span. The Temple's cleansing seems like such a perfect conclusion to the story that surely, modern readers might think, it must have marked a final victory in a decisive war of liberation. Actually, the process of winning national independence was a prolonged affair, with wars and crises enduring for a full generation. Far from ending his life as a lionized national liberator, Judah the Maccabee perished in a crushing defeat in 160. Peace of a kind followed shortly, as Seleucid leaders offered acceptable terms that ended religious intervention. Two of Judah's brothers succeeded him, Jonathan Apphus and Simon Thassi, whose campaigns merged into wider power struggles within the larger empire. Both men also perished violently, and the book of 1 Maccabees takes its story up to Simon's assassination in 134.

That chronology raises the question of just how the rebels could have succeeded against such a vast empire, particularly when Jews were themselves so bitterly divided. Fortunately, the Seleucids themselves faced severe problems that prevented them from focusing their power on suppressing Palestine for sustained periods. Outside forces pressed heavily against the empire. This included the long-standing rivalry with the Ptolemaic realm, but the Romans also intervened regularly to ensure that the Seleucids were observing their arms-control agreements. The Maccabees naturally sought support from these outside foes, and in 161 Judah reputedly made a treaty with Rome. Still more threatening was the rising power of eastern nations who sought to conquer the extensive eastern portions of the empire, the Parthians being the most effective. The first great Parthian ruler to operate largely free of Seleucid interference was Phraates I, in the 170s. Over the next thirty years, his brother Mithridates conquered much of the lands that had made up the old Persian Empire destroyed by Alexander, ranging from Afghanistan into Mesopotamia.[7]

The Parthian Empire persisted into the third century CE, and it often posed a deadly threat to Rome. That looming Parthian power would frequently influence the politics of Palestine and the Jewish people. We usually tell the Jewish story in terms of the growing power of great Mediterranean powers, especially that of Rome. Repeatedly, though, Jewish elites looked east as well as west and sought to use Parthian imperial power as a counterbalance to Rome.

Moreover, the Seleucids themselves faced deadly internal conflicts and civil wars. After Antiochus IV died in 164, he was followed by a series of weak kings and regents, with pretenders seeking to build a power base. These crises came together in 153 when the legitimate Seleucid emperor, Demetrius I, faced a simultaneous challenge from the kings of Egypt and Pergamon, who supported Alexander Balas, a pretender who claimed to be the son of Antiochus IV. Both emperor and pretender engaged in a bidding war for the support of Maccabean leader Jonathan Apphus. Ultimately, the imperial forces of Demetrius withdrew from most of Palestine, and Alexander appointed Jonathan as high priest. Jonathan's accession meant taking control of the institutional power of the Temple and its wealth, over and above its spiritual prestige; the title remained in his family until 37 BCE. The overthrow of the older high-priestly establishment echoed through the religion and its writings for decades to come.[8]

Only a series of critical events between 142 and 139 brought the Jews true independence. Jonathan's successor, Simon, in his turn, was a player in imperial politics, a valued royal ally during the rule of an unpopular boy king, Demetrius II, and a foe of new dissidents and pretenders. By 142 a grateful Demetrius remitted imperial taxes for the Jews and granted the right to mint coinage, effectively granting them full independence. Simon became governor, *hegoumenon*, and military commander, so that he alone would be entitled to wear the purple and gold ornaments. He also took control of the powerful citadel that was the heart of Seleucid power in Jerusalem, the Akra, and either occupied it himself or else destroyed it. With Demetrius's blessing, he also became high priest. Given his non-Zadokite status, he buttressed his position through a kind of public acclamation, in major assembly "of the priests and the people and of the elders of the land." He held his power under the (generous) condition that it would endure "forever, until a faithful prophet should arise" (1 Macc. 14:41). Simon presumably never lost a sleepless night worrying that the arrival of such an individual was at all imminent.[9]

Simon benefited from external circumstances. In 141 the Parthian king, Mithridates, conquered the imperial capital of Seleucia, in one of the epochal transitions of power in the Middle East. From that point, Seleucid attention would be directed eastward, leaving Palestine in decent obscurity. In 139 the Roman Senate acknowledged Simon's regime.

Even so, the Jewish state was still not wholly safe. Rarely receiving the historical attention it deserves was a new crisis in 135, when the emperor Antiochus VII besieged Jerusalem under its new ruler, Simon's son John Hyrcanus. Although at first sight this looks like just another episode in the endless cycle of wars and betrayals, its extreme seriousness is revealed by the desperate measures that John took to save the city, as he bought off the invaders with three thousand talents of treasure looted from King David's tomb. Greek historians report that Antiochus's advisers were pressing him to exterminate the Jews altogether as obnoxious enemies of humanity or at least to abolish their laws and customs. Antiochus VII resisted such calls, earning the gratitude of Jewish writers, but his reasons are uncertain. Perhaps he was a tolerant man by nature, but it is also possible that the Jewish polity by this point simply had no Hellenizers of the sort who had been so common a generation before, leaving the king no chance of building up a loyalist party. Hellenists had been suppressed in various forms, whether they were killed, exiled, converted, or simply terrified into silence. But the whole affair points to the existential dangers facing Jews thirty years after the depths of the Maccabean crisis. Even at this late stage, the Jewish kingdom endured a further few years as tributaries of the Seleucids, as John supplied contingents for a Seleucid war against the Parthians. That defeat, in 129, effectively ended Seleucid ambitions east of Syria.[10]

By Simon's time, the Hasmoneans held enormous power in Palestine as both princes and priests. They knew nothing of any separation between secular and spiritual authority, if indeed they could have grasped the modern concept of a "secular" sphere. Even with all this accumulated power, the Hasmoneans were slow to claim the title of king openly. For multiple reasons, they wanted to avoid provocative acts in a dangerous political environment, especially if that would stir Seleucid anger. Just how risky that environment was is suggested by the fate of the eight or so high priests who served between 185 and 135 BCE. (As we will see, the exact number of incumbents is uncertain.) All but one either died violently, by execution or assassination, or died in exile. The one exception was Alcimus, who died following a stroke in 159. Simon, accordingly, was never officially king, nor was his son John Hyrcanus, who ruled from 134 through 104. John in turn was followed by his son Aristoboulos, who in 104 finally did take the Greek title of king, *basileus*, complete with the royal diadem, and that was in addition to his high priesthood. Aristoboulos did not long remain in office, but his brother Alexander Jannaeus made the Jewish state a significant regional power (see Table 5.1).[11]

The family owed its power to a revolt against Hellenization, but it adopted both Greek names and Greek ambitions. The princely sons of John (Yohanan) adopted the names of Alexander (Yannai), Aristoboulos (Judah), and Antigonus (Mattathias). John himself minted coins with the inscription "High Priest, Council of the Jews." As king, though, Jannaeus's coins looked very Greek, with an eight-point sunburst within a diadem and an anchor symbol, a significant borrowing. The anchor had originally been used by the first Seleucus himself and subsequently became the logo of his dynasty.[12]

The Seleucid realm itself dissolved to the point of becoming merely a local Syrian statelet, so that a grandly named ruler of the 80s BCE like Antiochus XII Dionysus exercised little power beyond Damascus. The empire's fragmentation created a multipolar political scene. By this point, most of the eastern territories were under

TABLE 5.1.   HASMONEAN GENEALOGY

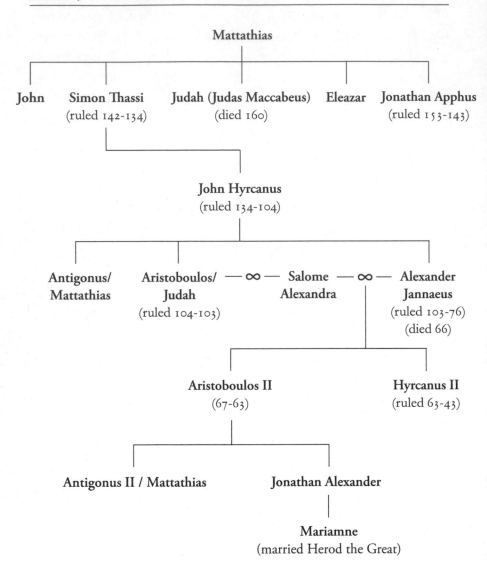

Mattathias

John | Simon Thassi (ruled 142-134) | Judah (Judas Maccabeus) (died 160) | Eleazar | Jonathan Apphus (ruled 153-143)

John Hyrcanus
(ruled 134-104)

Antigonus/ Mattathias | Aristoboulos/ Judah (ruled 104-103) | ∞ — Salome Alexandra — ∞ — Alexander Jannaeus (ruled 103-76) (died 66)

Aristoboulos II (67-63) | Hyrcanus II (ruled 63-43)

Antigonus II / Mattathias | Jonathan Alexander

Mariamne
(married Herod the Great)

Parthian sway, but several other parvenu states also grew and flourished. Briefly triumphant was Pontus, which under King Mithridates (120–63 BCE) ruled most of Asia Minor and became a lethally dangerous enemy of Rome. Under King Tigranes the Great (95–55 BCE), a reunited Armenia became a forceful player. At its height, this Armenian empire stretched from the Caucasus across most of eastern Asia Minor and northern Mesopotamia and incorporated Syria and Phoenicia. When Tigranes seized the city of Ptolemais, he seemed on the verge of annexing Palestine itself. It was the contests with these local empires—of Mithridates and Tigranes and then the Parthians—that brought the Romans ever deeper into the Middle East and to the gates of Jerusalem itself.[13]

It is in the context of these insurgent states that we should see Jewish rulers like John Hyrcanus. Under John the Hasmoneans launched their own wide-ranging campaigns of conquest and annexation, so large in fact as to recall the (likely mythical) dominion that the Bible attributes to David and Solomon centuries before. Although John began his rule with only Judea and the land of Perea, immediately across the Jordan, he more than doubled the size of his state by conquering Samaria and Idumea (Edom).[14]

That campaign meant the eclipse of the independent Samaritan cult, which for three centuries had maintained a parallel existence to the official Temple on Mount Zion. As a worthy king of his age, John was pledged to imperial expansion, but as high priest he also faced the biblical injunction to centralize the worship of the Hebrew people. In a campaign in 111, Hasmonean forces destroyed the Samaritan Temple at Mount Gerizim, sacked and enslaved the city of Samaria, and reduced Shechem to a village. Samaritans, moreover, were forbidden from restoring their Temple. These ruthless actions stirred furious resentment and contributed to the loathing that Jews and Samaritans felt for each other in New Testament times. The fact that Jerusalem's Temple now truly became the sole cult center in Palestine made it a national and international institution in a way it had not been since before the Exile. That epochal victory in turn added still further to the odds at stake in the control of Jerusalem.[15]

John's successor, Jannaeus, faced an even more encouraging political situation with the evaporation of Seleucid rivalry. He not only held on to John's conquests but also won major possessions across the Jordan, including Moab, Gilead, and Iturea. He also gained victories on the Mediterranean coast around Gaza and the

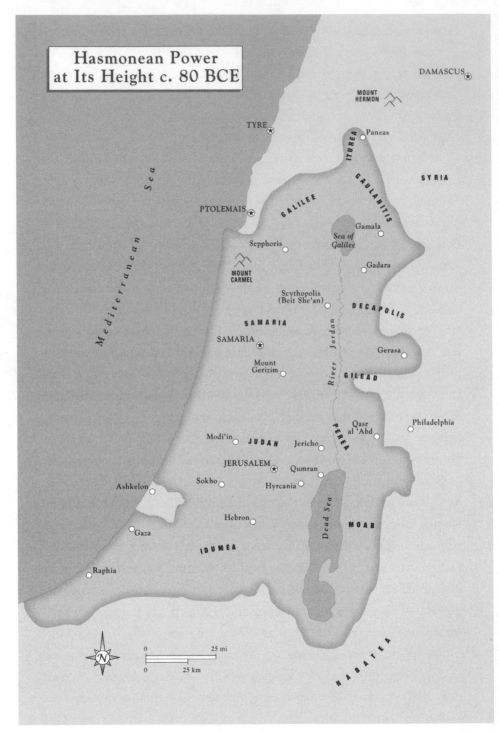

Hasmonean Power
at Its Height c. 80 BCE

DAMASCUS

MOUNT
HERMON

TYRE

SYRIA

Paneas

ITUREA

GAULANITIS

GALILEE

PTOLEMAIS

Gamala

Sea of
Galilee

Sepphoris

MOUNT
CARMEL

Gadara

Scythopolis
(Beit She'an)

DECAPOLIS

SAMARIA

SAMARIA

Gerasa

River Jordan

Mount
Gerizim

GILEAD

Philadelphia

Qasr
al 'Abd

PEREA

Modi'in

JUDAH

Jericho

JERUSALEM

Qumran

Ashkelon

Sokho

Hyrcania

Dead Sea

Hebron

MOAB

Gaza

IDUMEA

Raphia

Mediterranean Sea

0   25 mi

0   25 km

NABATEA

MAP 5.1.   HASMONEAN EXPANSION

ancient Philistine regions. In modern terms, he gained large portions of the nation of Jordan, and his power stretched deep into Syria.

Palestine was already a diverse land with substantial Gentile and Samaritan populations, but even the Jews of the era were by no means a simple category. Most, certainly, were the descendants of ancient tribes, but there were also newer converts. When Hasmonean rulers conquered neighboring lands like Idumea, they demanded conversion, insisting that conquered peoples accept circumcision and Jewish law. Enforcing a far-reaching act of conquest scarcely seems credible for the limited military resources available at the time. However, Idumeans and other local peoples found religious conformity a reasonable sacrifice to make in exchange for political protection and an alliance against their Greek-leaning neighbors. Whatever the roots of the religious change, there is no sign that occupied peoples abandoned their new identity when Hasmonean power collapsed. Judaism in this era was an expansionist and highly fluid religion.[16]

Although the Hasmonean state ceased to exist in the mid-first century BCE, their lost empire demarcated the Jewish and near-Jewish world of the later Second Temple era, the world known to Herod the Great and to Jesus's first followers. When New Testament figures, like Jesus's apostles themselves, speak of "restoring the kingdom to Israel," it was the Hasmonean era they had in mind. The problem was that this potent kingdom represented an unsustainable historical freak. The geography of Palestine meant that the land was at the pivot of major empires elsewhere in the region. It could escape their power only when those other states had their attention distracted elsewhere, or when dueling empires faced a delicate balance of power, making it convenient to permit an independent Jewish kingdom, however temporarily.

THE DEFEAT OF the radical Hellenizers meant that the holy city never became Antioch-in-Jerusalem, yet that salvation brought neither peace nor stability to the Jewish polity. Even when the Hasmoneans had secured themselves against foreign threats by the

140s, they presided over a deeply divided nation that was desperately riven between political/religious parties and factions. The causes of dissent were many. The Hasmoneans were controversial for their departure from traditional ideas of kingship and also for their adoption of Greek names and imperial styles. They combined in themselves the authority of worldly kings and religious high priests. So were they Jewish kings or Greek emperors? And could those roles be reconciled? Most damning for critics was the creation of a kingdom without Davidic credentials or any legitimacy beyond naked force. Critics also challenged their high-priestly authority and their displacement of the Aaronic succession.

So extreme were the conflicts of these years that modern observers would speak in terms of a revolutionary dictatorship dissolving into a failed state. Like any small post-Hellenistic state, the Hasmonean realm was riddled with elite feuds that made the country all but ungovernable. Royal families were large, and a king with several sons would likely face insurrection from at least one of the brood. When John Hyrcanus died in 104, he left five sons. His immediate successors were his two sons Aristoboulos and Antigonus, who jailed their younger brothers. Aristoboulos also imprisoned his mother and allowed her to starve to death before assassinating Antigonus—allegedly, at the instigation of his wife, Salome. Aristoboulos himself died shortly afterward, to be succeeded by his brother Jannaeus, who duly married Salome. Jannaeus's own father had hated him from the day of his birth and could never bear to have him in his company, all of which presumably contributed to the son's lifetime of notoriously heavy drinking. Vicious interfamily tensions constantly ran the risk of sparking civil wars and foreign interventions. At such times, each side sought support from one or another of the religious sects, which now became critical to political developments.[17]

It was around 150 BCE that three famous names were first recorded among the Jews. In his *Jewish War*, Josephus introduces us to three sects with very different opinions about the roots of human behavior, namely, the Pharisees, Sadducees, and Essenes, of whom he had more to say in the *Jewish Antiquities*. Josephus frames his description in terms of the groups' varying attitudes toward fate, determinism, and free will, but they had many other divisions, about theology, about the afterlife, about angels and the spiritual hierarchy. (Fortune, Tyche, was a dominant religious concept in Hellenistic culture at this time, usually imagined in terms of arbitrary chance.) The Pharisees held that Fate determined some actions, but not all, so that at least some actions remained open to free will. The Essenes held that Fate was absolute and shaped all human deeds. The Sadducees denied Fate altogether, so that all actions were subject to free will and human beings alone were responsible for whatever good or evil befell them.[18]

Josephus's philosophically focused description of the sects and their ideas sounds like excellent fodder for an academic seminar. We can question, though, whether those issues were actually their main concerns in the period he is describing rather than in the more recent era in which he had known them personally. In reality, the earlier movements were deeply and militantly political and activist. Pharisees were deeply committed to defending the Law as they understood it and to maintaining Jewish freedom and integrity. That did not extend to supporting the Hasmonean dynastic project, especially when royal actions seemed to threaten religious interests. Not only were these different sects immersed in public affairs—especially the Pharisees and Sadducees—but they also acted like quite recognizable political parties and were involved in protests and paramilitary activities over centuries. (In Chapter 7 we will look more closely at the Essenes, who played nothing like as active a role in factional politics.)

Modern scholars differ over the degree of power and influence that each of these movements had at any given time, and it would be wrong to suggest that their activities closely affected the mass of ordinary people. Most Jews of the time followed a standard core of beliefs and practices that is often called Common Judaism, which included practicing circumcision and observing dietary laws and the Sabbath, while following the usual round of ritual observances. Most did not formally adhere to sects or share their particular views. That said, each group had a solid power base of sympathizers in the community at large. The Pharisees were very much the popular party, with sizable influence over the masses. Meanwhile, the Sadducees drew their support from the rich, the aristocratic, and the priestly elites.[19] With their respective constituencies, Pharisees and Sadducees were key factions in the perennial civil wars that divided the Jewish kingdom.

KINGS SIDED WITH one of these factions or another, and when they shifted their allegiance, it was a major political event. One such transition occurred around 115, when John Hyrcanus defected to the Sadducees after previously following the Pharisees. According to Josephus, this shift supposedly resulted from an embarrassing clash at a social gathering, when one tactless or provocative Pharisee raised the lethally sensitive issue of John's supposed low birth. If in fact the Hasmoneans were descended from a captive woman, then she had likely been raped, making her offspring illegitimate and non-Jewish and invalidating the family's claims to exercise royal power. The enmity of the now out-of-favor Pharisees reverberated through the kingdom's politics for decades to come.[20]

During the ensuing struggles, the Hasmoneans were quite as likely to massacre or crucify their enemies as had Antiochus IV before them or Herod the Great and Pontius Pilate afterward. On occasion, they out-Heroded Herod. Especially under Jannaeus, Hasmonean rule was characterized by pathological violence. Like his father, Jannaeus himself favored the Sadducees; the Pharisees were his deadly enemies.

The country during his reign was in a near-permanent state of internecine war. After one defeat, Jannaeus tried to take refuge in Jerusalem, only to find the city in arms against him. A bloody six-year war followed, and relations between the two sides were venomous. When Jannaeus asked his Pharisee-led enemies what he could do to make peace, the best solution they could offer was that he should kill himself immediately. Those rebel subjects called for help from the Seleucid king Demetrius Eucaerus, who duly invaded. Jannaeus eventually regained control of the country and took reprisals that shocked even the hardened Josephus. With his concubines, the king held a public feast, at which the entertainment was the crucifixion of eight hundred Pharisee rebels. While those rebels were still living, their wives and children had their throats cut before the eyes of the men undergoing torment on crosses. In response to this atrocity, the king's enemies labeled him *Thrakidas*, a Thracian or wild barbarian, and, again, definitely a stranger to the house of Israel. But terror worked: thousands of his other opponents fled and remained in exile for the rest of his reign. It says much about our general ignorance of this period that such a gruesome career has not ended up more prominently in popular history.[21]

The rift between the Pharisees and the ruling dynasty was not healed until the 70s. Before his death, Jannaeus reportedly told his wife to make diplomatic overtures to the Pharisees, who were to organize his funeral. The queen, Salome Alexandra, not only accommodated the Pharisees but actually reigned through them, rewarding them with state patronage. According to later legend, the Pharisee leader at the time was noted scholar Simeon ben Shetach, who subsequently purged Sadducees from the council, the Sanhedrin, and replaced them with members of his own party, who were recalled from their exile in Alexandria. Salome drew the line at allowing the restored Pharisees to kill Jannaeus's servants, who had carried out some notorious massacres, although some of the most egregious offenders suffered vigilante reprisals. So successful was the queen's sectarian shift that she managed to rule the nation in reasonable peace for another decade—no small achievement given its chaotic recent history. In modern terms, it sounds like a state suffering a series of coups and countercoups, with the victims of one regime demanding retaliation against the killers and torturers of the previous government.[22]

Contemplating the succession of regimes from the Hasmoneans through the Herodians and the Romans, it seems that the region never knew anything vaguely like good government, as opposed to one capricious despotism after another. Given that long history of political disasters and the sectarian response, it is not difficult to appreciate the very negative perception of worldly governments in the New Testament or the desperate hope for divine rule that might offer justice—or at least ensure that violence was inflicted on our enemies rather than ourselves.

To ILLUSTRATE THE headlong pace of change in this era, we might look at the long life of one individual, namely, Queen Salome Alexandra herself, who lived from 143 through 67 BCE. When Salome Alexandra was born, Palestine was operating within the Seleucid Empire, which still controlled Babylon. Her life span included the rise of the Hasmonean state as well as its glory days and its sharp decline. In her last years, the main political question was just how long Jewish independence could be preserved and which of the various successor states might absorb it, whether Armenia, Pontus, Parthia, or Rome. Born under the Seleucids, she came close to dying under the Romans.

Hardly less than the political world, the religious universe had also changed dramatically during her lifetime, perhaps unrecognizably. The era of revolution and civil wars was marked by new religious concepts and schools of thought, fresh movements, and innovative genres of writing. The queen lived through one of the great tectonic shifts in religious history. In the following chapters, we will trace aspects of this transformation, which completely remade ideas of spiritual good and evil.[23]

Chapter 6

DANIEL'S REVOLUTION

Visions of Cosmic Warfare

=====

And in the days of these kings shall the God of heaven set up
a kingdom, which shall never be destroyed: and the kingdom
shall not be left to other people, but it shall break in pieces and
consume all these kingdoms, and it shall stand for ever.

DANIEL 2:44, KJV

WHEN ANTIOCHUS IV tried to stamp out Jewish customs, faithful Jews suffered en masse for their refusal to obey. The book of 2
Maccabees tells the story of a young man being tortured to death
for refusing to eat pork. With his last breath, he addresses his Greek
tormentors: "You accursed fiend, you are depriving us of this present life, but the king of the universe will raise us up to live again
forever, because we are dying for his laws" (2 Macc. 7:9). A modern
reader finds those heroic words a quite conventional sentiment. In
the context of the time, it was anything but that, with its declaration
of faith in the novel doctrine of individual resurrection for the righteous dead. We see here two ideas that have become central to the
modern religious worldview, which might be summarized as "The
world is not my home" and "Death is not the end."

Earthly conflicts during that nightmare century encouraged the
potent new belief in wars in the heavens. The worse the situation
appeared, the greater the despair about worldly outcomes, the more
fervently writers turned to visions of apocalyptic judgment and

rescue and, increasingly, to messianic hopes. Such motifs had been central to the Enochic literature, but they now became a major feature of Jewish thought. Out of these agonies came so many key beliefs of later religious movements, including the afterlife and resurrection.

THROUGH THE CENTURIES, prophets had envisioned the fate of the world through the microcosm of Jerusalem, the site of God's presence. God's anger or pleasure was reflected through the state of his holy city, and descriptions of the End Times were precise in their sense of the city's geography. When the prophet in Second Zechariah foretells the terminal crisis, he does not merely say that disaster will overwhelm Jerusalem. Rather, he proclaims very specifically, "the Mount of Olives shall cleave in the midst thereof toward the east and toward the west, and there shall be a very great valley; and half of the mountain shall remove toward the north, and half of it toward the south. . . . All the land shall be turned as a plain from Geba to Rimmon south of Jerusalem: and it shall be lifted up, and inhabited in her place, from Benjamin's gate unto the place of the first gate, unto the corner gate, and from the tower of Hananeel unto the king's winepresses" (14:4–10, KJV).

Under Antiochus IV, the material city was literally overcome by destruction quite as horrendous as the prophets had foreseen. In the Maccabean years, people saw the Temple plundered and ruined: "And when they saw the sanctuary desolate, and the altar profaned, and the gates burned up, and shrubs growing in the courts as in a forest, or in one of the mountains, yea, and the priests' chambers pulled down, they rent their clothes, and made great lamentation, and cast ashes upon their heads, and fell down flat to the ground upon their faces, and blew an alarm with the trumpets, and cried toward heaven" (1 Macc. 4:38–40, KJV). How could such a moment be understood except in cosmic terms?

Some incidents almost demanded a religious framing, and they easily lent themselves to apocalyptic readings. At one point during the Maccabean revolution, high priest Alcimus sought to divide the opposition by offering peace. Maccabee diehards resisted these blandishments, but others were open to negotiation. These included the scribes and the Hasideans, who were content to see a high priest of legitimate descent. Alcimus granted them safe conduct for the negotiation but then executed sixty of them in a single day. Reputedly, one of the victims was Yose ben Yoezer, one of the legendary sages of the time, who was celebrated as "the pious of the priesthood." Such atrocities were commonplace in ancient warfare, but in this instance the victims and their friends belonged to a literate class deeply immersed in scriptural interpretation and memory. Accordingly, they interpreted the massacre through the lens of Psalm 79, a plea for God to avenge the slaughter inflicted on Jerusalem, his Temple, and his holy people: "Their blood have they shed like water round about Jerusalem; and there was none to bury them" (3). That psalm ends with a cry for bloody vengeance against oppressors.[1]

As an imaginative exercise, let us suppose that Yose's friends had chosen to present their grief and anger in a somewhat different form and had used storytelling to convey theological argument. As we have seen from works like the book of the Giants, this was a culture that loved to tell stories and to elaborate on familiar tales and myths. As far as we know, no extant writing specifically refers to Alcimus's crime, but we can easily reconstruct what such a tract would have looked like. Instead of merely pleading for vengeance, the Hasideans would have portrayed a near-future divine intervention in which such vengeance would actually be inflicted. Such a work might be put in the words of some ancient seer foretelling the future, almost certainly through the revelation of some mighty angel. The hypothetical text would describe the history of future generations, until the rise of evil men serving foreign lords who slay the righteous. Many real individual characters would be represented by symbolic figures, commonly animals. Yose himself might have featured as a glorious lion. The work would end with a vision of the vindication of the slain righteous, whose enemies were consigned to everlasting torment. Although this particular apocalypse remains in the realm of fiction, it is very close to numerous works that actually did appear between 200 BCE and 200 CE.

Among the wave of actual pseudoprophecies and neoscriptures directly inspired by the Maccabean revolution, by far the most important was the book of Daniel. Daniel is, in fact, the charter text of later apocalyptic, as well as the foundation for so many later ideas about messianic figures, the Antichrist, and the Day of Judgment. Unlike many other compositions of these years, moreover, Daniel entered the biblical canons of both Jews and mainstream Christians. Similar ideas and images had already appeared in Deutero-Zechariah and 1 Enoch, but Daniel popularized these themes. Moreover, it did so in a unified and systematic form canonized in scripture.[2]

Because it was so significant, this multilayered work needs to be analyzed in some detail. In the usual translation, Daniel has twelve chapters. (That chapter division, of course, is not original.) Through the centuries, Daniel has circulated in various versions, some of which include extraneous material that has become attached to the text. The Greek version includes several short passages that are difficult to date, the so-called Greek Additions, which are accepted as canonical by Catholic and Orthodox churches but not, generally, by Protestants. We will return to them shortly.

The book's core is clearly divided into two sections. Most scholars agree that the first portion is older than the second, but it is not evident whether this means by a few years or by some decades. The early section tells of a group of aristocratic young Jews who are exiled to Babylon in the sixth century BCE together with the rest of their nation.

The stories concern Daniel himself but also three Hebrews named Shadrach, Meshach, and Abednego, and the different legends might have originally circulated independently. Together and separately, these Jewish heroes have many interactions with the kings of Babylonia Nebuchadnezzar and Belshazzar and their Persian successor Darius, most involving the Hebrews' ability to interpret royal dreams and visions. In the process, we encounter some of the Bible's most celebrated tales and some of those most often represented in visual art through the centuries. This includes Daniel in the lions' den (Dan. 6), the three Hebrews in the fiery furnace (Dan. 3), and the writing on the wall at the royal feast. The action throughout takes place in Babylon, which in this context has a double valence. Beyond being the center of the Exile in the sixth century, it also points to the strictly contemporary Seleucid metropolis. Contemporary analysis masquerades as historical narrative.

The stories suggest the debates over the Jewish relationship with Hellenism that were raging in the years before the great revolt. They show the Jews' superior wisdom and access to divine favor, allowing them to succeed where the collective pagan wisdom of Babylon has failed. In each case where the Hebrews counsel or assist a king, he comes to confess the mighty works of the God of Israel. That theme is familiar from many alternative writings in the Second Temple era, but there are also signs that Jewish life was facing an existential crisis at the time the book was written. Repeatedly, and unsubtly, the author uses his heroes as examples that faithful Jews should follow when facing pressure or persecution. Daniel stubbornly refuses to abandon his dietary restrictions in order to eat the rich food set before him at the Babylonian court. The three Hebrews are thrown into the furnace for their refusal to fall down and worship a golden idol.

That context becomes much more apparent in Daniel's second and more phantasmagoric section, which can be dated precisely to 165 BCE. Although nothing can be said about the book's authorship, it is tempting to see a connection with the Hasideans, who were both militant warriors and learned defenders of the Law.

Like its countless successors and imitators through the centuries, Daniel presented current events—wars, rumors of wars, revolutions—as precursors to titanic changes in the world order and God's judgment. The story is told throughout in allusive form, using animals to symbolize real individuals (8:5–9). Daniel, notionally writing in the mid-sixth century, claims to be baffled by the visions he receives of future events. What does it mean to say that there would be a mighty two-horned ram, which would in turn be overthrown by a shaggy goat? Or that after the goat, there would be four broken horns? Throughout, angels and other supernatural characters appear to expound the mysteries. The ram, they clarify, represents the kings of Media and Persia, while the goat is the king of Greece, that is, Alexander. The four lesser horns denote the successor kingdoms, none of which would ever fully reproduce his glory.

These histories form a prologue to the book's main subject, which is Antiochus IV himself and his hatred for Jews and Judaism. The prophecies warn of a future being, an evil king, a "horn," who "shall speak great words against the Most High, and shall wear out the saints of the most High, and think to change times and laws: and they shall be given into his hand until a time, and times, and the dividing of time" (7:25, KJV). The pseudoprophecy makes the king a diabolical figure, a master of deceit and deception. As such, Antiochus became the forefather of all later apocalyptic tyrants. He supplied the matrix into which Beastly villains like Herod, Nero, and Domitian could be fitted, not to mention such later candidates as the papacy, Stalin, Saddam Hussein, and, assuredly, other political leaders yet unborn. Antiochus's crimes would provoke the final catastrophe: "The end will come like a flood: War will continue until the end, and desolations have been decreed. He will confirm a covenant with many for one 'seven.' In the middle of the 'seven' he will put an end to sacrifice and offering. And at the temple he will set up an abomination that causes desolation, until the end that is decreed is poured out on him" (9:26–27, NIV).[3] The abomination alluded to here is the pagan altar that Seleucid forces erected in the Temple. Conceivably, too, the mysterious "covenant" cited here is the king's alliance with Hellenizing Jewish factions. (The enigmatic "sevens" are weeks or time periods, which the reader was meant to translate into actual dates.)

However dreadful the threat, however, God would intervene to help his people and establish his rule. The physical conflict in Palestine would escalate to a full-scale supernatural war, a moment of ultimate judgment and of bodily resurrection. Even after "a time of distress such as has not happened from the beginning of nations until then," there would still be hope for "every one that shall be found written in the book. And many of them that sleep in the dust of the earth shall awake, some to everlasting life, and some to shame and everlasting contempt. And they that be wise shall shine as the brightness of the firmament; and they that turn many to righteousness as the stars for ever and ever." Playing his role in the cosmic drama would be "Michael, the great prince who protects your people," while the angel Gabriel also counsels Daniel (12:1–3).

One key passage shows how, almost by accident, particular historical individuals gained a new significance in the universal scheme: "From the time the word goes out to restore and rebuild Jerusalem until the Anointed One, the ruler, comes, there will be seven 'sevens,' and sixty-two 'sevens.' . . . After the sixty-two 'sevens,' the Anointed One will be put to death and will have nothing. The people of the ruler who will come will destroy the city and the sanctuary" (9:25–26, NIV). The Anointed One is, literally, a messiah, and he will be put to death. Not surprisingly, later believers have found here a ringing prophecy of the Crucifixion; the King James Bible even uses the words "Messiah, the Prince." But the author of Daniel had no such messianic intentions. Rather, his retroactive prophecy concerns an individual who was a significant player in the affairs of his own time, but who today is recalled only by the very narrow band of specialists in that era. The reference is to the former high priest Onias III, who was murdered in 170 as a result of court intrigues. Because he had served as high priest, Onias was "anointed," the word translated as "messiah," so that the allusive passages describing his murder receive eschatological significance. This was by no means the only instance in which a sordid sectarian conflict was projected into cosmic affairs and remembered in that context for millennia afterward.

READING DANIEL TODAY, it is tempting to see analogies with modern-day anticolonial and anti-imperial writings. However different the settings, some of the characteristic features of such modern writings do apply remarkably well to the ancient examples. Then as now, occupied peoples reasserted their identity in the face of empires that claimed a universal authority and absolute cultural hegemony. As so often in modern contexts, the main arena of conflict was that of history or of competing histories. While imperial authorities presented themselves in terms of liberation and enlightenment, the underdogs reclaimed their own history by denigrating that of the masters. Far from bringing civilization, the empires in this vision were blundering, destructive beasts or mythical monsters. Not only were subject peoples morally superior to their masters, but the whole of history lay at the direction of their specific God, who would shortly restore the natural balance of the universe. Far from being "lesser breeds without the law," they actually had a monopoly on Law. History, in other words, was God's, and it was theirs. The apocalyptic framework was endlessly malleable and could be adjusted to accommodate each new horror or portent—the coming of the Romans, the Parthian wars, and ultimately the fall of the Second Temple.[4]

But the book of Daniel was not an isolated monument, nor was it the only work to present these emerging religious ideas. Several other scriptures of catastrophe have been assigned to these years, usually on the basis that the savage persecutions that they describe fit neatly into the revolution against Antiochus IV. Writing around 160, the author of Jubilees presented a trenchant manifesto for the Maccabean cause and a diatribe against Gentiles. He held ferocious views on the issue of circumcision, a detonator for the revolution, and he claimed to cite a prophecy from Abraham's time that foretold that "the children of Israel will not keep true to this ordinance, and they will not circumcise their sons according to all this law . . . and all of them, sons of Beliar, will leave their sons uncircumcised as they were born" (15:33). (Beliar is an Aramaic form of the name also encountered as Belial.) God's wrath would be turned against those who "have treated their members like the Gentiles, so that they may be removed and rooted out of the land." The main lesson that Jubilees draws from the story of the Garden of Eden is that Israelites should avoid nudity and cover themselves properly, as the Gentiles did not. We recall that public nudity in the gymnasium was a major grievance preceding the revolt.

On occasion, the accounts are allusive, and they could be just as applicable to any number of other people or episodes. Among the strongest candidates for a Maccabean date are some of the Greek additions originally written separately from Daniel but appended to that book in some traditions. One of these, Bel and the Dragon, mocks idolatry and the worship of pagan images. Using familiar arguments against graven images, Daniel easily convinces the Babylonian king that the image of the god Bel has no life of its own; only the deceit of the priests makes it appear that it eats and drinks the offerings set before it. Furious, the king kills the priests and their families. Although allegedly concerned with Babylonian affairs, the message would apply equally to Greek rulers and believers, especially those who tried to impose their false ideas on Jews.[5]

Another such Greek Addition is the Prayer of Azariah, which in some versions becomes part of the story of the fiery furnace. In his suffering, Azariah utters a psalm that would be singularly appropriate during the time of Antiochus IV. Bemoaning the sins of the Hebrew people, he admits that God has treated them justly by punishing them: "Thou hast given us into the hands of lawless enemies, most hateful rebels, and to an unjust king, the most wicked in all the world" (1:9). ("Lawless" was a standard way of denouncing the Hellenizers.)

Other evidence comes from the Sibylline Oracles, a source that is cryptic even in a literature that delights to mystify. In Roman and Greek lore, the sibyls were prophetic female figures who foretold coming events, and many of their oracles circulated through the centuries. A large surviving collection of these texts shows clear signs of Jewish and Christian influence, even if their actual date and origin has long been debated. Most were written between the second century BCE and the fifth century CE. As in the case of the Enochic writings, even some of the oracles that look explicitly messianic might in fact be pre-Christian in date, but this is difficult to determine with any certainty.[6]

For present purposes, the most significant sections of the Oracles are found in book 3, most of which was written by an Egyptian Jew in the mid-second century BCE. Conceivably, it might even be the work of that Onias who fled Jerusalem in order to establish a new Temple at Leontopolis. Like Daniel, this oracle offers a description of the Hellenistic empire, and it shows how deeply Seleucid aggression had aroused eschatological hopes and fears. The oracle portrays an imminent crisis and the destruction of invading pagan forces. When God uttered judgment with a mighty voice, all creation would tremble; mountains would be split asunder. All would end "by fire and by overwhelming storm, and brimstone there shall be from heaven:"[7]

> And all the unholy shall be bathed in blood;
> And earth herself shall also drink the blood
> Of the perishing, and beasts be gorged with flesh.[8]

But if cosmic warfare was indelibly established on the religious agenda, it was far less certain who the enemies of righteousness would be in such future struggles. Would it always be Gentiles, or might this language be applied to other Jews? As protest mounted during the Hasmonean era, so did the explicitly religious nature of rhetoric, as so many political battles occurred within a sacred context. In most conflicts, after all, control of the Temple was a primary goal, and priests and high priests were leading protagonists on both sides of partisan battles. In such a setting, writers denounced their (Jewish) opponents not merely as vicious and corrupt but as servants of Satan or the forces of Darkness. Each side in the deeply fractured Jewish polity read its rivals out of the Jewish world.[9]

Not all these polemical texts opposed the dynasty, and the author of Jubilees was sympathetic to the Hasmoneans. One of that book's stories tells of Levi's visit to Bethel: "Levi dreamed that they had ordained and made him the priest of the Most High God, him and his sons for ever." This seems like a standard expansion of the familiar biblical text, but the specific phrase "priest of the Most High God" was an official title claimed by the Hasmonean rulers. The author was thus giving ancient sanction to the regime and its sacred pretensions. Other texts were much more incendiary, using long-dead patriarchs and prophets as the ostensible authors of subversive tracts. In the first century BCE, the Hasmonean title appears again in the Testament of Moses, but this time in an unflattering context: "Then there shall be raised up unto them kings bearing rule, and they shall call themselves priests of the Most High God: they shall assuredly work iniquity in the Holy of Holies."[10]

Several other works demonstrate the use of apocalyptic and diabolical language against fellow Jews, and most derive from the century after the 160s BCE. Seditious words are found in the Testaments of the Twelve Patriarchs, a work with a very long history in Judaism and Christianity. Supposedly the last words of the sons of Jacob in around 1500 BCE, they were actually written in the century or two before the Common Era. Some, at least, were heavily Christianized, and in that form, they enjoyed a long afterlife in Christian Europe, where optimistic churchmen treated them as the authentic words of ancient patriarchs. Scholars debate to what extent the early Jewish originals can be reconstructed, but the presence of early materials is confirmed by the close resemblance between the Testaments and several writings from the Crucible years, including the Dead Sea Scrolls, the book of Jubilees, and the Enochic writings.[11]

The Testament of Levi attacks evil priests, in words that many modern editors apply to the priest-king Alexander Jannaeus, around 90 BCE. That would fit the charges of widespread sexual immorality with Jewish and Gentile women, as well as his alleged acts of theft and corruption. As Levi thunders, "And ye shall be puffed up because of your priesthood, lifting yourselves up against men, and not only so, but also against the commands of God. For ye shall contemn the holy things with jests and laughter."[12] If in fact that is the correct context for Levi, that would also provide a setting for the extensive apocalyptic themes that run through the work. The author saw the world as dominated by "the spirits of deceit and of Beliar" and knew that God and his angels would soon intervene against them: "Now, therefore, know that the Lord shall execute judgment upon the sons of men. Because when the rocks are being rent, and the sun quenched, and the waters dried up, and the fire cowering, and all creation troubled, and the invisible spirits melting away; and Hades [Sheol] takes spoils through the visitations of the Most High, men will be unbelieving and persist in their iniquity. On this account, with punishment shall they be judged."[13] As so often in these years, hatred of the oppressive dynasty justified extreme and apocalyptic language, and helped popularize the attendant religious system.

The Dead Sea Scrolls offer some of the clearest examples of this new religious approach, which was so rooted in the partisan conflicts of the day. Like the Testament of Levi, the Qumran sect looked harshly on the nation's rulers. As we will discuss in the next chapter, the Qumran movement owed its existence to a schism from the Hasmonean Temple order in the 150s. The group never reconciled themselves to what they saw as an irredeemably tainted institution. Around 90 BCE, one Qumran document denounced King Jannaeus the crucifier as a "Wrathful Lion . . . who hangs men alive." The sect developed elaborate theologies of holy warfare against enemies domestic and foreign, ideas that would become very influential during the era of Roman rule.[14]

AND WHAT OF the victims who fell in these struggles against God's enemies? The story of the young man defying his torturers points to the historically new concept of martyrdom, of righteous death in the service of God and his Law. Older Hebrew literature certainly had its stories of individuals who served God faithfully at the cost of their lives. Now, however, martyrdom and its rewards became a

central concern in ways that would be instantly comprehensible to
early Christians.

Alongside martyrdom there developed a much firmer and more
explicit belief in the afterlife and in the doctrine of future rewards
and punishments. Such ideas are not necessarily connected to martyrdom, and people might well lay down their lives for the general
good, without any hope of individual survival. Historically, though,
the ideas tended to evolve in close parallel. Especially during the Maccabean years, such beliefs offered hope for an individual to survive
death rather than merely forming part of a collective resurrection
of the entire people. This new hope resolved the ethical dilemma
of seeing so many heroic figures dying for the godly cause, whether
as soldiers or martyrs. Did these individuals really have no hope of
reward or vindication, beyond the collective good of the people? But
of course they did, if you assumed an afterlife and a resurrection to
Judgment. In the fourth century, a glorious afterlife was a distant
aspiration; by the second, the idea became an urgent necessity.[15]

The strongest evidence of these changing ideas about martyrdom
and the afterlife also emerges from the books of Maccabees. While
1 Maccabees pays virtually no attention to the supernatural, to the
point of not even using the word "God," 2 Maccabees is thoroughly
immersed in otherworldly interpretations, suffused with omens and
visions. When the Seleucid king sends his envoy Heliodorus to seize
Temple treasures, the attempt is thwarted by divine intervention,
manifested by a miraculous horseman and warriors, presumably
angels. Much like the pagan kings in the Greek Additions to Daniel,
Heliodorus now "recognized clearly the sovereign power of God,"
and he receives an angelic visitation (3:28).[16]

The book of 2 Maccabees recounts many stories of martyrdom,
lauding the righteous who laid down their lives for the wider community, in acts of vicarious sacrifice. When one martyr has his hands
severed, he declares that he will receive them again after his death.
His brother not only proclaims a similar faith, but warns his perse-
cutors that they, unlike he, will have no resurrection to life to which

they can look forward. As seven brothers are killed in turn, their mother urges them to remains constant so that one day they will all be reunited. The book's language of a "resurrection to life" (*anastasis eis zoen*) sounds very close to later Christian usage, but the author takes them for granted as standard Jewish beliefs of his own time (2 Macc. 7).

After Judas achieves victory, he collects money to be sent to the Temple for a sin-offering for those who had fallen in heroic battle. The author praises his deed, which he holds out as an example for others to follow: "For if he had not hoped that they that were slain should have risen again, it had been superfluous and vain to pray for the dead. And also in that he perceived that there was great favor laid up for those that died godly, it was a holy and good thought. Whereupon he made a reconciliation for the dead, that they might be delivered from sin" (12:44–45).[17] Alternatively, he "made atonement for the dead," but still with the goal of freeing the dead from their burden of sin. The doctrines expressed here are surprising in light of the Old Testament precedents we have seen that paid such scant attention to the afterlife. Remarkably, they rather sound akin to ideas of later Catholic Christianity, including the Communion of Saints and the practice of prayer for the dead.

Jubilees offers a like hope of future survival. After depicting a series of crises and disasters, God promises that "the righteous shall see and be thankful, and rejoice with joy for ever and ever, and shall see all their judgments and all their curses on their enemies. And their bones shall rest in the earth, and their spirits shall have much joy" (23:30–31). The promise of bodily resurrection is explicit in the Testament of Judah, in the context of a glorious future age. Again, it is specifically the martyrs who will win resurrection: "There shall be one people of the Lord, and one tongue; and there shall no more be a spirit of deceit of Beliar, for he shall be cast into the fire for ever. And they who have died in grief shall arise in joy, and they who have lived in poverty for the Lord's sake shall be made rich, and they who have been in want shall be filled, and they who have been weak shall be made strong, and they who have been put to death for the Lord's sake shall awake in life" (25). Those assurances about future rewards sound very close to the Beatitudes of Jesus, who may have been recalling an early version of this text.

BEYOND PROMISING ETERNAL life, these new doctrines elaborated on the nature of survival. What, exactly, could or did survive death? This question was of paramount importance in distinguishing among the Jewish sects, as each followed a doctrine born of its role in the conflicts of these years. Josephus summarizes one position when he writes about the Essenes, in the context of the Jewish War of the 60s CE. (At different times in his life, Josephus had been affiliated both with the Essenes and the Pharisees.) Whatever the horrors they faced, he reports, whatever tortures and threats of death, Essenes greeted them with scorn and even joy. They gave up their souls precisely because they knew they would receive them again. As he explains, Essenes believed that their bodies were corruptible and impermanent "but that the souls are immortal, and continue for ever; and . . . are united to their bodies as to prisons, into which they are drawn by a certain natural enticement; but that when they are set free from the bonds of the flesh, they then, as released from a long bondage, rejoice and mount upward."[18] That imagery of the body as prison and bondage suggests Greek and Platonic influence, and the idea would also be integral to later Christian and Gnostic theories.

Again according to Josephus, the Pharisees held that all souls are incorruptible (*aphtharton*) and that human beings would be resurrected. Those beliefs might have arisen either during the Maccabean conflicts or the decades-long Hasmonean persecutions, and it is open to debate whether those ideas borrowed from Greek philosophical concepts. As in the world of 2 Maccabees, the sect needed to justify and explain the deaths of so many of its ardent partisans, making the promise of an afterlife overwhelmingly tempting. By the turn of the Common Era, that belief was a defining characteristic of the group and a critical division from its rivals. As the New

Testament book of Acts noted, "The Sadducees say that there is no Resurrection, and that there are neither angels nor spirits, but the Pharisees believe all these things."

Christian writers long debated how the Sadducees could have formed their seemingly skeptical and materialist opinions. In fact, though, they were just following the older Jewish worldview described in the Hebrew Bible. It was the Pharisees who were the modernizers, who had absorbed all the innovations of the previous two centuries, especially the ideas associated with the Enochic writings. The Sadducees, by contrast, were conservatives who refused to accept those theological changes.[19]

Those partisan divisions also demonstrate the relative appeal of the different sets of beliefs. There is no doubt that it was the Pharisees who had the widest support beyond the elites. In religious terms, as much as any other, they were the People's Party. We can debate how they had won this position. Perhaps the masses responded enthusiastically to their message of angels, afterlife, and resurrection, which they found appealing and attractive. Alternatively, the Pharisees won support for other reasons, including their more liberal approach to matters of law and *halakhah* and their lenient approach to matters of ritual purity. They then used their prestige to promote the new spiritual ideas among the masses. Through whatever means, the revolutionary new themes became the ordinary currency of thought and belief for Jews and ultimately for Christians as well.

WHETHER EARTHLY OR spiritual, warfare can take many forms and know many degrees. The ancient world knew limited wars of conquest and annexation, and on rare occasions, it also experienced desperate wars of massacre and annihilation. In the case of supernatural conflict, though, the language of battle escalated to depict adversaries in terms of absolute evil, of enemies demanding annihilation. For some thinkers, that imagery extended to naked warfare between the forces of Light and Darkness.

Chapter 7

THE LIGHT AND THE LIFE

Wars of Light and Darkness

———————

> On the day when the Kittim fall there shall be a battle and hor-
> rible carnage before the God of Israel, for it is a day appoint-
> ed by Him from ancient times as a battle of annihilation for
> the Sons of Darkness. On that day, the congregation of the
> gods and the congregation of men shall engage one another,
> resulting in great carnage. The Sons of Light and the forces of
> Darkness shall fight together to show the strength of God with
> the roar of a great multitude and the shout of gods and men;
> a day of disaster.
>
> THE WAR SCROLL FROM QUMRAN

SINCE THEIR DISCOVERY in 1947, the Dead Sea Scrolls have transformed our knowledge of Jewish history and the development of
Jewish religious thought. Among other things, they reinforce what
we know about the atmosphere of savage partisanship in the century
or two before the Common Era. The Qumran group utterly rejected
any kind of accommodation or collaboration with the Gentile world
or indeed with most of their Jewish contemporaries.

Some documents go even beyond this rejection to frame those
confrontations in a quite new vision of universal realities. I have
quoted the War Scroll, an elaborate militaristic fantasy about how
the Sons of Light must prepare for combat against the Sons of
Darkness. Scholars disagree whether the evil enemies portrayed in
the text are more likely to be Seleucid Greeks or Romans. What is

new and striking, though, is the language of dualism, a system very different from anything found in the Hebrew Bible. Beyond positing a conflict of Light and Darkness, many items in the Scrolls divide humanity into two different camps, with the suggestion that such a division was determined or even predestined. Within a few decades, the universe was partitioned between the sons of justice, who walked on paths of Light, and the sons of deceit, who followed paths of Darkness.[1]

Although it never gained mainstream status in any existing world religion, that Crucible-era rhetoric of Light and Darkness became a surprisingly common strand of religious thought. Ideas akin to those of Qumran gained wide influence in the centuries around the Common Era, powerfully influencing early Christianity.[2]

THE LITERATURE SURROUNDING the Dead Sea Scrolls is fraught with controversy, and that debate extends to every aspect of the origins, identity, and influence of the people who produced them. It is not clear that the sect was as monastic or as strictly celibate as is sometimes claimed or if it was so completely isolated from the wider world. Nor is it certain how much of the hoard reflected ideas distinctive to the sect. The fact that something was found at Qumran does not necessarily mean that it reflected a common ideological approach. Sectarian groups can collect materials for polemical purposes in order to refute their ideas. A fair consensus today holds that the Scrolls represent a spectrum of thought: some of the texts were written at Qumran itself and reflected its distinctive doctrines, while others were of more general interest and application.[3]

Some points are however agreed widely, if not universally. Most scholars believe the community grew out of the Essene sect. We have already met the Essenes as a third strand or party in the Jewish religious spectrum, but the Qumran movement was a breakaway from that larger movement. Strictly speaking, there is no evidence for the existence of the Essenes before Josephus's description set around 150 BCE, but they already seem well established by that point.

Confirming that some kind of linkage did exist, Roman author Pliny (first century CE) describes an Essene settlement on the western shores of the Dead Sea, close to Qumran. The Qumran community itself would have existed from perhaps 150 BCE to 70 CE, a very long period in which ideas must have changed and evolved.[4]

The Essenes emerged early in the second century BCE. They may well have had precursors in the previous century, who were connected with the writing or editing of the Enochic documents around this time. For what it might be worth, the Damascus Document of the Qumran sect offers a historical framework for their sect in which God sends "a root of his planting" 390 years after the Babylonian capture of Jerusalem. If that date is to be taken literally rather than symbolically—and this is hotly debated—that would establish a foundation date for the Essenes, or a group like them, in 197 BCE. Such a chronology meshes well with the fraught political era at this time: the shift from Ptolemaic to Seleucid authority, the split within the Tobiad clan, and the civil war. Later in the century, the Qumran documents report that two factions struggled in Jerusalem. In reaction to an individual described as a Wicked Priest, a dissident priest challenged him and the Temple order, before leading a defection. (The term "Wicked Priest" uses a pun on the title of "high priest.") Breaking with its Essene parent stem, the dissident group—the Qumran sect—followed this man, whom they knew as the Teacher of Righteousness.[5]

The natural context for such a conflict would be in the revolutionary politics of the Maccabean years, which we encountered in Chapter 5 above, and one moment in particular looks very apposite. After the high priest Alcimus died in 159, no successor is recorded until 153, with the installation of Jonathan Apphus. That might mean that the office was indeed empty for those intervening six or so years, but that view is improbable for many reasons. More likely, there was indeed an incumbent, or perhaps even multiple claimants, and one of those, whose name has been lost or expunged from the records, was the Qumran sect's anonymous founder. If this reconstruction is sound, that would make Jonathan the Teacher's deadly foe, the "Wicked Priest" who serves Belial, which would make sense in terms of the bitter opposition to the Hasmonean seizure of the office. Both Jonathan and his successor, Simon Thassi, were of priestly descent, but neither was a Zadokite. The "Teacher" would thus have shared the widespread resentment to the new order but carried it to much greater extremes.[6]

Jonathan's accession thus split an older religious movement—Essenes or pre-Essenes—between accommodationist and diehard factions. Some partisans utterly rejected the legitimacy of the ruling regime and withdrew from a damned world, physically as well as symbolically. These rejectionists went to Qumran, where they claimed to follow the true Sons of Zadok. They venerated their Teacher, to the point of using near-messianic language. He was one "to whom God had made known all the mysteries of the words of his servants the prophets." The group's position as a sect within a sect explains their harshly confrontational view toward the outside world.[7]

To put him in cultural and political context, the Teacher would have been a near-exact contemporary of the author of Jubilees, as well as the pseudo-Daniel who wrote the apocalyptic sections of that book, and the creator of the Sibylline Oracles dating from this time. Also working at this time would have been some of the authors of the building blocks of 1 Enoch. This revolutionary generation was stunningly creative and obsessed with judgment and heavenly battle.[8]

The conflict that spawned the Qumran community began as a struggle of priestly elites, but it soon escalated to cosmic proportions. The sect taught a rigid separation from what they saw as a sinful and contaminated world. In their most extreme texts, they presented themselves as the true Sons of Light, while the official Temple cult was in the hands of these false Israelites, the Children of Darkness. The conflict, they wrote, would rage until it culminated with a divine intervention, a Judgment, which would annihilate the present world order; the fate of God's enemies is often described as extermination or annihilation. As one Qumran writer declared in a commentary on prophet Habakkuk, "On the day of Judgment, God will destroy completely all who serve the idols and the evil ones from the earth."[9]

THE TERM "DUALISM" has different meanings in different contexts. In the history of religion, dualistic ideas imply an eternal struggle between the equal forces of cosmic good and evil, a doctrine held today by none of the world's major religions. Both Christianity and Islam teach the existence of a devil, Satan, who is the enemy of God, but it is never implied that he is in any sense God's equal. He is a rebellious force whose continued existence God tolerates, for his own mysterious purposes. That is different from the mythological vision of the eternal conflict of Light and Darkness, which appears in versions of the Persian Zoroastrian faith and in the Manichaean religion that emerged in the third century CE.

As we will see, the Qumran texts—the Scrolls—make frequent reference to diabolical figures, usually Belial, who is seen as a very potent force in the world. That theme emerges in the Thanksgiving Hymns, which might conceivably be the work of the Teacher of Righteousness himself and which perhaps enjoyed canonical status at Qumran. These Hymns speak in the first person, and if they can in fact be linked to a real individual, then the voice in which they speak is both agonized and deeply paranoid. The speaker interprets every act and thought of his foes and critics as the plots of Belial, who constantly persecutes the virtuous and godly. He declares, "Brutal men seek my soul, while I hold fast to our covenant. They are the fraudulent council of Belial, they do not know that my office is from [God]." He refers often to the plots and conspiracies directed against him and fantasizes about the screams that the plotters will utter when divine vengeance overwhelms them. In contrast, the Hymnist himself (the Teacher?) proclaims that "my office is among the gods," again using near-messianic words.[10] If these are indeed the words of the Teacher, and debate rages about that point, then the attitudes of the sect on which he left his imprint can be easily understood.

At least some of the documents (by no means all) go even beyond that view of pervasive evil to offer an explicit statement of dualism. The War Scroll praised God, because "You appointed the Prince of Light [Michael] from old to assist us, for in his lot are all sons of righteousness and all spirits of truth are in his dominion. You yourself made Belial for the pit, an angel of malevolence, his dominion is in darkness, and his counsel is to condemn and convict." Belial was "a hostile angel: in darkness is his domination, his counsel is aimed towards wickedness and guiltiness. All the spirits of his lot, angels of destruction, are behaving according to the statutes of darkness: toward it is their one urge. . . . Of old you appointed for yourself a day of great battle . . . to support truth and to destroy iniquity, to bring darkness low and to lend might to light."[11] Not only do mighty angels serve the respective powers of good and evil, but the conflict between the two is a universal reality.

Another critical passage occurs in the sect's Community Rule, a fundamental statement of the group's ideals and practices, representing an advanced theological dualism. New members were instructed as follows:

Now, this God created man to rule the world, and appointed for him two spirits after whose direction he was to walk until the final Inquisition. They are the spirits of truth and perversity. The origin of truth lies in the fountain of light, and that of perversity in the wellspring of darkness. All who practice righteousness are under the domination of the prince of lights, and walk in ways of light; whereas all who practice perversity are under the domination of the angel of darkness, . . . the God of Israel and the angel of his truth are always there to help the sons of light. It is God that created these spirits of light and darkness and made them the basis of every act, the [instigators] of every deed and the direction and the directors of every thought.

Although it survives in the Community Rule, this actually derived from an older document that was subsequently incorporated into the group's instructional materials, and it is commonly titled the Treatise on the Two Spirits. It is difficult to determine just how much older it is than the rule, but it might be from the third century. As it is, it falls just short of true cosmic dualism, in that the two spiritual forces are not equal: God himself deliberately creates the evil force. Even so, that Two Spirits doctrine is a major departure from anything that might remotely be suspected from the older Jewish tradition.[12]

Another Qumran find was the Testament of Amram, credited to Moses's father, and it is thoroughly dualistic. It describes a vision in which two figures dispute over the speaker, asking him which he would follow. One is the ruler of wickedness, the dark angel Malki-Resha, who boasts, "We rule and have authority over all the human race." Of this figure, who is also named as Belial, it is explained that "all his deeds are darkness, and he dwells in darkness." Against him there stands a ruler of Light, here named both Michael and Melchizedek, "King of Righteousness," who explains the fates of the Children of Light and Darkness. In this vision, Belial was licensed by God to launch his war against the Sons of Light, which again falls short of absolute dualism. What it also shows is the group's rigid determinism, in that God plans and ordains all things, even those acts seemingly launched by the Devil. Unlike in 1 Enoch, this is not part of a spontaneous angelic mutiny but rather a part of God's plan.[13]

LATER DUALIST MOVEMENTS extended the struggle of Light and Darkness to propose a conflict between the realms of spirit and matter, one that often involved a rejection of sexuality. Such a view is rare in Judaism of any era, but Josephus does describe an Essene hostility to marriage and sexuality, which reflected suspicion of the material world. Such a view is not found explicitly in the Scrolls. Even so, the Thanksgiving Hymns teach a deep suspicion of the material creation that again departs from biblical understandings, and foreshadows that later dualism. At length, the Hymnist stresses the failings of his physical nature, which is less than dust. Repeatedly, he declares himself a mere vessel of clay. Only by receiving the spirit of God, the spirit of truth and light, can the body do anything right or virtuous.[14]

Despite their fragmentary state, other Qumran texts support such doctrines of a division of spirit and flesh, which perhaps dated back to the Creation. One puzzling tract is known by the technical title of 4QInstruction, most of which is standard Wisdom literature, in that it offered wise and pious sayings for the instruction of pupils. It differs from most of the genre in including apocalyptic materials and also contains what looks like a reference to a larger Creation myth. In an early Jewish legend, the children of the ancient patriarch Seth (Adam's third son) are said to have erected inscriptions to preserve their knowledge of the heavens. This story is the subject of a contorted part of 4QInstruction, which reads: "And as an inheritance he gave it to [Seth's son] Enosh together with the people of the spirit, because according to the blueprint of the holy ones he formed him but did not give 'murmuring' to the spirit of the flesh as it cannot distinguish between good and evil according to the judgment of its spirit." That is anything but lucid, but it seems to indicate a story of Creation through angelic beings, the "holy ones." There are two categories of being, the people of Spirit and of Flesh, and the latter are impaired because they do not understand the ways of Wisdom and the Law. The translator in this case has been restrained in his use of capitalization, but it would be tempting to render some of the words here as if they represented supernatural categories, such as the Holy Ones, the People of the Spirit, and the Flesh. The division between spiritual and fleshly foreshadowed the writings of Saint Paul, who announced that "to be carnally [fleshly] minded is death; but to be spiritually minded is life and peace" (Rom. 8:6).[15]

THE ATTENTION PAID to the Qumran writings is understandable, but we must be cautious about assuming just what impact the group had in its own day. Sectarian isolation created a hothouse atmosphere in which extraordinarily violent dreams and fantasies could flourish. Some might even take the position that the sect stood at the extreme margins of the culture of its time and was no more relevant to mainstream discourse than, say, a modern-day American commune movement living in remote rural isolation. Even so, throughout history, marginal and even cultish movements have served as laboratories for ideas and motifs that seemed extreme in their day but soon joined the religious mainstream. In the case of dualism, the Dead Sea discoveries focused new attention on other documents that were already well known but had been dismissed as much later concoctions. Now, though, we realize how closely they recalled themes from Qumran. Taken together, these writings confirm the presence of a diffusive dualism in many areas of Jewish culture of the Crucible era, to a degree that would not have been suspected before the discovery of the Scrolls. That fact fundamentally revises our understanding of developments during the early Common Era.[16]

Some of the best evidence for dualistic thought comes from that rich collection of pseudoscriptures called the Testaments of the Twelve Patriarchs (second or first century BCE), which we have already encountered. The Qumran texts included a number of early documents using the testament genre, one of which, the Aramaic Levi Document, provided inspiration for the Testament of Levi. Before Qumran the Testaments also have connections to the literature of 1 Enoch and Jubilees.[17] Recalling Qumran, the Testaments present the idea of the competing two spirits, which led a person to good or evil. In every human soul and mind, there were two paths. God's messengers would protect his elect and those who chose the right directions. In his supposed Testament, the ancient Asher declares that

> Two ways has God given to the sons of men, and two minds, and two doings, and two places, and two ends. Therefore all

things are by twos, one corresponding to the other. There are two ways of good and evil, with which are the two minds in our breasts distinguishing them. Therefore if the soul take pleasure in good, all its actions are in righteousness; and though it sin, it straightway repents. . . . But if his mind turn aside in evil, all his doings are in maliciousness, and he drives away the good, and takes unto him the evil, and is ruled by Beliar; and even though he work what is good, he perverts it in evil. For whenever he begins as though to do good, he brings the end of his doing to work evil, seeing that the treasure of the devil is filled with the poison of an evil spirit.

Levi urges his children to "choose therefore for yourselves either the darkness or the light, either the law of the Lord or the works of Beliar." Issachar warns his descendants that they must follow the commandments of God or pursue the way of Beliar. Naphtali says that a man's word might be "either in the law of the Lord or in the law of Beliar."[18]

A consistent theme in the various Testaments is how sternly they address issues of individual sinfulness. Believers must be constantly on their guard against the wiles of demonic forces who tempt them to sin. That did not mean offenses committed by communities or families, nor did it refer to ritual violations. If this sounds like the image of demonic tempters familiar from medieval Christian art, then that resemblance is made even clearer by the kind of sins at issue, sins such as lust, anger and envy, and roughly, the Seven Deadly Sins of later tradition. The Testament of Reuben specifically names seven evil spirits that lead people astray, namely, licentiousness, insatiability, contentiousness, flattery and hypocrisy, arrogance, lying, and injustice. All were bestowed by Beliar. The Testament of Dan reports that "one of the spirits of Beliar" tempted him to try to kill his brother Joseph. He warns of wrath and lying and the deep danger of combining the two offenses. "When the soul is continually disturbed, the Lord departs from it, and Beliar rules over it." No less medieval in tone is the vision of the individual soul as a battleground between angels and demons, as in the Testament of Benjamin: "The mind of the good man is not in the power of the deceit of the spirit of Beliar, for the angel of peace guides his soul." Such texts counsel constant introspection, of the kind to be expected from a monastic or eremitical setting.[19]

BESIDES THE GENERAL atmosphere of dualism, beliefs in determinism and predestination are also well documented. At the beginning of this book, I quoted Jesus's parable of the wheat and the tares, which implied not only a dualistic vision of the world but also that people were predetermined for either salvation or damnation, regardless of their individual will or inclination. Such texts support doctrines of predestination, which are difficult to find in the Old Testament, except through intense proof-texting. That influential idea had its roots in the preceding centuries and not just in the Scrolls. While Hellenistic cities placed their hope in the random power of Tyche (Fortune), at least some Jewish thinkers framed spiritual conflict in terms of determinism and explicit predestination.[20]

Such a division is already hinted at in 1 Enoch. One passage describes the two paths or ways that individuals might follow, "the paths of righteousness and the paths of violence. . . . For all who walk in the paths of unrighteousness shall perish for ever" (91:18). The text counsels the listeners ("my sons") to choose wisely between the ways, but already, other passages suggest that their ability to make such a decision was severely limited. The Parables tell us that God "knows before the world was created what is for ever, and what will be from generation unto generation" (39:11). The book of Sirach likewise points to the existence of deterministic ideas in the early second century CE. One curious verse protests that God has commanded no man to act wickedly, nor has he given anyone permission to commit sins (15:20). Such a rebuttal makes little sense unless somebody at the time was making just such arguments, and was attributing human evil to the deity.

It is, however, in the Qumran texts that such determinism emerges most powerfully. Josephus told us that the Essenes were strong believers in determinism, so that "nothing befalls men unless it be in accordance with her decree." Not surprisingly, the Scrolls were uncompromising in their ideas of absolute divine control. The *Pesher* (or interpretive commentary) on Habakkuk remarks, typically, that "all of God's periods will come according to their fixed order, as he decreed." The Treatise on the Two Spirits describes two hostile and competing realities, although it is not obvious whether these are actual cosmic beings or metaphors for human inclinations. But whatever their nature, the spiritual conflict is deeply laid. The Sons of Light needed to learn that

> from the God of knowledge stems all there is and all there shall be. Before they existed he established their entire design. And when they have come into being, at their appointed time, they will execute all their works according to his glorious design, without altering anything. . . . He created man to rule the world and placed within him two spirits so that he would walk with them until the moment of his visitation: they are the spirits of truth and of deceit. From the springs of light stem the generations of truth, and from the source of darkness the generations of deceit.

"[God] created the spirits of light and darkness and on them established every deed." That phrase recalls the division of the world between carnal and spiritual people taught in 4QInstruction.[21]

Predestinarian ideas are no less evident in the Thanksgiving Hymns. For the righteous man, "from the womb, [God] determined the time of approval, in order that he keep your covenant and walk in [it]." "But the wicked you created for [the time] of your [wrath] and from the womb you have vowed them to the Day of Massacre." Jubilees uses Qumran-like language about the Children of the Covenant and the Children of Destruction and actually sees circumcision as the factor dividing the two. That approach was more simplistic than that of the Qumran sectaries, who recognized that circumcision alone did not mark a man out as saved. In their view, plenty of so-called Jews were likewise destined for perdition.[22]

Deterministic ideas drew on the theme of heavenly writings and tablets, which are the eternal and absolute originals of earthly copies. Long before the Flood, Enoch was able to "read the book of all the deeds of mankind, and of all the children of flesh that shall be upon the earth to the remotest generations." Similarly, for Jubilees, the earthly Law is first written in heaven, and so are the deeds of individuals: "And the judgment of all is ordained and written on the heavenly tablets in righteousness—even [the judgment of] all who depart from the path which is ordained for them to walk in; and if they walk not therein, judgment is written down for every creature and for every kind. . . . [A]ll their judgments are ordained and written and engraved" (5:12–15).[23]

Individuals could actually join the Sons of Light or at least publicly align with the sect. The group made extensive use of rituals involving dipping or plunging in water with the goal of achieving ritual purity, acts that in Greek would be called baptism. Such acts intrigue scholars who wish to present the community as precursors of later Christianity, and again they draw comparisons between the Qumran sect and the Essenes, who had a similar ritual. Describing the Essenes in a later era, Josephus writes of the procedure by which candidates were tested through a probationary period, before receiving a kind of initiation, through what is variously translated as "waters of purification" or "the purer kind of holy water."[24]

The Qumran sect's Community Rule speaks of washings designed to remove ritual impurities, with the caveat that the person being treated thus must obey God's laws before he can expect true cleanness: "When his flesh is sprinkled with purifying water and sanctified by cleansing water, it shall be made clean by the humble submission of his soul to all the precepts of God." Coincidentally or not, that section of the rule leads directly into the famous Treatise on the Two Spirits, perhaps suggesting a linkage to the thought world of Light and Darkness. Tentatively, we might see the washing as a symbolic cleansing from darkness and evil. Another fragment from Qumran gives a series of set prayers and thanksgivings, in what some translators have described as a Baptismal Liturgy.[25]

Struggling to avoid excessive Christian interpretations, modern translators generally speak of such acts as ablutions, washings, or lustrations, but the term "baptism" is just as accurate. It was as if even Jews were being initiated into a new and more authentic covenant and prepared for spiritual combat during the forthcoming End Times. Nor did recruitment violate ideas of predestination: those new members were only discovering and acknowledging their status as Children of Light, which hitherto had been known only to God. But baptism, too, must be seen in this larger framework of spiritual warfare. It is an open question whether actual continuities to Christianity can be traced, but parallels are apparent. The Christian gospels begin with the mission of John the Baptist, whose reported career bore many resemblances to Qumran practice; it was even situated in the same geographical area. John, like the Qumran followers, offered a ritual washing for Jews, parallel to the rites used to bring Gentiles into Judaism.

So SUDDENLY DID the Qumran mythological framework appear, and in such fully developed form, that perhaps these various themes were imported in prefabricated form, rather than evolving locally. Through the decades, many scholars have turned eastward to find the origins of these ideas and located them in the great culture of Persia. Persia followed the religion founded by the prophet Zarathustra or Zoroaster, which at least in later times (and that distinction is important) was centrally concerned with dualistic themes. Palestine had been under Persian control during the Achaemenid era, from the 540s through the 330s BCE, some seven generations, so that a sizable Persian cultural inheritance might be expected. Apart from the Mesopotamian and Egyptian connections, Jewish apocalyptic has many points of contact with Persian notions. Persians too contemplated a day when those who betrayed or violated God's laws could be duly punished, while the righteous were vindicated. Beyond doubt, the Jews imported many ideas from the cultures with which they came into contact. But if Persian influences were certainly present, that does not mean that all the new ideas in Judaism were a Persian import. The spiritual revolution did not come intact from a Persian shelf.[26]

At different stages of its existence, Persian religion imagined mighty spiritual figures. The great God of Light, Ahura Mazda, battled the evil Angra Mainyu, or Ahriman. Persian religion also had its spirits, *ahuras* and *daevas*, much like their ancient Hindu counterparts. For Zarathustra, these figures became more dualistic in tone, with the good *ahuras* in combat with the evil *daevas*, and in retrospect, it is easy to read these as angels and demons. In some cases, borrowings are apparent. The demonic Persian figure of Aeshma, "Wrath," became Aeshma-Deva, who appears as Asmodeus in Tobit.[27]

Other suggested appropriations are convincing. Jews might just have evolved their own concept of the two spirits independently, but it is difficult not to see the influence of texts like this, from the Gathas attributed to Zarathustra: "Truly there are two primal Spirits, twins renowned to be in conflict. In thought and word, in action, they are two: the good and the bad. And those who act well have chosen rightly between these two, not so the evil-doers. And when these two Spirits encountered, they created life and not-life, and how at the end the Worst Existence [that is, Hell] shall be for the deceitful, but [the House of] Best Thought [that is, Heaven] for the just."[28] Explaining such influence would only require the travels of a handful of individuals or even the migration of some manuscripts. Once these ideas had been absorbed by one intellectual center, presumably Jerusalem, they could easily be transmitted elsewhere.

Qumran also produced other Persian-sounding concepts. Around 420 BCE, the traveler Herodotus stressed the Persian view of lying (*pseudesthai*) as an ultimate evil: "The most disgraceful thing in the world, they think, is to tell a lie." That may hint at a later Persian notion of the titanic struggle between competing forces, originally Truth and Falsehood, so that the world divided between followers of Truth and followers of the Lie. In later centuries, this was framed as a struggle between Light and Dark. The Qumran sect recalled this language when members denounced their enemies as "Man of the Lie" or "Spouter of the Lie." Jesus himself would later denounce the Devil as a liar (*pseustes*) and Father of Lies.[29]

But to acknowledge borrowings is not to accept that Jews imported a whole religious system intact. One obstacle to such a view is that of chronology. Although Persian rule over Palestine ended in the late fourth century, overtly dualist ideas are hard to find in the Jewish world until the post-170 era, and only in the following century do they become commonplace.

The other problem is in defining and dating the Persian ideas themselves. Nineteenth- and early-twentieth-century Western scholars were overconfident about what they could reasonably say about Zoroastrianism in those ancient eras, and they often back-projected from much later writings to understand primitive forms of the faith. For instance, the Zoroastrian tradition has a messianic figure, the Saoshyant, or Benefactor, who plays a special role in the apocalyptic renewing of all things, the Frashokereti, the day of Judgment and Resurrection. That seems to prefigure Enochic and Christian ideas, quite uncannily. But even if the term "Saoshyant" is ancient, the earliest scriptural references are scanty and lack the later mythological framework. The messianic association with a Judgment Day is chiefly found in medieval texts in Middle Persian, dating from long after the rise of Christianity and indeed Islam. Eschatological influences might even run from the Abrahamic religions to the Persian rather than the reverse.

Western scholars interpreted Zoroastrian scriptures with strongly Jewish or Christian eyes, making Zarathustra's doctrines resemble the beliefs they already knew. We see this problem with a particular group of Zoroastrian divine beings called the Amesha Spentas, or Bounteous Immortals, who at first sight look as if they must be the role models for the archangels we know from Judaism. The Persian exemplars were originally the six forces or divine sparks through which the good God, Ahura Mazda, created the world of Light, with names like Devotion, Purpose, and Wholeness. Yet these forces did not possess anything like the individual identity of, say, Gabriel and Michael, and they are represented not as individual spiritual beings but as character traits or virtues. Only in scholarly hindsight do they become the prototypes of the West's archangels.[30]

Zoroastrianism itself changed dramatically over time, so that the faith as it existed in, say, 400 BCE looked quite different from that of 200 or 500 CE. Although Zarathustra's system was accepted in Persia in Achaemenid times (550–330 BCE) and his deity Ahura Mazda was venerated, the prophet's name does not even appear in inscriptions from that era. Nor, in this early era, is there much evidence of the dualist mythology that is usually labeled as Zoroastrian. Relying on Herodotus alone, we would never suspect that Persia in his time held any dualist beliefs whatever. Herodotus offers not a word about dualism, Light and Darkness, the Last Judgment, any kind of Satanic figure, or a messiah. Reading Herodotus, in fact, Persian religious life emerges something more like Indian Vedic religion, which makes sense in that Zoroastrianism stems from that common Indo-Iranian origin. The name Zarathustra was attached to a faith of sacrifices and libations. It was especially during the much later Sassanian era, from the third century CE onward, that the Zoroastrian religion acquired the hard-edged dualist tone for which it became famous. Just because the religion looked very recognizable in Jewish or Christian terms in 500 CE does not mean that this was its form seven hundred years earlier or that we can trace a direct influence from Persia to Judea, from Persepolis to Qumran.

WITH THOSE CAVEATS in mind, we can legitimately seek Persian influences in Judaism, if not on such a massive scale as might once have been suspected. Nor were such influences early imports; many arrived as part of a broader Hellenistic worldview. Moreover, ideas of cosmic confrontation evolved independently and naturally in the Jewish world, assisted by the imagination of such critical spiritual entrepreneurs as Qumran's Teacher of Righteousness. This was an internal dynamic, with its own inexorable logic.

Whatever its origins, cosmic warfare beliefs became an integral part of the emerging Jewish synthesis of the Crucible years. And far from being confined to scholarly speculation, these ideas penetrated every aspect of daily life.

Chapter 8

THE POWERS ABOVE

How the Universe Filled with Angels and Demons

And there was war in heaven: Michael and his angels fought against the dragon, and the dragon fought and his angels, and prevailed not; neither was their place found any more in heaven.

REVELATION 12:7–8, KJV

NEAR GADARA IN the Decapolis, Jesus met a man possessed by many devils. Confronting the demons, Jesus learned that their name was Legion, because they were so many—which also, subtly, placed the characteristic military units of the Roman occupying army in a diabolical context. The demons agreed to be evicted from their host, but Jesus granted them the favor of transferring to a nearby herd of pigs, which duly drowned themselves in a lake (Matt. 8:28–34). Jesus's method of healing left readers no option but to see the man's illness in terms of real, objective demonic forces rather than any inner or psychological condition. Evil was an omnipresent reality, and so were the spirits who served the evil realm. Through signs, healings, and miracles, God's servants fought a holy war against these forces, and the world was their battlefield.[1]

In terms of the widespread perils of supernatural evil, that story of the Gadarene swine is typical of the world around the start of the Common Era, and it has its roots in the century or so after the Maccabean revolt. In this era, spiritual forces were personified in images that now occupied center stage in the religious narrative. Hell, Darkness, and the Devil now dominated religious thought, as they absolutely had not in the literature of the canonical Old Testament. In some accounts, the Devil was already becoming the lord of this world, with particular angels assigned hegemony over particular peoples and lands. Opposing him in the End Times struggles would be the leader of the forces of good, the Messiah. The heavens became densely populated as never before.

ANGELS ARE A lively presence in the New Testament. Jesus himself referred to them on many occasions, and the evangelist Luke reports that Jesus's birth was foretold by an angel with a specific name, Gabriel. So accustomed are we to those characters that it is easy to forget at how late a stage they appear in the Jewish story. In their familiar form, angels do not appear in Jewish texts that can plausibly be dated before the third century, but by about 200 BCE angelic mythology suddenly emerges fully formed in multiple texts. As we will see, the proliferation of angels in later years was a direct response to sea-changes in both religious thought and the larger Jewish culture, mainly in consequence of the endemic nature of conflict and confrontation. So florid was the growing interest in these princes of Heaven that a Jewish religious or pseudobiblical work can often be dated by the nature of its treatment of angels. The later it is, the greater the role that angels play and the more likely they are to be given names, identities, and specific tasks and functions.[2]

The practice of naming angels was a crucial marker in attitudes toward the supernatural realm. In earlier eras, attributing actions to the anonymous "angel of the Lord" commonly meant that God himself did something, with little attention paid to the nature of the messengers. They were just convenient faces of divine power. In one episode in the book of Judges (13), an angel tells Samson's parents about their unborn son. When the father asks the angel's name, he is rebuffed. Why do you want to know that, replies the angel, because it is a wonder (or beyond understanding)? Angelic names are beyond human comprehension, and there is no need to know them.

Actually naming such figures opened the way to formulating whole mythological systems and attributing agency to them in their own right. In the canonical Old Testament, named angels first appear in portions of Daniel written in the 160s, which mentions both Gabriel (8:15–16, 9:21) and Michael (10:13, 10:21, and 12:1). Conceivably, the practice of naming owed something to the influence of neighboring polytheistic societies, especially Babylonian and Egyptian, but it also followed logically from developments in Hebrew thought. In an age of such energetic literary creativity, those reconceived angels starred as vital figures in religious narratives, with extensive dialogue and even individual character development. In turn, the outburst of literary works further focused religious interest on those beings and prompted still other writings. Taking the numerous texts written between, say, 200 BCE and 200 CE would supply ample material for a literary biography of Michael or Gabriel. Before he was imagined as the sole God, YHWH originated as a deity surrounded by other colleagues in a heavenly court. The new emphasis on named angels and archangels again surrounded him with near-divine courtiers.[3]

INDISPUTABLY, ANGELS AS such feature in the Hebrew Bible. God placed cherubim with a flaming sword to guard the gates of the Garden of Eden, and angels visited Lot at Sodom. But these figures were far less frequent in later biblical texts. A standard English translation of the whole Bible contains 336 references to angels, a sizable majority of which (230) are found in the New Testament and the Deuterocanonical books, that is, chiefly from the period after about 200 BCE. (That figure does not include stories in which the text implies angelic activity or presence but without actually using the term.) When angels do appear in pre-Exilic texts, their function is to perform actions that would otherwise be attributed to God directly and personally. That is what would be expected of an increasingly monotheistic culture, in which writers were reluctant to involve God too directly in mundane functions.[4]

The Hebrew Bible offered two major accounts of a particular category of angelic figures, the seraphim and cherubim, but both chiefly refer to the symbolic images used to accompany the divine presence in the Temple. They are divine symbols or attributes rather than active creatures. One passage describes Isaiah's vision (6) of a divine appearance in the Temple, flanked by his six-winged seraphim. The other story is found in the opening chapter of the book of Ezekiel (10), which offers a terrifying vision of the divine chariot, *merkabah*, and the four living creatures surrounding it. These are the cherubim, and they are closely related to the human-headed animals often depicted in Assyrian art, the *karibu*. Although cherubim feature often in the Old Testament text, it is almost always in the context of the ornamental architectural figures used in the Ark and subsequently in the Temple itself. Even when Ezekiel sees them in living form, his cherubim neither act nor speak; instead, they just symbolize the active reality of YHWH.

Such passages are utterly different from the abundant depiction of angels in the subsequent history of Judaism and Christianity. The pioneering text for the new order was 1 Enoch, which enumerates both good and evil angels and identifies heavenly ranks and hierarchies. One passage in the Book of the Watchers lists the seven great archangels, each with his particular area of responsibility, including the following:

> Raphael, one of the holy angels, who is over the spirits of men . . .
>
> Michael, one of the holy angels, to wit, he that is set over the best part of mankind and over chaos . . .
>
> Gabriel, one of the holy angels, who is over Paradise and the serpents and the Cherubim.

The Book of the Watchers also presents several angelic names, grouped in a familiar pattern. It tells us of the sinful world before the Flood, "and then Michael, Uriel, Raphael, and Gabriel looked down from heaven and saw much blood being shed upon the earth, and all lawlessness being wrought upon the earth" (9:1–3).[5]

Surprisingly advanced theologizing about angels appears in Tobit, which was written around the same time as the earlier sections of 1 Enoch. Raphael introduces himself as "one of the seven holy angels who present the prayers of the saints and enter into the presence of the glory of the Holy One" (12:15). Raphael also tells his listeners that he has been intervening frequently throughout their adventures, offering healing and carrying their prayers, demonstrating the angelic role as intercessors. This is close to the concept of the guardian angel who protects individual people and families. In the Testaments of the Twelve Patriarchs, Dan urges his descendants to safeguard themselves from Satan: "Come close to God and to the angel who intercedes for you, for he is an intermediary between God and men for the peace of Israel, and he will stand up against the enemy's kingdom." We recall another form of heavenly intercession documented in the second century, with the prayer for the dead advocated in 2 Maccabees. Writers at this time were exploring the implications of a more interconnected and hierarchical universe, which contained not just angels and demons but also the souls of the dead.[6]

The celebrated names of these angels originated as divine qualities, or affirmations, and represented the presence of God in the world. Gabriel means "the Strength of God," Michael signifies "Who Is Like God," Raphael means "God Heals" or "God the Healer," and Uriel derives from "the Light of God" or "God Is My Light." Originally, perhaps, they represented indirect means of speaking of God, in an age increasingly nervous of mentioning his name or even invoking him directly. Over time, those qualities or titles came to be imagined as independent entities or persons, a process of personification that we will often observe in these centuries.[7] The dark angels experienced a similar evolution. Originally, the name Azazel was part of the ancient scapegoat ritual, by which the community selected goats to be sacrificed or exiled in order to carry away the sins of the community. These were to be consigned to "absolute removal," the word that became "Azazel." Eventually, that word became the personal name of a mighty archdemon, as in 1 Enoch. Originally, too, Belial likewise represented a title or quality, in this case "Without Worth." Concepts evolved into persons, who in turn became characters in a rapidly emerging mythology.[8]

So standard and orthodox did such angelic names become that later scholars were troubled by the lack of explicit identifications in the canonical Old Testament. As a result, they helpfully tried to supply angelic names retroactively. Genesis 18 records that three men visited Abraham. Their identity intrigued medieval Jewish scholars, who applied the then popular science of numerology to solving the problem. Each Hebrew letter in the text had a numerical value, as did each of the words that those letters made up. By piecing together the value of the words in the biblical text, then, scholars had no doubt that the visitors' names were Gabriel, Michael, and Raphael. That rendering became a standard part of biblical interpretation: the patriarch's visitors were not men but named archangels.[9]

THE GREAT ANGELS acquired specific roles that reflected new visions of the structure of the universe. Although Jubilees does not actually name individual angels, these holy paladins are a central part of the author's vision of the universe. In this work, in fact, Moses reveals words spoken to him not by God directly but by "the angel of the Presence." These angels fall into well-defined hierarchies:

For on the first day He created the heavens which are above and the earth and the waters and all the spirits which serve before him—the angels of the presence, and the angels of sanctification, and the angels [of the spirit of fire and the angels] of the spirit of the winds, and the angels of the spirit of the clouds, and of darkness, and of snow and of hail and of hoar frost, and the angels of the voices and of the thunder and of the lightning, and the angels of the spirits of cold and of heat, and of winter and of spring and of autumn and of summer and of all the spirits of his creatures which are in the heavens and on the earth.

Distinctive hierarchies also feature in the Parables of Enoch. There were Seraphim, Cherubim, and Ophannim: "And these are they who sleep not and guard the throne of His glory. And I saw angels who could not be counted, a thousand thousands, and ten thousand times ten thousand, encircling that house. And Michael, and Raphael, and Gabriel, and Phanuel, and the holy angels who are above the heavens go in and out of that house" (71:7–8).[10]

While the Hebrew Bible had described God's heavenly realms only in general terms, those heavens were now envisioned much more specifically, divided into specific layers (usually seven), each with its appropriate angels and guardians. The second century BCE brought the first of many accounts of heavenly visions and explorations, as particular prophets or sages recounted their experiences of travels through the spiritual regions, all the carefully categorized heavens and hells. Angels proliferated voluminously in such accounts, often as celestial guides and couriers.

In its catalog of the heavens, the Testament of Levi sketches an angelic hierarchy that would have been quite recognizable to medieval Christians. And of course, the heavens are seven in number:

The lowest is, for this cause, more gloomy, in that it is near all the iniquities of men.

The second hath fire, snow, ice, ready for the day of the ordinance of the Lord, in the righteous judgment of God: in it are all the spirits of the retributions for vengeance on the wicked.

In the third are the hosts of the armies which are ordained for the day of judgment, to work vengeance on the spirits of deceit and of Beliar.

And the heavens up to the fourth above these are holy, for in the highest of all dwells the Great Glory, in the holy of holies, far above all holiness.

In the heaven next to it are the angels of the presence of the Lord, who minister and make propitiation to the Lord for all the ignorances of the righteous; and they offer to the Lord a reasonable sweet-smelling savor, and a bloodless offering.

And in the heaven below this are the angels who bear the answers to the angels of the presence of the Lord.

And in the heaven next to this are thrones, dominions, in which hymns are ever offered to God.[11]

Dante's vision of the supernatural realms stood at the end of a tradition that was by then some fifteen hundred years old.

DURING THE SECOND century, angelic theories became ever more commonplace and mainstream. They were especially visible in three settings that were in their various ways very closely linked to cultural and political conflicts. One, as we have seen, was in the literature of apocalyptic, where angels conveyed heavenly messages to the sage or seer. Also, in the context of heavenly warfare, angels played a special role as God's soldiers, their hierarchies corresponding to the ranks of earthly forces. In heaven as on earth, there were generals and foot soldiers, all with their proper places in the chain of command. Third, angels appear as heavenly priests, or as transmitters of priestly authority, validating contested claims to religious power.

Angelic figures feature prominently in the Qumran sect's visions of holy warfare. The War Rule instructs the followers of righteousness to have no fear, because they follow a mighty leader: "Today is [God's] appointed time to subdue and to humiliate the prince of the realm of wickedness. He will send eternal support to the company of His redeemed by the power of the majestic angel of the authority of Michael. By eternal light He shall joyfully light up the covenant of Israel; peace and blessing for the lot of God, to exalt the authority of Michael among the gods and the dominion of Israel among all flesh. Righteousness shall rejoice on high, and all sons of His truth shall rejoice in eternal knowledge." Angels fight alongside God's warriors, who seek angelic protection. They would take refuge in fortified towers, and "upon all the shields of the tower soldiers, they shall write: on the first, Michael, on the second, Gabriel, on the third, Sariel, and on the fourth Raphael. Michael and Gabriel on the right, and Sariel and Raphael on the left." Readers of the War Rule would have been comfortable with Jesus's later references to the legions of angels whom God would send to defend his Son, should he so choose (Matt. 26:53). As in the rule, Jesus's angels are organized in military formation.[12]

The priestly context was critical in an age that was so divided over the credentials demanded of God's earthly servants and whether the Hasmoneans were properly qualified to exercise their high priesthood. Angels validated and sanctified the authority of earthly priests, just as they warranted the authenticity of apocalyptic texts. Who could challenge an ordination bestowed at the hands of an angel? This use of angelic figures meshed naturally with the common tendency in this era to project earthly institutions into a heavenly realm, so that, for example, the familiar Law was a reflection of words inscribed on heavenly tablets. Commonly too, the earthly Temple was portrayed as an imitation or shadow of a reality above, in which angels served just as priests did on earth, undertaking a similar sacrificial work.

That angelic association was obvious at Qumran, not surprisingly given the sect's ties to the Essene movement. The Essenes had had a special veneration for angels. After listing the requirements for membership in the sect, Josephus tells us that candidates swore to transmit faithfully the doctrines they had received and to avoid adultery and robbery, "and [they] will equally preserve the books belonging to their sect, and the names of the angels." Issues of priestly authority were especially sensitive at Qumran, given their continuing challenge to the legitimacy of the Jerusalem Temple. Indeed, the sect's whole raison d'être concerned the nature of authentic priesthood.[13]

Angels were ubiquitous in the Qumran documents, often in a priestly or liturgical context and commonly either possessing or transmitting heavenly writings. The concept of seven angels or archangels appeared in the Aramaic Levi Document, which was found at Qumran but predated the sect (it likely dates from the third century). This describes the group of heavenly beings who confirm Levi's appointment to the priesthood and outline his rights and privileges. In the related Testament of Levi, each angelic figure bears an aspect of priesthood:

> *And I saw seven men in white raiment saying to me,*
> *Arise, put on the robe of the priesthood,*
> *and the crown of righteousness,*
> *and the breastplate of understanding,*
> *and the garment of truth,*
> *and the diadem of faith,*
> *and the tiara of miracle,*
> *and the ephod of prophecy.*

In the lengthy Angelic Liturgy, seven angelic beings, godlike *elohim*, hold sacrifices in a heavenly Temple, with its seven sanctuaries. In his supposed Testament, similarly, Levi reports how "the angel opened the gates of heaven to me, and I saw the holy Temple, and the Most High on a glorious throne." That idea of the Temple above would have a profound impact on early Christianity, which viewed Christ as its eternal high priest. In the New Testament book of Acts, the martyr Stephen declares that angels had delivered the Law to the Jewish people, although they had forsaken it (7:53).[14]

Because they are so fragmentary, other references are harder to contextualize. They do, however, reveal an impressive range of theorizing and point to a once sizable speculative literature that is now wholly lost. One Qumran text imagines Michael in conversation with other angels, including Gabriel. In another fragment of a lost legend, Michael offers a covenant to Zedekiah, the last king of Judah before the Exile.[15]

ON EARTH ANGELS served as the leaders or rulers of particular nations or territories, and in this capacity they closely resembled the pagan gods of old. In fact, one passage in Deuteronomy shows a direct continuity in those ideas. In the original text, God assigned nations according to the number of "the sons of God," presumably an acknowledgment of the reality of rival deities. That nod to polytheism embarrassed later readers, and in the Septuagint translation God sets nations and boundaries "according to the number of the *angels* of God." Once upon a time there were gods, who were transformed into tutelary angels or spirits, who in turn became thoroughly godlike.[16]

This idea of national guardians is well developed in Daniel (10:13, 10:21, 12:1), where Michael is the special protector of the Jewish people but other nations have their own princes or protectors, including the guardians of Persia and Greece. So powerful is the prince of Persia, in fact, that it took the efforts of two mighty archangels, Michael and Gabriel, to overcome him. Sirach similarly notes that God "appointed a ruler for every nation, but Israel is the Lord's own portion" (17:17). It is not certain whether such other rulers represented a kind of rebellion against God, associated with Satanic forces, or if they were seen as tolerated provincial rulers within a wide empire under the suzerainty of YHWH.

Naturally enough, given its pervasive hostility toward Gentiles, it is Jubilees that presents these figures in the most sinister and exclusive terms. Yes, says the author, "there are many nations and many peoples, and all are His, and over all hath He placed spirits in authority to lead them astray from Him. But over Israel He did not appoint any angel or spirit, for He alone is their ruler, and He will preserve them and require them at the hand of His angels and His spirits."[17]

That ran against the common assumption that Israel did indeed have a tutelary figure, namely, Michael. But whatever the exact identity of such figures, the idea of territorial spirits lent itself to visions of earthly conflicts being mirrored in the heavens, to clashes of angelic and demonic beings.

Just how critically important these images became is revealed by a confrontation on the eve of the great Jewish insurrection of the 60s CE. Josephus reports how his friend Herod Agrippa II delivered a powerful speech urging the Jews not to revolt against Rome, listing the overwhelming odds they would face. He confirmed the truth of his statements by invoking the three most sacred things that Jews could value, namely, the Temple, God's holy angels, and the land all shared. In the hierarchy of sanctity, the angels stood between the Temple and the Land. They were the symbols of the nation, its chiefs, and its symbolic soul.[18]

As ANGELS OF Light and good proliferated, so also did their evil counterparts and in exactly the same years, from the third century onward. The image of a diabolical figure with his dark angels was widespread in the thought of the time. Michael and Gabriel served God; Azazel and Belial/Beliar rebelled against him. Soon, the chief force for evil would definitively be named as Satan.[19]

In Christian tradition, Satan or the Devil stands at the heart of a substantial mythology. As commonly understood, and as often remembered through Milton's *Paradise Lost*, Satan was originally a magnificent angel who rebelled against God. God punished him and his followers by casting them out of Heaven and confining them to the fires of Hell. Satan accepted his fate—in the words of Milton's Devil, "Better to reign in Hell than serve in Heaven"—and he pursued his war against God's Creation. Among other things, he poisoned God's human Creation by seducing Adam and Eve into disobedience and sin. The consequence of that encounter was that later human beings inherited inborn sinfulness, which consigned them to suffering and death. Satan's Fall from Heaven thus led inexorably to the Fall of Humanity. Satan, meanwhile, continues to rule his infernal dominion, from which base he and his demonic servants continue to patrol the world, to tempt humans into sin. Those who succumb will be eternally tormented.

In different forms, elements of that saga feature in countless works of literature and art, and it is difficult to imagine Christianity without such a Satanic figure. Yet Satan was by no means a major character in the canonical Old Testament. In every aspect of his story, he owes his origin to the Crucible years, especially to the time of the Enochic writings. Precisely in that era, the Devil enjoyed an impressive rise both in his professional status and in his assigned areas of responsibility. From being a minor official at the heavenly court, he rose to become a fully fledged adversary of God, almost an anti-God, the titanic Lord of Evil known through much of Christian history. Like God, he acquired his own institutional hierarchy of inferior angels, and many of those operatives also bore individual names and titles. Satan's authority extended to the material world, and he could rely on the faithful service of significant numbers of the human population. His history was retroactively rewritten to build up his role in historic events, especially the Fall of Man.

That initial remark about Satan's absence from the Old Testament may seem odd if the serpent in Eden should be taken as the Devil, but we have no justification for doing so, beyond much later commentaries. Nor is it obvious that many later texts that were subsequently applied to Satan were so intended at the time. Isaiah offers the famous line "How you have fallen from heaven, morning star, son of the dawn!" (14:12). That resonates wonderfully with our memories of the Satanic revolt in *Paradise Lost*. From its Latin Vulgate translation, that passage gives us the name Lucifer. Even so, the being whose fall is celebrated here is in no sense supernatural, but rather refers to the king of Babylon. Another text used to establish diabolical origins was the condemnation of the king of Tyre in Ezekiel 28, which medieval and modern Christians read as a portrait of Satan and his rebellion against God. The linkage initially sounds convincing enough, suggesting as it does a being who was originally heavenly and perfect but who fell through pride. There is even a reference to the king having been in Eden itself. Yet the text had no such diabolical connotations at the time of writing, and Jews historically understood the words to refer to Adam rather than Satan.[20]

When Satan actually does appear in the Old Testament, he is a marginal figure. For the book of Job, he is a divine servant, a kind of public prosecutor. Zechariah too portrays a member of the divine court (3:1), rather than a Satan in anything like his later devilish guise. Both Zechariah and Job use the term *ha-satan*, "the satan," and he is given a definite article rather than a personal name.

If Satan really had been a major figure in Hebrew thought during the First Temple era, it is astounding that he features scarcely at all in the quite extensive surviving writings of the prophets. Never do they denounce such enemy peoples as Edomites or Egyptians as "sons of Satan." (The book of Exodus recalls YHWH's conflict with "the gods of Egypt" without any implication that these were forces of cosmic evil [12:12].) If we relied on the canonical Hebrew Bible alone, without subsequent writing and commentary, our religious heritage would be Devil-free.

By the time of 1 Enoch, however, we have entered a different religious universe in which very potent evil forces exist and form part of a rival kingdom set against that of God. Among the evil angels who descended to earth to mate with human women can be found such later infamous names as Azazel. The evil they bring to the earth is cured only by the Great Flood, but evil continues to walk the restored earth. The Enochian mythology also appears in Jubilees, where Mastema ("Hostility") fills a role very close to that of the later Satan. Mastema is a transitional figure between the divine servant found in Job and the cosmic adversary of New Testament times, although the divine enemy is also titled Belial or Beliar. Moses prays that God will send his mercy upon the people, "and create in them an upright spirit, and let not the spirit of Beliar rule over them to accuse them before Thee, and to ensnare them from all the paths of righteousness."

The much greater availability of literary evidence from the mid-second century BCE demonstrates the breadth of concern about demonic and diabolical forces, due in part to the acute political divisions of the time. We have already seen the frequent references to Belial in multiple Qumran texts and the Testaments of the Twelve Patriarchs. Qumran's foundational Damascus Document declared simply that "in the present age, Belial is unrestrained in Israel." Jubilees, meanwhile, suggested that a whole category of humans, namely, uncircumcised Gentiles, were sons of Belial.[21]

Other figures too evolved from metaphors into personified forces of evil. The biblical book of Proverbs warns of the seductions of adulterous, wicked women who threatened to lead the virtuous into paths of disaster and even to the land of the dead. In that instance, the text is using rhetorical language to describe literal women. In an extended commentary on this passage, the much-discussed Qumran text known as 4Q184 turns the wayward woman into a monstrous demonic female who is nothing less than a personification of Death and Hell. A highly sexualized figure, indeed a prostitute, she foreshadows such figures of later Christian mythology as the Whore of Babylon in the book of Revelation.[22]

Satan himself became a familiar character in writings around the start of the Common Era. As the narrative of his rebellion and fall become better established in the overall mythology, so Satan became a powerful opponent of God rather than a wayward servant, and he was engaged in a mounting insurgency against divine order. The new synthesis was epitomized by the text the Life of Adam and Eve, which created much of the Devil mythology of later eras. This work was written in the first century CE and subsequently translated into many languages. This vastly influential text was widely read by Jews, Christians, and Muslims—it left its mark in the Qur'an—and it provided much of the story made famous in *Paradise Lost*. In the

Life of Adam and Eve, after the expulsion from Eden, the holy couple meet Satan, who describes the events leading to his own expulsion from Heaven. The Life then tells how this once gorgeous angel rebelled because he could not obey God's command to bow before the newly created Adam. Later in this same century, 2 Enoch tells of "the Watchers, who with their prince Satanail rejected the Lord of Light, and after them are those who are held in great darkness on the second heaven." In several texts, including the Assumption of Moses, the force of evil is usually counterposed by a good angel such as Michael, who leads the armies of Light.[23]

During these same centuries, Satan was credited with much greater direct power and capacity for independent action. One important source is the Martyrdom and Ascension of Isaiah, another Jewish text that was later edited and revised substantially by Christians. The Jewish original, which dated from the first century BCE, is notable for its strong views about devils and demons such as Sammael and Beliar, "the angel of lawlessness, who is the ruler of this world." Those words must give us pause for what they show about the utter rejection of "the world" as the Devil's realm, a weighty notion easily reconciled with dualistic readings. The Martyrdom and Ascension tells how Beliar possesses an evil king and through him drives Israel into apostasy, causing an upsurge of witchcraft and magic. As we have seen, the biblical book of Job depicts Satan as a diligent bureaucrat at the divine court, but a quite different image emerges in the much later Testament of Job, an elaborate expansion of the original narrative that probably dates from the first century BCE. Here, we find a Satan much more in line with the wholly evil image of later Christianity.[24]

ONCE SATAN HAD been identified and his kingdom established in the spiritual landscape, that mythology proved enormously convenient in understanding the canonical narrative of the Bible. Reading in hindsight, Satan or demons could be blamed for otherwise puzzling acts and commands previously attributed to God himself. That

trend is evident in several post-Exilic writings. In the earlier text of
2 Samuel, God inspires King David to conduct a census, a disastrous
decision with harmful effects. By the time the first book of Chronicles recounted that same narrative (21:1), in the fourth century,
blame for that action has firmly been relocated to Satan. The book
of Job demonstrates a tension here, in that the evils inflicted on the
virtuous man are apparently the work of Satan, but as the work pro-
ceeds, it is difficult not to see them as stemming from God himself.
Perhaps even there, "the Satan" was a later addition to an older story.

Such retroactive rewriting became more common in the second century BCE. It was strongly in evidence in Jubilees, which sys-
tematically rewrote biblical stories to shift the blame from God to
Mastema/Satan. One classic revision involved a dilemma that has
tormented believers through the centuries. According to Genesis,
God commanded Abraham that he should kill his son Isaac, only
to relent at the last moment. Many through history have agonized
over whether a benevolent deity could really have inflicted such a
brutal trick. Jubilees, though, finds no moral difficulty here, as Mastema bears the guilt of ordering the test and God appears as res-
cuer. Again, during Israel's captivity in Egypt, the canonical account
says that God hardened Pharaoh's heart to prevent him agreeing to
Moses's demand to free the Israelites, which almost suggests that
the resulting carnage and massacre were part of the divine plan. For
Jubilees, the evil advice stemmed not from God but from his evil
counterpart. The story culminates when "all the powers of Mastema
had been let loose to slay all the first-born in the land of Egypt."[25]

AS THE DEVIL became an anti-God, it was natural to divide his
realm likewise into multiple levels and to name its demonic guardians. Beyond the Devil proper, a whole mythology now described
the demons and evil spirits who walk the earth and who could be
blamed for any number of ills. The belief in evil forces grew out
of a kind of imaginative symmetry: if angels existed to bear God's
messages, then presumably they should have their evil counterparts,

demons or satans. In 1 Enoch, the prophet hears four heavenly voices praising God. "And I heard the fourth voice fending off the satans, and forbidding them to come before the Lord of Spirits to accuse them who dwell on the earth." Just as the Testament of Levi enumerated the angelic cohorts, so the Testament of his brother Reuben warned that "seven spirits were established by Beliar against man, and they are the beginning of the deeds of youth."[26]

Demons are a potent force in Jubilees, which draws its material from the book of Noah. I quote the summary of the pioneering scholar and translator R. H. Charles:

> The demons are the spirits which went forth from the souls of the giants who were the children of the fallen angels, *Jub. v. 7, 9.* These demons attacked men and ruled over them (*x. 3, 6*). Their purpose is to corrupt and lead astray and destroy the wicked (*x. 8*). They are subject to the prince Mastema *(x. 9)*, or Satan. Men sacrifice to them as gods (*xxii. 17*). They are to pursue their work of moral ruin till the judgment of Mastema (*x. 8*) or the setting up of the Messianic kingdom, when Satan will be no longer able to injure mankind (*xxiii. 29*).

That is an excellent summary of the concepts of Devil and devils known to subsequent Christianity.[27]

Demons served many practical functions for ordinary believers, in a world where God could no longer be readily invoked for the needs of everyday life. As in any premodern society, ordinary believers had a pressing need to seek protection from misfortune and harm by esoteric means, through amulets and magical texts, and it is in those contexts especially that exemplify the growing belief in angels and demons.[28]

Traditionally, scholars focused on "high" religion, favoring the theological and speculative over the vernacular and popular, and they drew a sharp distinction between religion and anything resembling magic or superstition. As we explore the realities of lived religion in the past, however, those lines become much fainter. In Hellenistic or Roman Egypt, a rich body of surviving documentation reveals what ordinary people believed, and this demonstrates the enormous presence of magical beliefs and an overwhelming need for amulets, curses, and exorcisms in daily life. Very thin boundaries separate magic and scriptural religion, even within a single text or tradition. The book of Tobit includes some glorious passages and prayers alongside very basic information about the best way of expelling demons, as passed on through an archangel: take a fish and burn its heart and liver. One Qumran text enumerates the enemies lying in wait for the righteous, who needed the skills of exorcism and protection: "All the spirits of the destroying angels, spirits of the bastards, demons, Lilith, howlers, and desert dwellers, and those which fall upon men without warning to lead them astray from a spirit of understanding." The community identified certain psalms as especially valuable weapons in this ongoing warfare with demonic forces, and one in particular—Psalm 91—became a mainstay for later exorcists and healers. The Aramaic Levi Document includes a typical prayer: "And let not any satan have power over me, to make me stray from your path."[29]

This magical element is strongly apparent in Noah, Giants, and other Enochic writings. These texts might have answered philosophical or spiritual questions about the origin of evil, but they also served as highly practical manuals. Together, they reveal a world obsessed with spiritual evil as an all too worldly presence, an impression that also emerges from the New Testament. This was, after all, a world that drew few distinctions between supernatural possession and illness in body and mind.[30]

Much of the book of Noah seems designed for a community deeply concerned with different forms of protective magic, and security against demonic forces. Technically, this is known as apotropaic magic, and it is usually manifested in charms, spells, and amulets. (The word is from the Greek for "turn away.") It usually involves heavy use of sacred or demonic names. Individuals could invoke archangels for protection, seek defense against particular named demons or monsters, or even (a different kind of magic altogether) call on the demons for their own nefarious purposes. Exorcism demanded knowing the individual name of the spirit to be evicted. In later times, both New Testament and rabbinic writings would condemn the actual worship or invocation of angels.[31]

One story in the book of Noah traces the origins of these apotropaic powers. Noah pleads with God to be protected from demons, who should be imprisoned in Hell. In response to this petition, Mastema agrees that nine-tenths of the evil spirits should be confined forever in Hell, or a similarly far removed spiritual dungeon, while the remaining tenth remain on earth to serve the forces of evil. "And we explained to Noah all the medicines of their diseases, together with their seductions, how he might heal them with herbs of the earth. And Noah wrote down all things in a book as we instructed him concerning every kind of medicine. Thus the evil spirits were precluded from (hurting) the sons of Noah. And he gave all that he had written to Shem, his eldest son; for he loved him exceedingly above all his sons."[32]

Readers of those texts could turn to Noah's tradition for healing from the ills of body, mind, or spirit and for protection against that feral remnant of demons that continues on the earth. Based on many later analogies, the passage sounds like an origin legend for the skills of fighting and resisting evil forces. It also resembles a thousand later *grimoires*, manuals of thaumaturgy and ritual magic. As so often in later centuries, literate religious figures had to walk a narrow line. Their official task was to record and preserve officially approved texts, but at the same time, they faced overwhelming demand to supply popular needs in the general area of magic and spells.

BESIDES ANGELS AND demons, the Messiah himself now became another central figure in the Jewish and Christian spiritual narrative. During the second century, messianic ideas not only emerged but rapidly took something very much like the diverse forms apparent in the New Testament and in rabbinic Judaism.

The word "messiah" stems from the Hebrew "anointed," which in Greek is rendered *christos*. Christians, by definition, are followers of the Messiah, and in Islamic tradition, Jesus is known as Jesus the Messiah, *Isa al-Masih*. In the Jewish context, the word implies a human figure who would appear to usher in the end of the present world order, to bring in a new era of holiness, justice, and divine rule. Commonly, this person is portrayed as a descendant of David's line, and he might be seen as either royal or priestly.[33]

Several Old Testament passages in particular are often quoted as messianic prophecies. The book of Isaiah was especially fruitful for these purposes. Hebrew prophets were thrilled by the decision of the Persian king Cyrus to allow the Jews to return from Babylon in the 530s. For great prophets like Second Isaiah, Cyrus's actions proved the universal nature of God's rule and his ability to use outside peoples and individuals to exercise his will. Christians read such texts retroactively, seeking prophecies that could be applied to Jesus, while both Jews and Christians assimilated prophecies of coming times of peace and prosperity to a general messianic scheme. Read through the eyes of faith, these were understood to predict a coming individual messiah on the familiar pattern. Apart from Second Isaiah, appropriate texts were easily found in Psalms, Zechariah, and Ezekiel. Yet the fact that scriptures were read in this way does not mean that the writers of particular texts intended such End Times readings. The Old Testament never uses the word "messiah" in this sense of a future individual, with the debatable exception of the book of Daniel, to be discussed shortly. As the *Encyclopedia Judaica* remarks, "One can, therefore, only speak of the biblical prehistory of messianism." If we imagine an encounter with a Jewish thinker of around 400 BCE, it would not have been easy to convey later meanings of the messianic idea. Even in the decades before Jesus's birth, the idea was still a work in progress.[34]

Plenty of Second Temple books looked to the End Times as a glorious age of restoration and salvation, a time when Diaspora exiles would return home and all nations would acknowledge Israel's God. This hope is evident, for instance, in Tobit and Sirach. In none of these cases, though, is this expectation linked to a specific individual. Not until after 200 do we find the "classic" image of the messiah as a mighty charismatic king who brings in the End Times.

In the canonical Bible itself, the best evidence for messianic beliefs comes from Daniel, in the sections dating from the 160s. Since early times, Christians have found images of Jesus Christ throughout Daniel, although it is doubtful that they are accurately reading the author's intentions. In the story of the fiery furnace, the king's servants are amazed to see the three Hebrews accompanied by a fourth figure, a *bar elahin*. That literally means a son of the gods, but Christians knew only one person who came close to filling that role, so that the King James English translation renders it "the form of the fourth is like the Son of God" (capitalized thus) (3:25). The original text depicts rather "one in divine form," and it refers to an angel, reflecting a new universe in which God's agents intervened directly to guard his true followers. Even so, it opened the way for far more exalted readings.

Cryptic figures abound in Daniel's second section, which begins with a classic vision of the Ancient of Days, *Atik Yomin*, God himself, clad all in white and reigning from a burning throne, standing by a river of fire. He is richly attended by angelic courtiers and supporters: "Thousands upon thousands attended him; ten thousand times ten thousand stood before him. The court was seated, and the books were opened." But accompanying God stands another being, portrayed in words that Christians have savored for millennia and indeed adapted in poetry and music. This other being was "one like the Son of man [who] came with the clouds of heaven, and came to the Ancient of Days, and they brought him near before him. And there was given him dominion, and glory, and a kingdom, that all people,

nations, and languages, should serve him: his dominion is an everlasting dominion, which shall not pass away, and his kingdom that which
shall not be destroyed" (7:9–14). As it stands, the phrase "one like a/
the son of man" (*bar enash*) simply means one in human form, and it
may well refer to an angelic figure in the shape of a human, such as
Michael. More likely, it is a metaphor for the whole people of Israel,
a reading confirmed by a later identification with "the people of the
saints of the Most High." It is another example of the kind of cosmic projection seen in other contexts in this era, by which an earthly
being or institution is imagined in archetypal or heavenly form. But
the language proved tempting for later writers, as did the concept of
the Son of Man as a literal and specific individual.[35]

By the first century BCE, the Son of Man figure acquired strongly
messianic implications, which are highly developed in Enoch's Parables. In the End Times, the Son of Man "shall raise up the kings
and the mighty from their seats, [and the strong from their thrones]
and shall loosen the reins of the strong, and break the teeth of the
sinners." Like many other passages, that sounds strongly Christian,
and it has close echoes in the Magnificat spoken by Mary in Luke's
gospel in the New Testament. That certainly does not mean that
the ideas were derived from Christian sources, however. The Son of
Man references are numerous and pervasive in the Parables (46:1–4,
48:2–7, 69.26–29), and they are integral to the work's argument. This
figure was more ancient than the Creation, "For from the beginning
the Son of Man was hidden, and the Most High preserved him in
the presence of His might, and revealed him to the elect" (62:7). He
predated Creation:

> *Yea, before the sun and the signs were created,*
> *Before the stars of the heaven were made,*
> *His name was named before the Lord of Spirits. . . .*
> *And for this reason hath he been chosen and hidden before Him,*
> *Before the creation of the world and for evermore. (48:3, 6)*

This awe-inspiring figure would fulfill a role in the judgment at the End of Days and would sit on a throne of glory.

The identity of this individual is often misunderstood. Scholarly translations of the original text leave no doubt that Enoch was not just witnessing the Son of Man; rather, he himself fulfilled that role. Quite rapidly, that identification was forgotten or muddied, to make the Son of Man a freestanding character in the End Times drama, which is how the term is employed in at least some of the usages of the phrase in the New Testament. Potential Christian interpretations were vastly enhanced by the appearance of Daniel's messianic reference to the Anointed Prince, only a few lines after the Son of Man text. Even if, as seems certain, that "anointed" figure was a specific priestly figure, Daniel was providing rich resources for future readers, who found here an extensive cast of supernatural characters crying out to be supplied with human faces.[36]

But the Son of Man was not the only messianic image that came to the fore in these years. Nor was he the only one who helps shape the New Testament worldview. From the mid-second century onward, the Qumran texts are prolific in messianic images and themes, and these provide critical context to the concept of messiahship presented in the New Testament.[37]

As they speculated about the End Times, the Qumran sect wrote extensively about messianic figures, although in ways that differed from later Christian interpretation. The Qumran believers enthusiastically mapped their plans and hopes for coming messianic figures, who would lead their cause to victory, but those figures were plural rather than singular. At least three figures in the Scrolls generally fit the messianic definition, including a prophet, a priest, and a king. The Damascus Covenant, for instance, refers to the messiah(s) from Aaron and Israel. Arguably, these figures corresponded to such Old Testament celebrities as Moses (the prophet) and Elijah (the priest).[38]

Underlying these speculations were the political circumstances of the time in which Hasmonean rulers served as both kings and priests, notionally thus heirs to both Aaron and David. For the dissidents at Qumran, both offices would need to be redeemed and purified separately, with distinct messiahs. Broadly, then, the Scrolls offer a diarchical scheme, dual messianism, with two key figures, so that the messiah of Aaron is a priestly counterpart to this royal Davidic messiah. This owes something to a mysterious passage in First Zechariah, which was read as predicting one or more messianic figures. The Genesis Pesher (commentary) includes the words "until the Messiah of Righteousness comes, the Branch of David." One unique text speaks of messiahs, in the plural: judgment would last until the coming of the prophet and "the messiahs of Aaron and Israel." Other texts assume the simultaneous appearance of royal and priestly messiahs, with the king messiah of Israel subordinate to the priest.[39]

Some controversial texts seem to bring Qumran teachings strikingly close to later Christian language. One passage reads, "He will be called the Son of God, and they will call him the Son of the Most High." In view of later Christian interpretations, this seems explosive, even if the implications are not quite clear-cut. Some scholars think the words might apply not to a future messiah but rather to a contemporary ruler. In the Prayer of Enosh, someone is compared to God's "First Born Son," but a great deal of biblical evidence suggests that the designation is meant to apply to Israel as a whole. We are still a good way from the Christian identification of the individual messiah with the Son of God.[40]

Also notable in light of Christian origins is the text 4Q521, a "Messianic Apocalypse," which specifically mentions the messiah and describes his healing ministry. It also refers to resurrection, with the messiah serving as God's agent. Such words come close to the expectations of Jesus's contemporaries, particularly when the text describes God releasing captives, giving sight to the blind, and raising up those who are bowed down. That recalls the gospel of Luke, in which John the Baptist sends messengers to Jesus to ask his real identity. He replies with the message that "the blind receive sight, the lame walk, those who have leprosy are cleansed, the deaf hear,

the dead are raised, and the good news is proclaimed to the poor."
If not a quotation from the Messianic Apocalypse itself, these words
belong to the same literary universe: these were the mighty deeds
that a messiah was meant to do. Another fiercely debated text is the
"War of the Messiah," which some read to describe "piercing" in
the context of the messiah. Depending on our reading, that might
refer to his slaying his enemies or else being pierced, in the victim
sense of Christian theology. The text is too short and cryptic to
build much of significance upon it, but it does hint at the revolutionary implications that might be found in these documents. Whether
or not direct influence can be proved, we must be less struck by
what might initially appear as the revolutionary novelty of the claims
made for Jesus's messianic role.[41]

CONCEIVED AND IMAGINED in many diverse ways, the messiah
quite suddenly became a major source of interest in the Jewish sectarian world in the century and a half before Jesus's time. Together
with the explosion of angelic and demonic images, the sheer pro-
fusion of such visions provides striking testimony to the scale and
popularity of End Times concerns in this era.

Chapter 9

THE WORD WAS WITH GOD

Rethinking the World's Creation

_____

Wisdom is more mobile than any motion; because of her pureness she pervades and penetrates all things. For she is a breath of the power of God, and a pure emanation of the glory of the Almighty; therefore nothing defiled gains entrance into her. For she is a reflection of eternal light, a spotless mirror of the working of God, and an image of his goodness.

BOOK OF WISDOM 7:24–25

POPULAR VISIONS OF Jesus's era portray the Jewish world of his time as overrun with doomsday cults, as a desperate people awaited each new prophetic revelation. In such accounts, the main debate appears to be over which of the various messianic candidates was authentic and how occupying regimes might be overthrown. Yet alongside all the overheated talk of revolution and apocalypse, this same era also witnessed far-reaching philosophical and mystical speculations.

Parallel to the obsession with the End Times was a passionate exploration of the very beginnings of the universe and of humanity. That issue might not seem too mysterious given the explicit statements found at the very start of all Bibles, in the book of Genesis. In Hebrew that book takes its name from its opening word _Bereshith_, "In the beginning," and it tells how God created Heaven and earth and all living creatures before forming humanity. The story then moves immediately to those first humans and how they were expelled from the idyllic Garden. Once we get to the story of humanity, the account is much more open to interpretation, and Jews do not accept the Christian concept of Adam's Fall. But the basic story of "In the Beginning" was, surely, clear and consistent in its emphasis on God's guiding role.

However straightforward that all seemed, very few aspects of that Creation story could easily withstand the intellectual challenges that arose from Greek philosophy during the Crucible era. In multiple ways, Greek assumptions made it unthinkable that a single transcendent deity could have created the material universe in anything like the way portrayed in Genesis. But if not the one true God, who or what might have performed the act of Creation? Was it possible to tell the Creation story in an intellectually credible way without hypothesizing another lesser Creator figure, who would in effect become a second God? Similarly, the biblical story told of a perfect Creation that had fallen into sin, but again such a story invited mockery in the Greek intellectual ambience. The whole idea of creating humanity had to be rethought in an age that increasingly separated material and spiritual realities and viewed matter as inferior. Surely, one good God could not really have created both aspects of humanity, the noble spirit and the defective material flesh? Must we then imagine a second Adam as well as a second God?

In order to defend their religion in a cosmopolitan world, Jews had to reimagine that Genesis story in wholly new ways, applying new intellectual categories. As elements of the biblical story were thoroughly reinterpreted, they gained a fundamental importance that they had previously never held. The once marginal mythology of Adam, his family, and the Garden of Eden moved to center stage in religious discourse. The long-popular genre of Wisdom literature, which had taught ethical precepts and practical ways of living, now evolved to give divine Wisdom an essential intermediary role in the Creation.

At first sight, these philosophical speculations seem to belong to a different intellectual universe from the apocalyptic writings, but in fact they did not. Often, the two themes were explored in nearly related works, so that wisdom and apocalyptic were often closely, and surprisingly, intertwined. Viewing matters through the new Greek philosophical lens, moreover, gave a vast additional significance to such concepts as angels, the Messiah, and Satan. Those very different concerns ultimately merged to create the worldview that survives especially in Christianity, but was once still more widespread. No later than the first century BCE, we can already trace most of the motifs and controversies that would dominate Jewish and Christian theologies and controversies over the coming centuries.[1]

PREVIOUS CHAPTERS HAVE stressed the role of political conflict in forcing the rapid development of End Times imagery. But other confrontations demanded the thorough revision of assumptions about the Creation, with all the theological rethinking such a task demanded. In this instance, the transformation of Jewish thought cannot solely be explained in terms of internal evolution. Encounters with Greek culture brought confrontations of philosophy and language, posing challenges that destabilized the intellectual status quo.[2]

The heady new doctrines and approaches to religious life grew out of the conflict between Jewish and Greek understandings, but these interactions were quite different from how they are imagined in modern stereotypes. Modern-day Christians and Jews imagine their ancient predecessors trying to take their exalted view of the one true God to ignorant polytheists and trying to rid them of their silly pagan superstitions. For the educated Greek world, though, it was rather the conventional construction of the Jewish (and later Christian) deity that was so self-evidently primitive as to be embarrassing. The problem did not lie with accepting the reality of such familiar figures of popular religion as Zeus, Dionysus, and Herakles. At this time, any learned Greek would have happily accepted that these figures were symbolic manifestations of the divine, just handy totems of vulgar faith. The real problem was more fundamental. Greek philosophy made it all but impossible to reconcile the transcendence of God, as they understood it, with a deity who created and ruled the material universe—in short, with a deity anything like that portrayed in the Hebrew Bible.

The ambitious intellectual advances of the Hellenistic era were nowhere more evident than in philosophy. The most influential thinker of the time was Plato (ca. 428–348 BCE). After his death, his Academy lasted into the first century CE. Platonism moved through various phases, as identified and named by modern scholars. Middle Platonism, which prevailed from the end of the second century BCE through the early third century CE, was an eclectic system that built on the insights of other schools of thought, including the Stoics, Pythagoreans, and Aristotelians. The greatest representative of this school was Plutarch in the first century CE.[3]

These schools developed core themes that stemmed from Plato's writings. Most centrally, this meant the novel and revolutionary distinction that Plato had drawn between worldly reality, the world of the body and perception, and the nonvisible nonmaterial realm of Ideas. Humans have both a visible material body and an incorporeal soul. So fundamental has that matter-spirit distinction become to us that it seems incredible that anyone could ever have invented it at a given historical moment. Linked to this Platonic approach is the theme of the soul being imprisoned in the body, from which it needs liberation. Plato's thought portrayed hierarchies of reality and perfection, the idea that the visible, changeable, material world is only an image of a higher and authentic reality, which does not change. Visible things are images of higher Forms. Platonic writings are suffused with the language of images and shadows, reflections and resemblances.

Greek thinkers in this era had no difficulty accepting views that to us seem like pure monotheism, imagining one transcendent deity over all things. There was an absolute One that could only be described in terms of negatives—immovable, impassible, unchangeable—and material things existed only as shadow images of ideal forms within that One. But the One was not a creator. Of its unchangeable and immovable nature, the transcendent One could have had nothing to do with the lower realms of change and motion. Plato portrayed the creation of the world through a lesser being, the Craftsman or Demiurge (*demiourgos*), who shaped the material world. The Demiurge also created a world-soul (*psyche tou kosmou*). That Demiurge was neither evil nor malicious, but because he was in motion, he was inferior to the perfect First God, and that accounted for the imperfection of his material creation. The universe was derived from these two principles: the One, God or the Monad, and the Dyad, which is matter. Such lesser figures as the Demiurge and the World-Soul were divine but not absolute, and that distinction was unavoidable.[4]

But could this be reconciled with the strict monotheism that was, and is, the absolute foundation of Judaism? The Bible made it easy to identify the Jewish God as the transcendent One who reigned above all, and Jews had no hesitation in claiming that identification. But that same Bible also declared that that same God was directly involved in creation and interfered in that worldly process, personally and repeatedly. God acted in history. From a Greek perspective, this was not merely absurd but actively scandalous. Worse, this same deity was so far from being impassible and unchangeable that he actually felt emotions. That was the behavior of a primitive tribal god, who might similarly show anger, jealousy, or affection. It was much like treating the Greek fables of Zeus or Hera as serious theology. Jews could, of course, ignore Platonism and the other Greek philosophies, but if they did, they were abandoning any claim to a place in civilized society—not in Alexandria or Antioch or in many lesser cities. And the Maccabean revolution, which rejected assimilation, assuredly did not end the appeal of Greek learning for large sections of the elites within Jerusalem itself.

Somehow, Jewish thinkers had to find ways of reconciling competing views of the divine, and two solutions offered themselves: either they had to portray God in a Platonic mode yet somehow explain how he could have created the material universe, or, alternatively, they must deny God's responsibility for that Creation. At different times, thinkers followed both courses. However radical it may sound, some did teach a denial of divine responsibility (we will return to these ideas in Chapter 11). Such theories would become the basis of outright Gnostic and dualist movements that preached a conflict between Spirit and Matter.[5]

A more popular option postulated aspects of the deity that could serve as creator and as intermediary. That meshed well with trends in Middle Platonism, as Plutarch himself portrayed a God who ruled through subordinate creatures or intermediaries, daimons, that is, gods or spirits. The only way to reach the highest good, the One, was through these intermediary forces. Plutarch also believed in divine interventions in the material world through revelation and prophecy, which made accommodation of Jewish traditions easier. Jews, though, still had to construct an intermediary figure without its acquiring divine qualities in its own right and thereby contaminating the monotheist proclamation.

IN SEEKING AN intermediary Creator, two closely related candidates readily came to mind, namely, Wisdom and the Word. The figure of Wisdom was well known in the literatures of most Near Eastern societies, usually as the source of proverbial sayings and aphorisms that to modern eyes often look conventional and staid. Egypt had its wisdom literature, as did Babylonia, and so too did the Hebrews. In each case, Wisdom usually meant the sound practical knowledge of the world acquired through lengthy experience. Over time, Wisdom (*hokmah*) became a much more exalted figure in the Jewish context and was moreover represented as an individual force or figure, closely associated with God himself and with the act of Creation. Sometimes the writer is using that personification as a simple metaphor, but from the fourth and third centuries BCE onward, Wisdom acquires a more substantial identity as a real being, and moreover as a feminine figure. It is rarely easy to distinguish between these varied uses and implications of the Wisdom figure, all the more so as some of the more mystical "Wisdom" texts also continue to present the old saws and aphorisms.[6]

This dilemma is evident in the biblical book of Proverbs, which originated in the fourth or third centuries BCE and which later writers attributed to Solomon. Most of the book consists of proverbs in our common sense of the term, many of which entered conventional language ("As a dog returns to his vomit, so a fool returns to his folly" [26:11]). Unfortunately, at least a half-dozen passages from Proverbs have been cited through the centuries as justifying or demanding the corporal punishment of children, which makes the text unattractive to modern readers ("He that spareth his rod hateth his son"). Yet amid the clichés, the text gloriously proclaims, "The Lord by wisdom hath founded the earth; by understanding hath he established the heavens." In a famous poem in the book's eighth chapter, Wisdom declares:

> *The Lord possessed me in the beginning of his way, before his works of old.*
>
> *I was set up from everlasting, from the beginning, or ever the earth was. . . .*
>
> *When he prepared the heavens, I was there: when he set a compass upon the face of the depth:*
>
> *When he established the clouds above: when he strengthened the fountains of the deep:*
>
> *When he gave to the sea his decree, that the waters should not pass his commandment: when he appointed the foundations of the earth:*
>
> *Then I was by him, as one brought up with him: and I was daily his delight, rejoicing always before him. (8:22–31, KJV)*

In the context, the author is using metaphor to stress the radiant and fundamental nature of divine Wisdom. It would be easy, however, to read the passage as if Wisdom were a cosmic being in her own right who was already present at the Creation. Many later

Christians have read the Proverbs text as if the words were spoken by Christ himself.

The poem has many parallels in the literature of neighboring pagan societies, where the figure proclaiming his or her virtues and achievements is a deity. So common are such recitations of virtues (Greek, *arete*) that this genre of sacred boasting has its own name, *aretalogy*. At very much this same time, aretalogies were a popular genre in Ptolemaic Egypt, where the speaker was usually the goddess Isis.[7]

Wisdom language became a mainstay of Jewish thought from the third century onward. That was natural in an age when readers had to choose between competing and equally tempting forms of Wisdom, the debate we have seen played out in the context of 1 Enoch. From around the same date, the book of Sirach associated Wisdom with God Himself in the act of Creation. As Sirach declares, "Wisdom was created before all other things, and prudent understanding from eternity" (1:4). That certainly sounds as if the Wisdom language has moved from the realm of metaphor to that of cosmology. An aretalogy in this book describes how Wisdom made her abode among the nation of Israel, alone of all the nations of the earth, and made her home on Mount Zion. Sirach makes Wisdom at once the Creator figure and the essence of the Torah (Sirach 24). Such a view foreshadows the later rabbinic beliefs we have already encountered about the eternal, heavenly Torah that existed before the Creation. In terms of its format, a contemporary pagan would have easily read this text as a declaration by a creator goddess and would likely have assumed that the Jews venerated their own version of Isis.[8]

Wisdom is no less exalted in the book of Baruch, a puzzling text that dates to the second century BCE. Like Sirach, Baruch proclaims Wisdom's role as the possession of Israel and emphasizes this negatively by listing the glorious and powerful beings from whom it has been withheld (3:24–28). Those groups who lacked Wisdom include princes, great merchants, and also the famous giants of old, who perished because "Those did not the Lord choose, neither gave he the way of knowledge unto them" (3:27). That reference to the giants points to the overlap of the Wisdom literature with Enochic traditions. In the Parables of Enoch, Wisdom is very close to a divine female force. Wisdom "went forth to make her dwelling among the children of men, and found no dwelling-place: Wisdom returned to her place, and took her seat among the angels" (1 Enoch 42).

The sense of dealing with an objective being is evident in the Wisdom of Solomon, written in the late first century BCE, which I cited at the start of this chapter. "Solomon" describes the scope of what he has learned at the hands of Wisdom, a compendium of natural science as well as philosophy. Such an expansive list of intellectual boasts perfectly recalls the breadth of knowledge and interests that is expounded in the Enochic writings: "namely, to know how the world was made, and the operation of the elements: the beginning, ending, and midst of the times: the alterations of the turning of the sun, and the change of seasons: the circuits of years, and the positions of stars: the natures of living creatures, and the furies of wild beasts: the violence of winds, and the reasonings of men: the diversities of plants and the virtues of roots: and all such things as are either secret or manifest, them I know" (7:17–21, KJV). Beyond this, Wisdom was essential to the act of Creation. She was the one who knows God's works, who was with him when he made the world. "Solomon" then lists the works of Wisdom through history, from watching over Adam to protecting the Israelites through the Exodus and the years in the Wilderness. At every point, Wisdom is credited with deeds that the Bible attributes to God himself. "Although she is compared with the Light, she is greater" (7:29).[9]

As this work survives only in Greek, Wisdom's name appears as Sophia, and as such she sounds very much like a figure in contemporary Greek philosophy. In that context, she would be an intermediary between the unchangeable transcendent Monad, the One, and the material creation. The same text is densely packed with technical terms and concepts from contemporary Platonism. Wisdom is characterized as "a *reflection* of eternal light, a spotless *mirror* of the working of God, and an *image* of his goodness" (7:26; emphasis added).

The altar in Solomon's Temple is a "resemblance" (*mimema*) of the original Tabernacle.[10]

Wisdom, Sophia, was approaching divine status in Jewish thought, an angelic figure at least, and likely more than that. She was the vehicle through whom God created the world, almost his divine representative in the world.[11]

OF THE THINKERS who tried to reconcile Jewish and Greek thought-worlds, the most celebrated was Philo of Alexandria (25 BCE–50 CE), whose life overlapped with those of Jesus and Paul. Like his Jewish contemporaries, Philo encountered the common difficulty that Platonic philosophical assumptions were so thoroughly infused into Greek culture and thought that it was impossible to separate the two. It was difficult in this era to write or speak Greek without "speaking Platonic" or absorbing Platonic insights. The process of Bible translation contributed to this intermingling of worldviews. From the third century BCE, Jews had access to their scriptures in Greek, especially the immensely popular Septuagint. As they read the sacred text, they found words and concepts that had particular resonance within the contemporary philosophical framework, not least potent words like *ikon* (image) or *gnosis* (knowledge). The Septuagint invited and provoked Greek philosophical readings, if it did not actually demand them.[12]

Such discoveries came from the very start of the sacred text. In Genesis 1, Philo read that God made man "according to the image of God" (*eikona theou*), wording that justified a whole Platonic reconstruction of the creation. Not just for Philo, such interpretations made it both easy and tempting to assimilate the biblical stories to Greek philosophical views. Septuagint translations also opened the way to imagining other divine beings. In Psalm 82, God stands in the assembly of gods, *synagoge theon*. I am using the lowercase g for "gods" in order to distinguish between the great God of heaven and minor deities, though the Greek implies no such difference.[13]

At first sight, Philo presents God in a way instantly recognizable to a contemporary Platonist. God is unchangeable, without
name, without relation to any other being, and humanity cannot
perceive him. Philo briskly rejected the Bible's anthropomorphism,
its description of a deity with hands or eyes, with a face and "back
parts" (Exod. 33:23). As he argued, such words were all symbolic
and metaphorical expressions used by biblical authors, and only a
very simple reader would treat them seriously.

Having all but excluded God from the world, Philo used a Stoic
concept to bring him back, and he often ran into serious contradictions in doing so. God was transcendent, argued Philo, but also
thoroughly immanent, a constant creative force in all things. As a
Platonist, Philo explained creation as the work not of a God sepa
rated from the world but of divine powers or attributes. The most
important of these powers that lay between perfect Form and imperfect matter was the Logos, Reason, God's firstborn, which is equivalent to Plato's creative Demiurge. The Logos concept stemmed
from Stoic thought and was also current in other Greek schools. In
the Hebrew tradition, it corresponds to the Word of God that is so
frequently mentioned throughout the Bible, as in the revelations to
prophets. Beyond argument, the biblical God had spoken, and used
words, and that fact now gave warrant to philosophical doctrines. As
Sirach had observed, "By the word of the Lord, his works are made"
(42:15). The book of Wisdom praised God, who made all things with
his *logos*, "and ordained man through thy wisdom [*sophia*]" (9:1–2).[14]

Seeking to integrate ideas from multiple traditions, Philo is
none too specific about how his Logos relates to the divine Wisdom or which emanates from which. He understands the Logos as
"the image of God," as mentioned in the Septuagint translation of
Genesis, almost as the shadow of God's perfection. Following the
angelic theorizing of his time, he identifies the Logos with the Angel
of the Lord, who is mentioned periodically throughout the Bible.
Philo presents the Logos as the archetype of things, including the

human mind, and the creator of all. As he wrote, "The Logos of the living God is the bond of everything, holding all things together and binding all the parts, and prevents them from being dissolved and separated." It is difficult to read such words without invoking later Christian theology and especially the prologue to John's gospel, which proclaimed, "In the beginning was the Word [Logos], and the Word was with God, and the Word was God. The same was in the beginning with God." (The first words here explicitly recall the opening of Genesis as they appeared in the Septuagint Greek, *En arche*.) Scholar James H. Charlesworth remarked acutely that "God's word is seen first as the word of God, then the word from God, and finally, perhaps in only a very few circles, as 'the Word.'" Philo demonstrates the near impossibility of merging Judaism and Platonism without creating another figure who is, more or less, another manifestation of God. In the Christian tradition, that Word became identified with the Son of God, who became incarnate as Jesus Christ.[15]

Just how firmly thinkers of this age held to pure monotheism is controversial. Studying the views of some heterodox and "sectarian" Jewish thinkers early in the Common Era, a number of scholars have proposed that some Jews at least taught the existence of two Powers in heaven. That idea was quite independent of Christian theories about the divine nature of Jesus Christ. If that is correct, then perhaps Christian Trinitarianism was not a departure from strict monotheism but rather an evolution from Jewish precedent. What we can say confidently is that a Creator or intermediary figures who stood even higher than the angels were proliferating around the start of the Common Era. Apart from Wisdom and the Logos, there were hints of other such individuals in the Qumran texts and elsewhere. Despite all the qualms about compromising God's absolute unity, cultural and intellectual pressures were demanding more flexible solutions. Those efforts would have an incalculable impact on the making of Christianity and on Christian theology.[16]

WHETHER BY MEANS of Word or Wisdom, God created the world. But the presence of sin and evil in that world still demanded explanation. The Jewish interaction with newer philosophical ideas made the issue of theodicy—that is, the question of why God allows evil—still more intense and troubling. The evolving ideas and debates demonstrate a common concern with ideas of perfection, perfectibility, and the relationship between spiritual and material realities. Whether or not they explicitly cite Greek philosophers, Jewish thinkers were at every stage responding to the challenges those foreign sages had posed. And as in the case of Creation itself, the resulting controversies left a deep imprint on Christianity.

The reality of evil forces was unavoidable to anyone who experienced the oppression of the Crucible age. But the Bible made it clear that originally, humanity—Adam—possessed perfection as the image of God. How, then, had Creation thus fallen? For later Christians, that problem is resolved easily by invoking the story of the Garden of Eden and the Serpent and the fall of Adam and Eve, which left the taint of Original Sin upon all their descendants. Yet however fundamental that idea seems, it receives meager treatment in the Hebrew Bible. After its appearance in Genesis 1–3, the Fall story makes no impact in that text.[17]

Ancient Hebrews were thoroughly familiar with the concept of sin, which could be collective or hereditary, but the canonical Old Testament does not say that Adam's disobedience corrupted humanity as a whole. In Psalm 51, the speaker declares his utter sinfulness, to the point that he was born in iniquity, and even conceived in sin, but this looks more like literary hyperbole than a theological or biblical statement (5). We look in vain for any reference to Adam or a Fall. Conversely, Psalm 8 celebrates the glory of humanity, of *ben-'adam*, the son of Man (or son of Adam): "For thou hast made him a little lower than the angels [alternatively, "little less than God"], and hast crowned him with glory and honor. Thou madest him to have dominion over the works of thy hands; thou hast put all things under his feet" (5–6). The second sentence here links the human figure to Adam himself, to whom God gave dominion over the beasts, and commentators generally identified Adam as the main subject. Even so, for all we know from this joyous text, the Fall might never have occurred. (We will return to this psalm later, as it was such a critical source for doctrine and controversy during the Crucible years.) The idea of original sin never features in the words of prophets who otherwise had no problem whatever in denouncing the manifold sins of a community. And although some much later Talmudic scholars favored the original sin motif, it never became part of rabbinic Judaism. Surprisingly for many Christians, the idea makes no appearance in the gospels, and Jesus himself never cites either Adam or original sin.

The most influential exposition of the Eden story is in the New Testament letters of Saint Paul, especially as they were expanded and cultivated by the Latin church father Augustine, around 400 CE. By the 50s CE, the story of Adam and the Fall was central to Paul's theology, which ultimately became the essential core of all Christian orthodoxy. In this view, Christ took human form so that through his sacrificial death, he might reverse the Adamic taint of sin and death. (Different churches would long debate the exact method or rationale of this transaction.) To quote *Paradise Lost* once again, Paul's theology told

> *Of Man's first disobedience, and the fruit*
> *Of that forbidden tree whose mortal taste*
> *Brought death into the World, and all our woe,*
> *With loss of Eden, till one greater Man*
> *Restore us, and regain the blissful Seat.*

Paul, though, was no isolated spiritual entrepreneur. Rather, he was invoking ideas about Adam and the Fall that were already well known to his readers in Corinth and elsewhere (see Rom. 5:12–14;

and 1 Cor. 15). He was using ideas that were under vigorous discussion during the Crucible years.

ONLY GRADUALLY AND tentatively did the image of the Garden of Eden emerge during the Second Temple era. Ezekiel (28:13) and other prophets refer to Eden as God's garden but never in the context of the Fall. The literature of those earlier years had much to say about the origins of humanity, the sources of human sinfulness, and temptations by diabolic forces, but the biblical passage under discussion was usually the Genesis story of the Watchers. The Fall in question was thus the events preceding Noah's Flood rather than the expulsion from Eden. The book of 1 Enoch has nothing at all to say about the Eden story, and Adam features only as a name in genealogies.[18]

But if the classic Christian interpretation of the Fall was not in view, individual actors in the drama certainly were. We have already observed the "rise of Satan" from the third century onward, but Adam himself was rising from near invisibility in the canonical Bible to play a critical role in Jewish thought and writing. Very much like his foe Satan, and in just the same years, Adam now entered center stage. The growth of Adam's role follows a pattern that we have often remarked on, by which ideas first developed independently within Jewish circles but were then vastly elaborated in dialogue with outside influences, in this case Greek philosophy.[19]

From around 200 BCE, references to Adam begin to appear in ways that imply the existence of larger discussions on the subject that are now lost to us. Much of this new interest grew out of exegesis of Psalm 8, with its vision of a humanity created a little lower than the angels. In its Greek Septuagint translation, this short psalm abounds with words that in the context of the time had potent messianic implications. Man (or the son of man) is "crowned with glory and honor," and all things are set under his feet. The book of Tobit lauds God: "You made Adam and gave him Eve his wife as a helper and support. From them the race of mankind has sprung" (8:6). But the theological framework is thin, and there are no references to a Fall. Yet not long afterward, and seemingly out of nowhere, Sirach declares, "No one like Enoch has been created on earth, for he was taken up from the earth. . . . Shem and Seth were honored among men, and Adam above every living being in the creation" (49:14–16). Within a couple of verses, the intriguing group of pre-Flood heroes who were so central to the later pseudepigraphic literature are mentioned, with Adam as the greatest among them.[20]

Jubilees, too, stands witness to Adam's dramatic enhancement. As a greatly augmented commentary on the book of Genesis, it naturally tells the story of the expulsion from Eden, with much noncanonical legend and lore about Adam's children and family and their fates. Even for Jubilees, though, the Fall receives little weight as the source of later evil and sinfulness, which is instead blamed on the Watchers.[21]

A similar emphasis on the Watchers is found in the Qumran sect, which was obsessed with matters of sin, impurity, and evil. In its foundational Damascus Document, evil is traced no further than the fall of those guardian angels. In later documents, Adam himself becomes much more prominent, sometimes in the context of the Fall and redemption, and such discussions usually arise from readings of Psalm 8. He is commemorated in the very fragmentary liturgy known as the Words of the Luminaries. The work celebrates God's mighty deeds, which include forming Adam "in the image of your glory." Another text imagines the purified Jewish sanctuary that would be restored in the eschatological age, which would reverse the damage done by the Fall. The authors thus use the Adam story to shape later understanding of Jewish law in matters such as ritual purity. This text does contain one intriguing element, in terms of what exactly is to be restored or renewed. Translators differ whether a certain phrase should read "sanctuary of men" or else the "Temple of Adam"—that is, the Garden of Eden. That vision of a restored and purified Garden of Eden resonates with many later Christian and Jewish speculations.[22]

From the second century onward, the linkage between Adam, Eden, and the Fall became commonplace, as did the idea of reversing that Fall and returning to primeval perfection. Some of the most significant texts derive from after the end of the Crucible period as I have defined it, but their ideas follow naturally and logically from that era. We have already seen Philo's use of the Creation story in the first chapter of Genesis and the appearance of Adam in "the image of God." But the opening of Genesis actually includes two originally separate Creation stories, each with its own slant on human origins. In the second story, in what is now the book's second chapter, Philo found a "man of dust" mentioned as the first human creature (2:7). So was this being the same as the divine image in the previous section or something altogether distinct? Some passages in Philo suggest that the two Adams were identical, while others did not. The most likely interpretation suggests that a divine or supernatural Man preceded or coexisted with the material human being, standing parallel to frail humanity. That in turn offered a way of understanding the Fall and sinfulness, as the ideal Adam must somehow have been reduced to the sinful and corruptible material reality.

SIMILARLY PLATONIC IN its approach was the book of Wisdom. Unusually for Jewish writings of any period, Wisdom teaches a strict separation of mind and body, and even a conflict between the two, and that schism accounts for human frailty and failures: "A perishable body weighs down the soul, and this earthy tent burdens the thoughtful mind." The key word here is *phtharton*, which means "corruptible" or "perishable." Another passage in Wisdom describes the origin of this lamentable human state. According to this text, "God created man to be immortal [*aphtharsía*, not-corruptible], and made him to be an image of his own eternity. Nevertheless, through envy of the devil [*phthono de diabolou*] came death into the world: and they that do hold of his side do find it" (2:23–24). (Alternatively, "they who are allied with him experience it.") The brief reference implies the existence of an already well-known mythology about Satan and the Fall.

Through the wiles of the Devil, then, humanity has lost its pristine perfection. Such a view fitted perfectly with the common dualistic ideas of the time about the warfare between the forces of good and evil. In Eden Satan had won a spectacular victory, which later humanity must seek to reverse. Such words appear familiar from a Christian perspective, but they are a massive departure from earlier Jewish views of the origins of death and sinfulness. Indeed, the Wisdom passage sounds surprisingly close to the medieval formulation of the enemies of the human soul, namely, the World, the Flesh, and the Devil. Yet Wisdom was definitely written from a strictly Jewish point of view, without any Christian influence.

We have already encountered the influential Life of Adam and Eve, which no later than the first century CE drew together the various strands of the Eden and Fall mythology, including a definitive account of Satan. Separately, in this story, Adam and Eve supply their own accounts of the Fall, emphasizing the hope that God would ultimately restore and heal the Edenic world. The book also addresses the question of the bodies that Adam and Eve had before the Fall, when they more closely resembled the angels. In both Jewish and Christian tradition, this allusion inspired mystical ideas of reversing the Fall and returning to those exalted states.[23]

Underlying the surging interest in Adam and the Fall were the new attitudes to resurrection and the afterlife, which were evolving so rapidly from the mid-second century BCE onward. Josephus's account of the Pharisees and Essenes described their firm belief in the indestructible and incorruptible nature of the soul, and the language he uses echoes that of Philo and Wisdom. The Pharisees, moreover, preached resurrection. But if resurrection was such an article of faith, believers had to address the question of exactly what was to be raised from the dead. Would a corpse simply reanimate, or did resurrection mean rising in a new and glorified body? What, if anything, would be restored in the Last Times? (For Josephus, see Chapter 6.)

Understanding the different images of Adam contributed powerfully to understanding these questions. If in fact God had intended Adam to attain such a perfect and incorruptible state, only a little lower than the angels, then surely that would be the condition to which all humanity would be restored in the last days. Such a view of the nature of resurrection is the immediate cause of Paul's profound exposition in 1 Corinthians 15, one of the most influential passages in Christian theology. Christ, he declared, was the second Adam, the new Adam, and "as in Adam all die, even so in Christ shall all be made alive." Resurrection, Paul taught, would mean rising in a body that was new, incorruptible, and immortal.

BY THE LATE first century CE, these various themes—Adam, Eden, the Fall, original sin, resurrection—were thoroughly integrated and popularized. Around this time, Adam is repeatedly mentioned in the apocalyptic pseudoscripture called 2 Esdras (or 4 Ezra), which explicitly draws a connection with the Fall. God created Adam in perfection, but he violated the commandment to love God's way, and that inflicted death not just on the patriarch but on all his descendants. "The first Adam bearing a wicked heart transgressed, and was overcome; and so be all they that are born of him. . . . For the grain of evil seed hath been sown in the heart of Adam from the beginning." Those successors pursued their sinful ways until they were wiped out in the Flood. "As death was to Adam, so was the Flood to these" (3:5–7, 21–22, 30, KJV).

That is close to the view of Paul, who told in the Epistle to the Romans how "sin came into the world through one man and death through sin, and so death spread to all men because all men sinned." Yet although 2 Esdras is later than Paul, there is no suggestion that the author knew Pauline writings or ideas. By this stage, Adamic speculations were becoming almost too commonplace to be singled out. Rarely noticed by Christian readers, Luke's gospel (ca. 100 CE) even describes Adam as "Son of God," making him a counterpart and predecessor of Christ himself (3:38). The Paul who wrote the great Epistles may have been expressing radical views, but he was no eccentric outlier to the Jewish thought of his time. Oddly, he was even riding a fashionable wave.

Just as the Christ of early Christianity came to be seen as the manifestation of the creative Word or Wisdom, so he was also portrayed as a new and greater Adam. All those once disparate images united and assimilated in a way that seems quite natural in Christian retrospect, but they involved some daring intellectual speculations.

By the opening years of the Common Era, the religious themes that had emerged in the previous two centuries or so now became common currency in the Jewish and near-Jewish world. Just as the spiritual revolution received its greatest impetus from the political crisis of the Hellenization crisis, so another series of wars and catastrophes fundamentally reshaped the movement and brought it into the international arena.

Chapter 10

SMASHING GOD'S HOUSE

How Apocalyptic and Messianic Ideas
Drove Political Action

———

The crucible is for silver, and the furnace is for gold, and the
Lord tries hearts.

PROVERBS 17:3, RSV

WHEN JESUS TRAVELED to Jerusalem to take part in the feast of
Passover, he arranged a symbolically laden entry into the city, in
which he rode on an ass. While his disciples strewed palm leaves in
front of him, they cried slogans praising the return of the Davidic
kingdom. Such a display infuriated the Temple authorities, who
decided to move against the new sect. Jesus was arrested, and during
his trial he was asked whether he claimed to be the Messiah. According to some accounts, Jesus uttered the fateful words "I am, and you
will see the Son of Man sitting at the right hand of the Mighty One
and coming on the clouds of heaven" (Mark 14:62). His condemnation inevitably followed.

The fact that the authorities were so profoundly sensitive to any
hint of insurgency can only be understood against the background
of the previous 250 years, which had so popularized apocalyptic and
messianic ideas. Whatever Jesus actually said or did, his followers
knew precisely which scripts were being enacted and the appropriate biblical texts to cite in his support. When he invoked the Son

of Man, he was echoing Daniel or 1 Enoch, and the cryptic narrative of the Wicked Shepherd in Second Zechariah decisively shaped accounts of his final weeks. Moreover, the spiritual revolution of the Crucible Years had created a near-perfect revolutionary religious and political ideology. It not only justified and demanded resistance to illegitimate authority, but also offered supernatural scenarios that gave the hope of inevitable victory.

Through the first century CE, political events moved toward catastrophe with what in hindsight looks like the inevitability of a mighty tragedy, which climaxed with full-scale revolution and civil war in the 60s. But although the Jewish nationalist movement ended in cataclysm, the underlying ideas survived and prospered, laying the foundation for new and world-changing religious structures.

JUST HOW THOROUGHLY the new religious synthesis was shaping political action may be seen from some sensational events that occurred in 4 BCE. That may also have been the date that Jesus was born.

In that year, the city of Jerusalem was, yet again, in a state of turmoil. On the basis of false rumors that King Herod the Great—the Roman client king of Judea—had died, revolutionary nationalists decided to strike a blow for Jewish independence and freedom, for the rebirth of a purified Jewish state. Two suicidally brave scholars, Mattathias and Judah, destroyed an imperial Roman eagle that Herod had ordered erected at the Temple gate. They proudly admitted to royal officials that they had done it, even though they faced death on the pyre. Basing themselves in the theories of martyrdom that had emerged in the previous two centuries, the men asked why should they not exult. "It was a glorious thing to die for the laws of their country; because the soul was immortal, and an eternal enjoyment of happiness did await such as died on that account." Even so, the campaign they launched failed badly. Far from being dead, Herod was still sufficiently in control to strike forcefully at the perpetrators.[1]

Herod actually did die shortly afterward, preventing him from taking full revenge on his countless enemies, and there were high hopes of a new, less exploitative regime under his teenage successor, Archelaus. According to Josephus, "the people" assembled to demand that the new ruler implement a new regime, but Archelaus was terrified of the crowds flocking into the city for the Passover feast. He ordered his soldiers to attack protesters, reportedly killing three thousand in or near the Temple. The next major feast of Pentecost brought new disasters, as the city was flooded by "a great number of Galileans, and Idumeans, and many men from Jericho, and others who had passed over the river Jordan, and inhabited those parts." The mob besieged the Roman garrison, leading to another bloody battle, in which the Jews were alarmingly undaunted by their Roman enemies. Chaos spread far afield, "with ten thousand other disorders in Judea," as at least three (unrelated) popular leaders emerged to claim the role of messianic king. The Romans sought help from the governor of Syria, Quintilius Varus, who in turn called on his fierce Arabian allies. After the rising was suppressed, with extreme bloodshed, Varus crucified some two thousand rebels.[2]

The crisis of Varus's War demonstrated the wild hopes and expectations that now drove political actions and the absolute and uncompromising views that inspired political activism. Historians tend to use events like Varus's War, revolutionary moments of change and crisis, as key markers in the development of societies. In the Jewish case, the problem is that such outbreaks were so common and regular in this era as to appear the norm rather than the exception. What was new was the increasingly supernatural interpretations through which such events were understood.

POLITICAL PEACE SEEMED a distant dream. The last decades of the Hasmonean era were tempestuous, and the 60s BCE witnessed a perfect storm of political chaos. Salome Alexandra provided competent rule until her death in 67, but crisis followed. Her two sons by

Jannaeus, Hyrcanus II and Aristoboulos II, contested the throne and the high priesthood, and each fought with the support of one of the main religious factions, the Pharisees or Sadducees. At one stage, the losing side provoked a full-scale Nabatean (Arab) invasion of Judea.[3]

This series of catastrophes opened the way to Roman invasion. The general Pompey was operating in the region, initially against the Pontic kingdom of Mithridates, and he reorganized the vestiges of the Seleucid Empire into a new Roman province of Syria. After such triumphs, his move into Judea came almost as an afterthought. In 63 BCE, he besieged and occupied Jerusalem, even entering the Temple's Holy of Holies. Pompey dismembered the Hasmonean kingdom, severing coastal regions from its control and placing the Gentile region of Decapolis under separate rule. Hyrcanus II was made high priest and ethnarch ("ruler of the nation"), but not granted the more splendid title of king. Meanwhile, the non-Hasmonean warlord Antipater was a growing force at court. Under Alexander Jannaeus, he had originally served as governor of his home territory of Idumea, and he later gravitated toward the rising stars in the Roman elite, making himself a special favorite of Julius Caesar. In 47 Caesar made Antipater the first Roman procurator of the new province of Judea and poured honors on his family. Antipater's historical reputation was soon eclipsed by that of his son, Herod the Great (74–4 BCE).[4]

The last gasp of Hasmonean power came in 40 BCE, with Antigonus, the son of Aristoboulos II. He made himself king, briefly, by agreeing to serve as a puppet of the Parthians, who duly invaded the country and briefly threatened to conquer the whole region. Antigonus deposed and mutilated his uncle Hyrcanus II, whom the Parthians carried off into Babylonian captivity. (Reputedly, Antigonus bit off his uncle's ears.) That Parthian entanglement was too much for Roman warlord Marc Antony and his Herodian allies, who not only deposed Antigonus but killed him, perhaps by the degrading method of crucifixion. Herod, meanwhile, received the royal title as the gift of the Roman Senate, and he ruled from 37 to 4 BCE. In order to cement his position among the local population, he married a Hasmonean princess, though he later had her executed. In 30 BCE, he also executed Hyrcanus II, the last Hasmonean ruler, after persuading the Parthians to return him from exile.[5]

Roman power spread rapidly over the rest of the region, culminating in the annexation of Egypt in 30 BCE. At that point, Palestine was a critical component of their burgeoning imperial structure, especially given the repeated rivalries with the rising Parthian Empire to the east. While insisting on maintaining control of the country, the Romans acknowledged Jewish sensitivities by ruling through their faithful Herodian friends. Any direct Roman presence was as far as possible kept out of sight in order to minimize potential insults to the religion and the Temple. The Romans established their main administrative center at the nearby city of Caesarea Maritima rather than Jerusalem, and the Roman governor restricted his visits to the great city to times of special tension or danger, such as the major feasts. The Romans avoided making the imperial cult as visible as it was elsewhere, even though the Temple offered sacrifices for the emperor twice daily. Generally, these compromises achieved their goal.

Although Rome maintained order, and generally respected local traditions, the occupations served as a focus for local grievances and divisions. If the Jewish world had always been under foreign subjection, then presumably its people would have found the means to cope with this new situation. Under Roman rule, however, they had very recent memories of being part of an aggressive free state that developed its own empire. That recollection made its subject status that much harder to bear. Occupation added one more degree of fury to the troubled conditions that already existed in the land.[6]

HEROD RETAINED POWER because he knew how to exploit his ability to get along with successive Roman regimes. Even so, from the beginning, Herodian rule was driven by a sense of potential threat and instability. As king of Judea, Herod the Great thoroughly remodeled and rebuilt the country, constructing or expanding a series of fortresses, ports, and cities. This building boom transformed the landscape of Palestine, and his successors continued his efforts. Those activities partly reflected an all too real sense that volatile Jerusalem might at any time fall out of the dynasty's control, so that the regime would need an extremely strong network of defensive positions from which to reconquer the land—hence the bastions at Antonia, in Jerusalem itself, at Samaria (Sebaste), at Machaerus, and at Caesarea Maritima. Beyond defense, those cities gave Palestine an excellent vision of the latest styles in Roman cities. Caesarea especially had its modern fortifications, but also its palace, its theater and amphitheater, its lighthouse tower, and its efficient systems for water supply and sewage disposal. Naturally, the city had a special devotion to Tyche (Fortune).[7]

Herod's efforts created a whole new material landscape. When John's gospel reports Jesus's doings on the Sea of Tiberias, that name was anything but ancient, referring as it did to a city that Herod Antipas had constructed around 20 CE, in honor of the emperor Tiberius. (Antipas was the son of Herod the Great, and brother of Archelaus.) The world simply looked physically different from what it had been a few decades earlier, promoting a sense of rapid change and dislocation. The new material world even suggested the potential for re-creating the whole world afresh.[8]

Beyond being an organizational genius, Herod the Great was a capricious tyrant, whose career was bloody and paranoid even by the standards of Hellenistic monarchies. He killed multiple members of his family, and in the final year of his life he was in the process of trying (and eventually executing) his son Antipater for alleged treason. Palace intrigues need not have a wider public impact, but Herod's growing paranoia and mental illness were becoming a scandal among other rulers and were well known to any educated member of the Jewish elite. The hatred he aroused is evident from this pseudoprophetic tirade in the Testament of Moses, which is not subtle in its references to Herod:

And an insolent king shall succeed them, who will not be of the race of the priests, a man bold and shameless, and he shall judge them as they shall deserve. And he shall cut off their chief men with the sword, and shall destroy them in secret places, so that no one may know where their bodies are. He shall slay the old and the young, and he shall not spare. Then the fear of him shall be bitter unto them in their land. And he shall execute judgments on them as the Egyptians executed upon them, during thirty and four years, and he shall punish them.[9]

Adding to the complexity of the situation was the half-foreign nature of Herod's family. When the Hasmoneans conquered Idumea (Edom) and enforced conversion to Judaism, one of those converts was Antipater, who married a Nabatean woman. Their child was Herod the Great, and he was therefore of mixed ethnic and religious background. Only someone with those dubious credentials would have been so fanatically determined to prove his Jewish authenticity, which was best symbolized by his rebuilding the Temple on a phenomenal scale.[10]

In truth, however, Herod's own background made him a highly appropriate ruler for the remarkably diverse land that he ruled. At the height of his power, Herod ruled not only most of the modern areas of Israel/Palestine, but also much of what today would be called Jordan, Syria, and Lebanon. These realms had extensive Gentile and pagan populations, not just in the lands beyond Palestine proper. With its pagan temples and baths, a city like Ptolemais/Akko was virtually a Diaspora city for Jews. Another potent symbol of the Gentile presence was the thriving Greek city of Sepphoris, which was rebuilt by Herod Antipas and which boasted a theater, bathhouses, and mosaic floors. In tribute to the emperor Augustus, the city was briefly renamed Autocratoris, and it would likely have supported a sacrificial cult to that ruler. Although it stands just a few miles from Nazareth, it is never mentioned in the New Testament itself. However accessible one community might be from another—Nazareth from Sepphoris, say—the de facto walls were very high, dividing people by language, dress, custom, faith, and (above all) the mode of eating and drinking. Palestine in this era was a patchwork of these microcultures, which were separated by so little and so very much. During times of tension and crisis, one never needed to look far to find behaviors and symbols that could outrage and infuriate and ultimately provoke open warfare.[11]

THE MAP OF Herodian possessions might imply that the Jews had maintained and expanded their empire from Hasmonean days, but of course they had not. The Romans had no interest in identifying any one ruler with the Jewish people, if only to prevent him becoming a national leader, and they indiscriminately expanded Herodian power over Jewish, Samaritan, and Gentile populations. (The dynasty retained its power until the end of the first century CE.) Even so, the map of where Herodian power expanded does give some sense of the wider sphere of influence extending beyond Jerusalem. Herod simply could not rule solely as Jewish monarch, although at the same time, he could never ignore that fundamental dimension of his power.[12]

Throughout his rule, Herod had to manage a nearly impossible balancing act, ruling at once as a Jewish king, but also a Mediterranean monarch, who had to support the public symbols and spectacular performances that that entailed. The kingly honor of Herod and his descendants obliged them to maintain the appropriate range of shows, games, and public works, all with their extensive pagan accoutrements. The Herodian regime perfectly epitomized the conflicting and perhaps irreconcilable values and traditions to be found within the Jewish realm. That was nowhere more apparent than in the Roman eagle mounted at the entrance to the Temple, which faithful Jews viewed as at best a symbol of blasphemous arrogance, at worst an idol.[13]

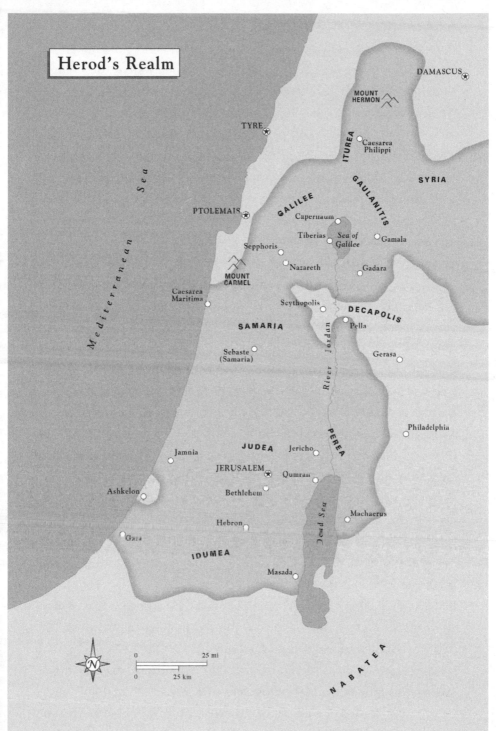

Herod's Realm

DAMASCUS

MOUNT
HERMON

TYRE

ITUREA

Caesarea
Philippi

SYRIA

Mediterranean Sea

PTOLEMAIS

GALILEE

Capernaum

GAULANITIS

Tiberias

*Sea of
Galilee*

Gamala

Sepphoris

Nazareth

Gadara

MOUNT
CARMEL

Caesarea
Maritima

Scythopolis

DECAPOLIS

SAMARIA

River Jordan

Pella

Sebaste
(Samaria)

Gerasa

Philadelphia

JUDEA

Jericho

PEREA

Jamnia

JERUSALEM

Qumran

Ashkelon

Bethlehem

Machaerus

Hebron

Dead Sea

Gaza

IDUMEA

Masada

N

0   25 mi

0   25 km

NABATEA

MAP 10.1.   HEROD'S REALM

BASED ON THE Christian gospels, later readers might be puzzled by the seemingly excessive reaction of both Jewish and Roman authorities to Jesus's activities as preacher and healer as well as their failure to comprehend his purely religious intentions. At the time, in an age when revolutionary ideas had gained such a following, the boundaries between religious and political activism were close to invisible. Modern historians are cautious about using words like "nationalism" in an ancient context, because it often means back-projecting post-Enlightenment ideas into a world that lacked most of the trappings of that ideology. Yet the very strong linkage between religious and ethnic identity in the Jewish case makes the language difficult to avoid.

By the end of the Crucible years, revolutionary activism was increasingly deployed in religious language, and it took scriptural forms. Those new texts included the psalms credited to the ancient king Solomon that were actually written in the 50s BCE, in the latter days of the Hasmoneans. "Solomon" laments the dreadful things that will befall his people when the rightful Davidic line is displaced by evil usurpers who are the Hasmoneans themselves: "Thou, O Lord, didst choose David (to be) king over Israel, and swore to him touching his seed that never should his kingdom fail before Thee. But, for our sins, sinners rose up against us; they assailed us and thrust us out; What Thou hadst not promised to them, they took away [from us] with violence. . . . They set a [worldly] monarchy in place of [that which was] their excellency; they laid waste the throne of David in tumultuous arrogance" (17). A more recent translation of the last verse proclaims that "With pomp they set up a monarchy because of their arrogance; they despoiled the throne of David with arrogant shouting." No better are the pagan Romans, who had so brutally conquered and sacked Jerusalem.[14]

Beyond merely condemning and complaining, such texts move swiftly and inevitably to the language of messianism and apocalyptic, offering readers a glimpse of a better future when their current oppressors would be punished and the righteous would be rewarded.

In the same psalm (17), Solomon offers an extended hymn to a coming king, a son of David, who would "shatter unrighteous rulers, and . . . purge Jerusalem from nations that trample (her) down to destruction":

> *He shall destroy the godless nations with the word of his mouth;*
> *At his rebuke nations shall flee before him,*
> *And he shall reprove sinners for the thoughts of their heart.*
> *And he shall gather together a holy people, whom he shall lead in*
>   *righteousness,*
> *And he shall judge the tribes of the people that has been sanctified by*
>   *the Lord his God.*

Aliens and sojourners would no longer be tolerated in the land. The king would rule from a purged and purified Jerusalem, and he would be a mighty judge and conqueror.

THE SUBSTANCE OF politics was changing, and the scale of that change was already evident by the latter stages of Herod's own rule. The extent of disaffection in 4 BCE, the upsurge of military messianism, shows just how widespread discontent had been beneath the seemingly tranquil surface of Herod's rule. Among other elements, the new openness to martyrdom reduced the likelihood that formidable Roman resources would be enough to hold radicals in check. Josephus specifically tells us that Judas and Mattathias, the two firebrands of 4 BCE, had taught their doctrines to audiences of eager young men. At some point in the first century CE, a collection of Lives of the Prophets offered multiple examples of noble martyrdom, adding to the popular literature on heroic death in God's service. Reputedly, six of the historic prophets suffered that fate, and the accounts of their deaths closely resemble the better-known stories of the early Christian sufferers. The implication is that martyrdom was a natural and glorious consequence of faithfully serving God and his Law.[15]

Revolutionary ideas had become vernacular and popular, the pre-serve of mass movements rather than just theorists or elite factions. Crowds and mobs were waiting to be mobilized, and the city of Jerusalem itself perfectly symbolizes the real and potential chaos of these years. The crisis of the Varus War showed the extreme diffi-culty of controlling the city in the face of armed and dedicated mili-tants. This was hard even for the very well-equipped and well-trained Romans, and their garrison came close to destruction. In Jerusalem above all, Demos—the People—had arrived on the political scene.

The Romans and the high priestly elites were right, then, to be worried about the turbulence of Jerusalem. Just in the first century BCE, acts of extreme violence included the massacres of rivals by king Jannaeus, the conquest of the city in 63 and 37 BCE, and the multiple acts of bloodshed in the year 4 BCE. Each of these instances reputedly claimed multiple thousands of lives. Extrapolating from that history, Jerusalem in Jesus's time was a generation overdue for an explosion, a fact known all too well by the Temple establishment. The pilgrim feasts were times of special concern. At such times, the city filled with tens of thousands of outside visitors, many filled with religious zeal and easily open to revolutionary manipulation. Making Jerusalem even more sensitive politically was its central role in so many prophecies and apocalypses, canonical or otherwise. The End Times were destined to begin within the city's walls.

Urban dissidents also knew they could draw on support from the wider territory. The decisive lurch to outright revolt at Pentecost in 4 BCE was sparked by the influx from the small towns and villages of Galilee, Idumea, and Perea. There were worrying parallels to the Maccabean revolt, when country dwellers rose against the Helleniz-ing slant of the urban elite. In these later years, one additional factor making these areas even more turbulent was the constant frictions with neighboring Gentile areas.[16]

Local militant and anti-Roman movements also demonstrated deep continuities. In the 40s BCE, Herod captured and killed a Gal-ilean bandit named Hezekiah, who had been raiding into Syria. Or, at least, Hezekiah is remembered as a simple bandit: perhaps he saw himself as a patriotic revolutionary or holy warrior, even a new Phinehas like the Maccabees before him. Hezekiah's son Judas was one of the popular revolutionary kings of 4 BCE, who mounted an insurrection in Galilee, operating within a few miles of Nazareth. Presumably, his origins were not far away from that center. He was later credited as the founder of what would become the insurrectionary Zealot movement, in which his family were unofficial royalty. Two of his sons were crucified in the 40s; another relative—a grandson?—led the terrorist Sicarii movement of the 50s and 60s. This demonstrates the deeply rooted nature of local opposition cultures and of religious-based extremism. In the 60s, as in Varus's time, Galilee and Idumea were notorious bastions of sedition.[17]

Besides the overtly political groups, religious disaffection was growing apace. Between the 30s and the 50s CE, several self-proclaimed prophets alarmed the established authorities by attracting a devoted following, and also for their messianic pretensions. Quite apart from his notorious actions against Jesus, Pontius Pilate had to send military forces against the hordes following a Samaritan prophet. In the 40s, one Theudas was executed after promising to divide the waters of the Jordan for his faithful followers; some years afterward, an Egyptian prophet persuaded some thousands to join him at the Mount of Olives, in preparation for his miraculous conquest of Jerusalem. As Josephus complains, such false prophets were even more wicked than the Sicarii. They "deceived and deluded the people under pretense of divine inspiration, but were for procuring innovations and changes of the government; and these prevailed with the multitude to act like madmen, and went before them into the wilderness, as pretending that God would there show them the signals of liberty." A less damning translation of the phrase here given as "act like madmen" would be that they would "abandon themselves to divine powers."[18]

Even without the revolutionary prophets, there were still abundant reasons to fear discontent. By no means all Jewish militants in

this era were explicitly apocalyptic or otherworldly in their motiva-
tion. As the Maccabees had shown in their day, there were plenty of
thoroughly secular ways of asserting nationhood without expecting
divine intervention. The Seleucid experience had shown that even
empires that on the face of things appeared all-powerful might
collapse more or less overnight. For all their rhetoric about divine
intentions, religious-motivated revolutionaries were not necessarily
dreamy fantasists aiming for pie in the sky. The movements they
stirred could be thoroughly practical and surprisingly effective.[19]

So STRONG, IN fact, is the evidence for political conflict and revolutionary activism that it is difficult to recall how much was taking
place in the Herodian years that had little or nothing to do with what
can sometimes seem like the main narrative, the high road to open
revolution. Yet these other developments mattered enormously in
showing the absorption of the ideas and beliefs from the Crucible
years and, critically, how these would allow Judaism to survive overwhelming catastrophe.

Much as many loathed Herod, his reign also marked a fundamental restructuring of Judaism and the creation of many critically
important institutions. The greatest new symbol of the material
world of Judaism was Herod's rebuilding of the Second Temple,
which began in 20 BCE and was substantially completed by the mid-
20s CE, so that the edifice that filled Jesus's disciples with such awe
was a very new (and indeed ongoing) project.

But at humbler levels too, we now for the first time see the emergence of local prayer houses, synagogues. The New Testament
makes these institutions sound like such familiar parts of the landscape that it is easy to forget just how new these places were, and
how they revolutionized piety and practice at the level of local communities. Appropriately, given the cultural interactions of the time,
"synagogue" is a Greek word for a thoroughly Jewish institution,
which were also known by the term *proseuche*, house of prayer.[20]

The centrality of prayer to religious life was in itself quite revolutionary. In biblical times, prayer was something that was used as needed, but in the Crucible years Jews developed a regimen of daily prayers. The first evidence of such practice comes from Qumran, with the collection known as the Words of the Luminaries. This does not mean that Qumran itself invented the daily prayer institution; rather, the practice was known at or before the sect's foundation. Together with reading from sacred scriptures, such prayers represented the core practice of the synagogues, and this marked Judaism out as utterly different from most of the religions that Romans and Greeks encountered. How, wondered pagans, could a place of worship not involve sacrifice? Still more surprising, texts written while the Temple was still standing were already proclaiming that sacrifice was not necessarily greater than other religious duties that could be fulfilled in the synagogue or in private life—duties such as daily prayer, giving charity, and generally fulfilling the commandments.[21]

In this way, synagogues marked the culmination of the shift toward the textualization of religion, toward faith being something communicated through reading and writing. These prayer houses also demanded training in reading, through schools. The structure of prayers, worship, and structured services that evolved in early synagogues lies at the root of all later Christian liturgy, including the Mass and Eucharistic rites. Synagogues permitted the faith to continue even after the cessation of the sacrificial system that had for so long been its bedrock. When the Temple fell, the text endured.[22]

This was also a truly distinguished age for scholars and jurists, and we are much better informed about these illustrious figures than the earlier generations around whom so many legends have accumulated. The sages who composed the Mishnah and Talmud looked especially to such leaders of this time as Hillel the Elder, who lived at the start of the Common Era. Alongside such spiritual celebrities, there now appeared local spiritual leaders, the teachers or rabbis, and the ordinary scribes who were so central to the production and consumption of written materials during the ages of Jesus and Hillel. A strong and diverse institutional framework now supported the outpouring of written materials of all kinds during the first century CE, of which the Christian gospels, epistles, and revelations are only the best-known peak of a substantial iceberg. Such works show how thoroughly the worldview of the Crucible years had established itself in popular thought and culture. They also point to the existence of a substantial reading public with an appetite for Jewish-related themes, virtually always in Greek.[23]

Some of these texts were apocalyptic in tone, and such writings gained a heartrending quality during the Jewish War itself. Besides serious texts, other works were designed to be read for pleasure and for amusement, and it is presumably for that reason that they are not better known. One example is the Testament of Abraham, which is an apocryphal expansion on the life of a biblical patriarch, with major interventions by the archangel Michael. What we do not expect is just how funny it is. Michael is deputed to tell Abraham of his approaching death, but each time he is about to pass on the message, he is overcome by Abraham's wonderful hospitality and reneges on his mission. In order to communicate with God without Abraham realizing his identity, Michael has to pretend to need to leave the tent in order to urinate.[24]

Also from this era is the romantic novella Joseph and Aseneth, about the affair between the patriarch Joseph and the daughter of an Egyptian high priest. Naturally enough, given its date, an archangel is the critical intermediary between the two parties. He introduces himself as "commander of the Lord's house, and chief captain of all the host of the Most High," so presumably Michael was making another of his many literary appearances.[25]

Geographically, these works were produced in any number of centers, from Babylon to Alexandria to Rome, and they circulated easily throughout a Jewish world that stretched farther than ever before. Diaspora communities were stronger and more widespread, largely owing to the growth of Roman power, but many communities also existed east of the Roman frontier, in Babylonia and beyond. Jewish influence was particularly strong in the border states and petty kingdoms separating Parthia and Rome, in lands such as Osrhoene (Edessa) and Adiabene (Arbela), in what are today eastern Syria and northern Iraq. In the first century CE, the king of Adiabene even converted to Judaism.

That incident also points to another force for change in these years. As Jews assimilated into the wider culture, a significant number of outsiders were drawn to Judaism, either as full converts or as fellow travelers, including the "God-fearers" who feature in the book of Acts. Although Jews did not undertake widespread proselytization, many communities welcomed these seekers and inquirers, who brought with them their distinctive concerns and interests. Such Judaizers spread Jewish themes and attitudes in the larger culture.[26]

Those diverse communities served as an open door to ever-new waves of influence and ideas, which spread throughout the larger world of Judaism. Apart from travel related to trade or commerce, attendance at the great Jerusalem feasts ensured that Jews from various parts of the Diaspora maintained these cultural contacts. By the first century CE, major synagogues flourished in Syrian Antioch, in Egyptian Alexandria, and in Italy (Rome and Ostia), quite apart from the many lesser prayer houses recorded in the New Testament. However strong the political pressures building in Jerusalem, Judaism seemed ever more closely integrated into the wider Mediterranean society.[27]

FEW HISTORICAL SOURCES allow us to reconstruct the ideas of ordinary nonelite Jews at this time, but there is one obvious exception: the New Testament. At many points in the present book, any modern reader is likely to think of the life and times of Jesus and the origins of early Christianity and to relate every point in mainstream history to those very well-known events. That approach runs the risk of giving that Christian story far more significance than it would have actually had at the time. Even so, the New Testament offers a detailed and wide-ranging source for understanding the Jewish world at this time.[28]

What we know about Jesus was written and recorded by his followers who may well have adjusted those stories to fit the needs of their own times. Fortunately, that fact poses no great problems for our present purposes. Regardless of whether Jesus himself did not say or think such things—if, say, he did not actually preach particular parables—then those ideas were certainly present in the minds of his Jewish followers a decade or two afterward. And those writers presented their material in terms that they assumed would speak to the needs and interests of their mainly Jewish audience.

The first members of the Jesus movement were in every sense heirs to the revolutionary developments of the previous two centuries, as was Jesus himself. Such a cultural genealogy is anything but a new insight. Long before the discovery of the Dead Sea Scrolls, writers had linked both John the Baptist and Jesus to the Essene sect as described by Josephus. Ernest Renan, author of the pioneering nineteenth-century *Life of Jesus*, proclaimed that Christianity was simply a version of Essenism that happened to have survived. As early as 1875, long before the finding of the Dead Sea Scrolls, biblical critic J. B. Lightfoot complained, "It has become a common practice with a certain class of writers to call Essenism to their aid in accounting for any distinctive features of Christianity, which they are unable to explain in any other way." (Essenes served a similar explanatory role for other movements besides Christianity, including Gnosticism.) The Qumran finds of the 1940s created new interest in that connection and encouraged many overambitious theories about "Jesus the Essene." Setting aside such far-reaching claims, the Qumran materials often do help us understand Jesus's world, and especially the precursor movement led by John the Baptist. If they do not link Jesus to the sect itself, they show how strongly his ideas resonated with the spiritual insights of the two centuries before his time and its scriptural understandings.[29]

Echoes of the Crucible years appear on every page of the canonical gospels. Jesus was above all a prophet of Judgment and apocalypse. On the coming Day of Judgment, he said, the world's people "will see the Son of Man coming in clouds with great power and glory. And then he will send out the angels, and gather his elect from the four winds, from the ends of the earth to the ends of heaven" (Mark 13:26–27). Jesus's world was dominated by a belief in the afterlife and Resurrection, in future rewards and punishments. He warned of an Enochian Hell, "where their worm does not die, and the fire is not quenched" (Mark 9:48). However often the gospels disparage the Pharisees, Jesus was closely aligned with their way of thinking. On occasion, his ideas met opposition, chiefly from Sadducees, but usually he was speaking the commonplaces of the time.[30]

Jesus confronted Satan and he battled demons. In a famous passage, Satan encounters Jesus in the Wilderness and presents him with several temptations (Luke 4). That includes granting Jesus all the authority and splendor of the kingdoms of the world, which the Devil could hardly do unless they were already in his own claws. On several occasions, Jesus identified the prince or ruler (*archon*) of this world as his enemy, who would be judged or overthrown as a consequence of his mission (John 12:31, 14:30, 16:11). Jesus reportedly knew the story of Satan's expulsion from the heavenly court, as recounted in the Adam literature: at least, he declared that "I saw Satan fall like lightning from heaven" (Luke 10:18). Jesus also attributed some or all disease and human misfortune to demonic activities. He once healed a Jewish woman who had long been severely crippled—or, as he reportedly described her, "a daughter of Abraham whom Satan bound for eighteen years" (Luke 13:16).[31]

In his role as prophet too, Jesus was no less a product of the spiritual revolution of the Crucible years. Unlike the ancient prophets, who chiefly proclaimed the word of God and called for repentance, the newer emphasis was on charismatic figures who earned their reputation as wonder workers and healers. Many people suspected or feared that John the Baptist and Jesus himself were prophets, on the basis of the healings and wonders for which they have become famous.[32]

For his followers, Jesus was the Messiah, Christ, a term that had been comprehensively redefined in the previous two centuries. So thoroughly did that concept describe his role that in his writings, Paul virtually never speaks of "Jesus" alone but always "Christ" or "Christ Jesus." But what exactly did the word mean? Generations of Christian sermons have stressed that, in his weakness and apparent worldly failure, Jesus represented a truly odd candidate for messiahship and that in his very rejection of earthly glories, we see his true heavenly character.[33] As we have seen from Qumran, the story is more nuanced than this account would suggest, and messianic images were multiform. Whether or not there was any direct influence from Qumran or other sectarian circles, we must be less struck by what initially appear to be the revolutionary novelty of the claims made for Jesus's messianic role.[34]

Jesus seemingly stood apart from his contemporaries in his pacifism and rejection of worldly politics, in contrast to insurrectionists like the Egyptian Prophet or even his Zealot near neighbors. Later generations of Christians accept that stance as a fundamental part of Jesus's mission, although some scholars through the years have doubted whether the written records concerning Jesus can in fact be trusted in this regard. The gospels were written in the aftermath of the Jewish War, when Roman authorities were extremely sensitive about any movement that might be regarded as seditious, leaving early Christians little option but to present their founder in the most pacific and apolitical terms. Just how accurate that picture actually was remains open to discussion. From their point of view at least, the Romans of his time had reasonable grounds to link Jesus with a host of similar figures in these same years.

Even if the Jesus movement was a tiny sect within the larger Jewish world, few of the group's ideas marked them off significantly from the thought-world of their Jewish contemporaries. In so many of their beliefs, especially about issues of apocalyptic, prophecy, and messianism, Jesus's first followers were absolutely Jewish men and women of their time.

BY THE 60s, religious nationalist sentiment was growing, to the point of demanding an outright break with Roman authority. Little more was needed to ignite a full-scale revolt. Much like the Maccabean revolt, the Jewish rising that actually did occur in the 60s is usually portrayed in terms of a united patriotic effort of oppressed Jews against a pagan occupier. Like that earlier movement, though, the later rising was also a complex affair, setting different internal factions and ethnic groups against each other.

Interethnic tensions in fact provided the immediate spark for the revolt. Caesarea had long been a microcosm of the region's divisions. Jews claimed the city as their own, because it had been built by Herod, a Jew. The Gentiles and "Syrians" conceded that fact, but protested that the city was so full of pagan temples and statues that it obviously could not have been intended for Jews. (Reading such exchanges, we realize how far removed we are from any modern sense of peaceful coexistence, still less multiculturalism.) Some Greeks sacrificed doves outside a synagogue, and the offense that that caused was magnified when Roman authorities failed to intervene. Fighting spread until the governor of the Jerusalem Temple took the insurrectionary step of ending the service of sacrifice and prayers for the emperor. Roman troops entered the Temple to seize its wealth, which had the effect of focusing popular unrest on burdensome Roman taxation. This event incited outright revolution, as nationalist forces seized Jerusalem, overrunning the Roman garrisons as they had failed to do in 4 BCE. Roman authorities in Syria sent in a major army—again, closely following the script of Varus's time—but this force were defeated in one of the worst disasters that insurgents ever inflicted on imperial forces. In response, Rome appointed one of its toughest and most competent generals, Vespasian, to lead the reconquest, beginning in the most radicalized insurgent zone of all, the Galilee.[35]

In retrospect, we know that the Jewish Revolt was doomed and was bound to destroy the land and its society. Even at the time, a little history should have taught the rebels just how far-fetched their cause really was. Rome might indeed be challenged, but only provided that its empire and army were fatally divided and failing, or if rebels had the support of some mighty external power. For a brief period, internal Roman divisions seemed very promising for the Jewish cause, and Nero's death in 68 was followed by an intense civil war. The year 69, in fact, is remembered as the Year of Four Emperors, and the chaos naturally slowed the reconquest of Judea. Even so, one of those battling candidates, Vespasian himself, won the imperial crown, and his son Titus led the final assault against the Jewish insurgents. (The former rebel leader Josephus saved his own skin with a well-timed prophecy that Vespasian would be the prophesied world ruler who would come out of Judea—a devious reworking of the then-current Jewish obsession with messianic prophecies.) However disastrous they seemed at the time, then, Roman weaknesses were never grave enough to provide the conditions for a Jewish victory.

The Jews themselves were at least as badly divided. As in any revolution, radicals often found themselves at odds with more moderate groups, but the Jewish case was made much worse by the struggles between old-established sects. In 67 CE, the Roman conquest of Galilee forced thousands of Zealots to flee into Judea, where they confronted the Sadducees who were entrenched in Jerusalem itself. That conflict developed into an outright civil war among the Jews, which persisted into 69. Each side sought to eliminate its rivals by assassination and execution, with the Zealots particularly ruthless against anyone who contemplated surrender to the Romans. Meanwhile, people flocked into the city to aid the rival forces, each under its own warlords. Reliably fervent as ever, Idumeans swelled the Zealot army.

The war reached its climax in 70, when the Romans recaptured and massacred the insurgent city of Jerusalem, in the process destroying the Second Temple. The great Menorah and other sacred vessels were taken to Rome for display during a magnificent Triumph, which is commemorated in a famous and much-reproduced carving on the Roman Arch of Titus, erected around 82. (Another Roman arch erected in Titus's honor made the extraordinary claim that he was the first ever to have conquered the city, a statement that would have surprised earlier victors like Pompey, among others.) The smashing of God's House marked the end of the millennium-old sacrificial cult and the devastation of Judean society. The number of dead ran into the hundreds of thousands. Apart from the Temple, the Qumran community itself now came to an end, and the lesser Temple at Leontopolis, in Egypt, fell a few years afterward. A pseudoprophecy in Mark's gospel has Jesus echoing Daniel in warning about those years, "Those will be days of distress unequaled from the beginning, when God created the world, until now—and never to be equaled again" (13:19).[36]

THE RESULTING CONFLICT was indeed savage at the local level. Across Palestine and the wider Near East, the revolution was marked by intercommunal massacres and ethnic cleansing, and the redrawing of religious and cultural boundaries. This horrific era fundamentally changed the relationship between Gentile and Jewish communities and consequently altered the nature of Judaism itself. Memories of such atrocities poisoned intercommunal relations for decades.

As so often in such instances, we can rarely tell just who started a cycle of massacres and tit-for-tat revenge. After the radical coup in Jerusalem in 66, the people of Caesarea slaughtered their Jews, reputedly twenty thousand of them. Jews then retaliated against Gentile settlements across the country, devastating the villages and towns of the "Syrians" and burning and massacring across the Decapolis. Gentiles struck back against Jewish communities that they feared might be nurturing potential rebels and *genocidaires* in their midst. The insanity spilled outside Palestine's borders. Intercommunal rioting in Alexandria escalated until the Romans sent in regular forces, who massacred the substantial Jewish Quarter. Damascus slaughtered its Jews, allegedly ten thousand in number.[37]

After striking the Jews, the Gentiles targeted the Judaizers, *tous Ioudaizontas*, an intriguing word. It might refer to Gentiles sympathetic toward Judaism who had not undergone full conversion, but it might also include Gentiles attracted to the rising Jesus movement, which at the time was viewed as a Jewish sect. This was neither the time nor the place for people who straddled the religious and political boundary and wanted no part in the reciprocal mass murder.[38]

Obviously, even such disasters did not entirely destroy the Jewish world or its Christian offshoots. Reportedly, the early Christian church of Jerusalem responded to the crisis by relocating across the Jordan, to the Decapolis city of Pella. Other sectarian movements likely followed similar eastward routes, including the Jewish Christian baptismal sects. Nor did the violence actually end Diaspora communities, which in some ways were actually enhanced as they were strengthened by refugees and exiles from Palestine itself. Even so, it is hard to exaggerate the scale of the catastrophe at all levels, cultural, political, and religious. The war transformed the religious world, wrecking many older institutions and movements beyond repair.

Contemporary observers could have been forgiven for seeing the Jewish War as the end of the Jewish people, a cosmic catastrophe even worse than the Babylonian exile six centuries before. In fact, of course, it was no such thing. Judaism itself underwent a fundamental reconstruction, while the associated movements now developed their ideas on a much larger global canvas.

Chapter 11

MAKING FAITHS

The Making of World Religions

<hr />

And the Lord said unto me: "This city shall be delivered up for
a time, and the people shall be chastened during a time, and the
world will not be given over to oblivion."

2 BARUCH 4:1

ABOUT 120 CE, Basilides of Alexandria was one of the brightest
lights of the new Christian movement, although later generations
marginalized him as a Gnostic. Among his influential theories, he
described "those angels who occupy the lowest heaven, that, namely,
which is visible to us, [who] formed all the things which are in the
world, and made allotments among themselves of the earth and of
those nations which are upon it. The chief of them is he who is
thought to be the God of the Jews; and inasmuch as he desired to
render the other nations subject to his own people, that is, the Jews,
all the other princes resisted and opposed him. Wherefore all other
nations were at enmity with his nation." According to Basilides, only
by deception and error was this angel mistaken for God, and he
became the deity of the Old Testament. But the true and supreme
God, the Father, sent a redeemer to rescue people from this evil Creator deity. This savior was "his own first-begotten Nous [Mind], (he
it is who is called Christ) to bestow deliverance on them that believe
in him, from the power of those who made the world."[1]

In every particular, Basilides was imagining a universe derived from Jewish speculations of the Crucible years, with its heavenly hierarchies and its angels and the sense that the world was under the sway of these lesser divine beings. Even the idea of deities being allocated their own particular territories ultimately comes from Deuteronomy. But if the approaches were unmistakably Jewish, the conclusions were anti-Judaic, if not anti-Semitic. I will discuss this paradox shortly, but the case of Basilides illustrates just how thoroughly leading thinkers and theologians had borrowed their worldview and the cast of spiritual characters from those Jewish predecessors. They preached not just anti-Judaism but rather an "inverted Judaism." And these ideas developed within the familiar Hellenistic Triangle, that cultural region that looked to Alexandria, Antioch, and Seleucia-Ctesiphon.[2]

By the time of Jesus and Paul, the spiritual revolution was well advanced, although its victory was not quite assured, and it was still far from clear how those new insights would be institutionalized in the form of religions. Some movements acknowledged their Jewish heritage, while others actively rejected it. In hindsight, we know that Christianity and Judaism would be the two great heirs, but other claimants existed. Some ideas survived and flourished, others faded to the margins or vanished altogether, but all were manifestations of a wider and potent spiritual impulse. When modern scholars write the histories of such major faiths and sects as Jews, Christians, Gnostics, dualists, and Manichaeans, they are applying those terms retroactively, to groups that should be placed on a single continuum. All were heirs of the same religious revolution and shared very similar beliefs about the spiritual universe.

EVEN THE FALL of the Temple in 70 did not end the agonizing violence that had begun with the Jewish Revolt: further political disasters followed in the coming decades, reaching a climax in the 130s. The intervening years were an interwar period, one that lived with the aftereffects of one disaster while grimly awaiting the near-inevitable second phase. That whole period, from 70 through 135, not only marks a crisis within Judaism itself but among the various religious movements that had grown up within the Jewish framework.[3]

Earlier, I used the example of Queen Salome Alexandra to show how many tumultuous events could occur within a single lifetime. If we imagine another Jewish girl born in 70 CE, one blessed with around three score and ten years, then she likewise would until her dying day witness disasters and national calamities. Apart from brutal political and religious divisions, she would see recurrent famines and subsistence crises like the brutal one of the 90s that inspired the writing of the book of Revelation. From her earliest years too, her family would be subjected to the onerous Jewish Tax, the *fiscus judaicus,* which the Romans imposed as a collective punishment for the great revolt.[4]

In 115 she would hear of a new wave of Jewish revolts that began in Egypt and spread across much of the Near East, almost constituting a second Roman-Jewish War. Because the Roman commander Lusius Quietus played such a prominent role in suppressing this insurgency, the events are known as the Kitos War. The most traumatic events occurred in Egypt, where a Jewish revolt in Alexandria was followed by a Roman reaction that uprooted an ancient and crucial community. Reprisals were savage and involved executions and confiscations. Jewish life in the city, and in Egypt more generally, never fully recovered. That was vastly significant given Alexandria's role as a second Jewish capital and a primary center of Christian thought and innovation. In the 130s, our imaginary woman would hear of a new Jewish revolt in Palestine itself, led by one Simeon bar-Koseva, who took the messianic name Bar-Kokhba, Son of a Star. (A passage in the book of Numbers foretold the rise of "a star out of Jacob," and the Qumran War Scroll had already quoted this as a messianic prophecy.) But as in the 60s, the new revolt was totally defeated, and Jewish casualties were heavy. The Romans responded by the mass expulsion of Jews from the city of Jerusalem, which was renamed Aelia Capitolina, after the family name of the emperor Hadrian. The name of Judea vanished from the map, and the province was renamed Syria Palaestina.[5]

It is tempting to describe such repeated conflicts and bloodshed as "apocalyptic," but that term is wearyingly appropriate in these circumstances. Our Jewish woman likely died in the despairing belief that she had seen the end of the Jewish realm—Israel, or Judea—and the obliteration of Jerusalem.

THE INTERWAR CRISES inspired many writings, as Jews and Christians alike tried to make sense of the disasters around them, and many did so through the apocalyptic and messianic tradition that had emerged in the previous three centuries. The era between 70 and 135 was a golden age of apocalyptic.

The best-known example was the Revelation (Apocalypse) of John, which has exercised an incalculable influence on Western religion and culture, not to mention the visual arts. It was not unique in its day, and other Christian revelations such as that credited to Peter were also once celebrated. But John's text is the great survivor. At every stage, the book shows the pervasive influence of such seminal books as 1 Enoch and Daniel, while Second Zechariah provides the organizing framework of the whole vision. Revelation is centrally focused on the Judgment and the events and struggles preceding that ultimate historical climax. This is Doomsday, using the old English word for "law" or "judgment." Heaven and Hell are both very material realities. The greatest truths, moreover, are preserved in heavenly writings and mystic scrolls, as well as the books of life that record all human deeds. As this is an apocalypse, rather than a traditional prophecy, angels play a critical role in transmitting these messages and pronouncements.[6]

Revelation depicts a world ruled by the forces of sin and evil, in which God's people represent a tiny persecuted minority deeply at odds with all institutions and ideologies. Matters grow steadily worse under the rule of a number of evil figures who represent or serve the Devil—the Great Beast, the Whore, the Antichrist. Satanic forces exercise power through their control of worldly empires, above all the titanic power of Rome. Evil forces demand that believers choose between collaboration and martyrdom, until the powers of good intervene—Christ and the angelic legions, led by Michael. Great battles and tribulations devastate the world until divine forces decisively defeat the powers of evil, following the battle of Armageddon. The story culminates in Christ's millenarian reign on earth and the creation of an ideal New Jerusalem.[7]

Revelation shows how the political and religious crisis forced believers (Christians and Jews alike) to resort to these End Times visions to comprehend what was, evidently, the ruinous end of a world that had existed for centuries. Apocalyptic prophecy was the best way to understand the sober politics of the era. Less famous than Revelation are two Jewish works—2 Baruch and 2 Esdras—written at almost exactly the same time and responding to similar circumstances and theological quandaries. Such writings struggled to imagine how the Jewish people could survive in a world bereft of an institution as fundamental as the Temple. Was this the end of a faith, a race, even a world? Yet there were new hopes, new visions, even dreams of how God would restore his creation.[8]

The book of 2 Baruch shares many assumptions with Revelation and occupies a near identical spiritual universe.[9] Angels proliferate throughout the work, and one of them, Ramiel, provides advice and explication to the prophet, Baruch. Both Revelation and 2 Baruch imagine the opening of heavenly books as a portent of the coming End. Both also treat actual cities like Rome and Jerusalem in symbolic or spiritualized form, and both use Babylon as a coded way of referring to Rome. But the resemblances to Revelation go far beyond these specifics. Both are grounded in their belief in the imminent coming of the Messiah and the Judgment of the world. That cataclysm will be followed by a general resurrection and the reward or punishment of the restored dead. Baruch asks God the agonized questions that Jews must have asked after 70:

What, therefore, will there be after these things? For if you destroy Your city, and deliver up Your land to those that hate us,
how shall the name of Israel be again remembered? Or how
shall one speak of Your praises? Or to whom shall that which is
in Your Law be explained? Or shall the world return to its nature
of aforetime, and the age revert to primeval silence? And shall
the multitude of souls be taken away, and the nature of man
not again be named? And where is all that which you did say
regarding us?[10]

This is a work of lament, of grief, to the point of asking whether
a man would not have been better off not being born. Even so, God
responds with a message of hope. The destruction, he says, was
done with his approval, in order to hasten the coming of the Judgment. "Therefore have I now taken away Zion, that I may the more
speedily visit the world in its season" (20:2). Baruch describes the
coming Judgment, which will be preceded by wars and chaos. On the
great day, "the books shall be opened in which are written the sins
of all those who have sinned, and again also the treasuries in which
the righteousness of all those who have been righteous in creation
is gathered" (24:1). The righteous would be resurrected in glory; the
wicked would suffer torment and perdition.

The Latin Apocalypse of Ezra assumes a comparably Enochian
universe. This again dates from around 100 and is presented in the
form of visions received by the prophet Ezra during the Babylonian
exile. Like Baruch, Ezra too gropes to find meaning in the sack of
the city, after "our sanctuary is laid waste, our altar broken down, our
temple destroyed" (10:21). God sends an angel, in this case Uriel,
to explain the signs of the times. In passages recalling the book of
Job, Uriel explains that humanity cannot fully understand God's purposes. Even so, the apparent catastrophe is a harbinger of the imminent End Times. The theme of judgment runs through the work,
as does the doctrine of future rewards and punishments. "For after
death shall the judgment come, when we shall live again: and then

shall the names of the righteous be manifest, and the works of the ungodly shall be declared" (14:35).[11]

Like Revelation, Ezra's Apocalypse imagines cosmic visions in animal form, and in this case the Roman Empire is portrayed as an eagle, confronted and destroyed by a lion. Recalling Enoch's Son of Man, Ezra sees the Messiah as a "man from the sea," who eliminates Gentile enemies without bothering to raise a sword or weapon. "He sent out of his mouth as it had been a blast of fire, and out of his lips a flaming breath, and out of his tongue he cast out sparks and tempests" (13:10). After the struggle, a New Jerusalem would arise.

BUT IF CHRISTIANS and Jews at this stage thought and wrote in such close parallel, the differences between the two groups grew enormously over time. In the process, each side built on that Crucible inheritance while divesting itself of particular aspects of that legacy.

Jews, of course, had to reconstruct and redefine their faith, which involved a fundamental shift of emphasis from the now impossible Temple sacrifices to prayer and study in the synagogue. That change also transferred power and prestige from the old priestly elites to new categories of scholars, sages, and teachers or rabbis. We are observing the emergence of Rabbinic Judaism. The emphasis on texts and scholarship, rather than sacrifice, allowed the community to survive far beyond its original geographical home. *Ioudaios* now meant Jew rather than literally Judean, while "Judaism" denoted an ethnic and religious concept separated from any homeland.[12]

From the late first century CE, rabbis and scholars undertook the immense project of debating and expounding Jewish law and practice, a process that involved literally centuries of study and argument. Of course, the scholars reaffirmed the central truths of Jewish identity—the Law, the Covenant, Sabbath observance, dietary laws, circumcision, and the sacred bond with the land—but they also expounded just how the biblical commandments offered a total and demanding framework for every aspect of daily life. Between 180 and 220 CE, the sages compiled the oral Torah in the great collection called the Mishnah, which was assembled in Palestine. Further commentaries and elucidations appeared in the Jerusalem Talmud in the fourth century. Finally, chiefly between the fifth and seventh centuries, the heart of intellectual life moved eastward, as Mesopotamia became the indisputable intellectual center of Judaism, with the flourishing of the Talmudic (Geonic) academies. Scholars in this region compiled the Babylonian Talmud, the *Bavli*. That text itself noted that "The Holy One, blessed be He, knows that Israel is unable to endure the cruel decrees of Edom [Rome], therefore He exiled them to Babylonia."[13]

Not only did rabbinic Judaism triumph, but over time histories were written to assert that this was the inevitable goal toward which earlier developments had inevitably been tending. Rival forms of Judaism were written out of the story, and some were all but forgotten until modern times. This was partly because some older movements and factions had suffered so heavily in the wars or been discredited. Both Sadducees and Essenes vanished from debate, leaving the field to the heirs of the Pharisaic tradition. Overtly Essene and Enochic sources are conspicuously absent in the founding texts of rabbinic Judaism from the late second century onward.

That purge profoundly reshaped attitudes to scripture and to pseudoscriptural works. The scale of the task that the rabbis faced is apparent from the passages in Ezra's Apocalypse about the restoration of scripture and also its limits. God appears to the scribe and orders him and his assistants to write down the visions they had received (14:45). The result is ninety-four books, twenty-four of which represent the standard number for the canonical Old Testament, and these were to be read by worthy and unworthy alike. The other seventy were to be delivered only to the wise. Presumably, that vast additional library signifies a range of noncanonical and pseudepigraphic works of the sort that had proliferated since the time of 1 Enoch.

Despite "Ezra's" vision, those works remained very controversial for Jews, all the more so given the political and intellectual dangers of the time. In the aftermath of the twin disasters of 70 and 135, that meant deep suspicion about any texts or traditions hinting at political messianism or apocalyptic. Also, Jewish leaders were increasingly aware of the rival movement of Christianity, which divided so many communities and synagogues. The minority sect was now definitively excluded from synagogues and its members persecuted. Hostility grew as Christianity became a potent presence across the whole Mediterranean world in the third century and after it gained the active support of the Roman Empire in the fourth.[14]

Jewish scholars reacted viscerally against beliefs and texts that were favored by Christians, a reaction that went far beyond the messianic ideal itself. That reaction shaped attitudes to Enochic ideas and texts and to many of the once influential pseudepigrapha. The second century CE text known as the Dialogue with Trypho reports a Jewish apologist citing a well-known tale from Enoch to complain about how gullible Christians were in accepting falsehoods, "nay, even blasphemies, for you assert that angels sinned and revolted from God." Christian claims to a continuing tradition of charismatic prophecy made Jews suspicious of such doctrines, especially when prophetic revelations threatened to supersede canonical scripture. Contemporary visionary claims of heavenly journeys were treated with just as much disdain. More basically, the Christian predilection for the Septuagint encouraged Jews to reject that version and the additional books that it contained over and above Hebrew versions.[15]

Rabbinic Judaism strictly defined the limits of scripture, to the point of suppressing most noncanonical texts. In many cases, that meant eliminating the Hebrew or Aramaic originals of pseudoscriptures, which survived only in Christian contexts or in other languages. The Apocalypse of Ezra mainly survives in Latin, the Testaments of the Twelve Patriarchs in Greek. Gradually, Christian churches themselves became hostile to some of these writings, which survived only in peripheral regions and isolated churches. Only in Ethiopia did Christians not just carry on reading 1 Enoch and Jubilees but still regarded them as canonical scripture. A whole library of ancient

Jewish texts was preserved in the Slavonic-speaking churches of eastern Europe, where such long-forgotten works as 2 Enoch and the Apocalypse of Abraham have been rediscovered in modern times. Other texts were recovered only gradually, and partially, at Qumran and elsewhere.[16]

Of course, reconstructed Judaism did not altogether lose access to mystical and esoteric ideas, although it is difficult to trace the exact means by which older ideas survived. However thoroughly these were (notionally) suppressed, medieval Jewish sages still referred obliquely to texts like Jubilees. In addition, a whole genre of visionary literature, the *Hekhalot*, harks back to Enochic stories of heavenly ascents. (The word *Hekhalot* refers to the temples or palaces above.) Other forms of historical Jewish mysticism retained their own memories of sectarian ideas from the Crucible years. The very influential Qabalistic tradition powerfully recalls Gnosticism, even though issues of chronology make it difficult to see direct linkages. The most ancient Qabalistic texts were written down long after the disappearance of active Gnostic communities, no earlier than the sixth century CE. Even so, much of that tradition sounds like a close facsimile of ancient Gnostic and Neoplatonic schools. Perhaps Jewish thinkers were drawing on sectarian traditions of a kind that also, separately, contributed to making Gnosticism. Strongly recalling the Crucible years was the central role of Adam in Qabalistic thought— or rather, of the two Adams, both the heavenly and spiritual Primal Man, as well as the flawed and fleshly ancestor of humanity. Connections between Qabala and the older sectarian world are highly likely, even if we cannot plainly see the intervening stages.[17]

THE CRISIS OF Judaism reverberated throughout the religious world. The collapse of central control allowed the upsurge of many previously minor groups, especially the nascent Jesus movement. Within that new sect, the multiple crises caused a major rupture in the historical continuity from the earliest church. The ensuing debates form much of the subject matter of the New Testament epistles, and the same years also witnessed the composition of the gospels.

In retrospect, knowing as we do the subsequent development of the two faiths, we often assume that both Judaism and Christianity achieved their own distinctive identities very early on, leaving obscure sects of "Jewish Christians" as a heretical curiosity. But even speaking of Jewish Christians is misleading, as it would be impossible at this time to have a kind of Christianity that was not essentially Jewish, or grounded in the Jewish world of the previous three centuries. Even the New Testament doctrines that at first sight most strongly signal Greek or non-Jewish influences can be traced directly to the Jewish world of the Crucible years.[18]

Later Jews, of course, were scandalized by the messianic claims made for Jesus and appalled when these advanced to assert his divine status. But throughout that process, Christians were drawing faithfully on ideas that were quite familiar within the Jewish world, albeit within forms of Judaism that were now tainted as sectarian. At an early stage in the story, Christian thinkers explored some of the intermediary figures that Jewish thinkers had devised to explain God's interactions with the world. Might Jesus have been an angel? One interpretation of the Son of Man passages in Daniel understood the heavenly creature in human form to be an angel or archangel. When gospel writers describe Jesus's ascension to heaven following his resurrection, the passage draws heavily on the scene in the book of Tobit when another archangel, Raphael, returns to the heavenly realms (12:16–22).

Other writers turned to the idea of Wisdom (Sophia) and to Philo's theory of the Logos to explain the divine nature of Christ. Like so many Jewish contemporaries, New Testament authors were well acquainted with Platonic language, none more so than in the Epistle to the Hebrews. In a typical passage, the Epistle states, "The Law is only a shadow [*skia*] of the good things that are coming—not the realities themselves" (10:1). The earthly sanctuary is "a copy and a shadow" of a heavenly Temple, where Jesus serves as eternal high priest (8:5). The heavenly city is a type, a pattern, of its earthly manifestation. At the end of the first century CE, the gospel of John described the Logos, the Word, as the means by which God created the world and affirmed moreover that this same Logos had taken flesh as Jesus Christ himself. Paul's Letter to the Colossians proclaims Christ as "the image [*eikon*] of the invisible God, the firstborn of all creation; for in him all things were created, in heaven and on earth, visible and invisible. . . . He is before all things, and in him all things hold together" (1:15–17).

Generations of scholars viewed such texts almost as a Hellenistic excrescence, an infusion of alien philosophies that departed sadly from the Jewish thought world of the pristine early Christian church. Yet such ideas had long been thoroughly absorbed into that Jewish world, as was the dualistic language of Light and Darkness that John's Jesus so often employed. Jesus proclaimed himself "the Light of the World," and he promised that his followers would not walk in darkness but have the Light of life. In the earliest surviving Christian text, 1 Thessalonians, Paul offered this theme of Christ's followers as children of Light, who belong neither to the night nor to Darkness (see 1 Thess. 5:5 and Eph. 8:5). Paul may have been a Pharisee, but he really does sound like a Qumran adherent when he warns his readers, "Do not be unequally yoked with unbelievers. For what partnership has righteousness with lawlessness? Or what fellowship has light with darkness? What accord has Christ [the Messiah] with Belial?" (2 Cor. 6:14). Early in the second century, an unknown Christian who probably lived in Alexandria wrote a tract called the Epistle of Barnabas, which came close to being included in the canonical New Testament. One section of Barnabas includes a lengthy disquisition on the Two Ways, which likewise reads as if it could have come directly from Qumran: "There are two ways of teaching and of power, the one of Light and the other of Darkness; and there is a great difference between the two ways. For on the one are stationed the light-giving angels of God, on the other the angels of Satan."[19]

The separation of Judaism and Christianity was slow and gradual, spread over the seventy years or so following the Fall of the Temple. Before about 120 CE, it is exceedingly difficult to draw sharp lines between the Jesus movement and Judaism broadly defined, and examples of hostility and exclusion in one region did not necessarily apply elsewhere. Particularly in key regions outside Palestine, the real split with Judaism came in the mid-second century CE rather than in the first. Across the Near East, anti-Judaism became rife following the Kitos War of 115–17, and so did critical attitudes toward Jewish claims to exclusivism. Another decisive break came in the 130s with the desperate nationalist revolt led by Bar-Kokhba, which we have already encountered. The total failure of that movement discredited nationalist militancy, but the affair also further alienated Christians from the Jewish mainstream: Bar-Kokhba, "Son of the Star," himself had made messianic claims, and his forces persecuted the followers of Jesus. The resulting hostility shaped the church's bitter memory of the event, as recorded by the later Christian historian Eusebius. Bar-Kokhba, he said, "possessed the character of a robber and a murderer, but nevertheless, relying upon his name, boasted to them, as if they were slaves, that he possessed wonderful powers; and he pretended that he was a star that had come down to them out of heaven to bring them light in the midst of their misfortunes."[20]

What was rapidly becoming the mainstream of the Great Church had to acknowledge the new realities, the new schism.

BUT EVEN AFTER Jews and Christians had become more delineated, the two groups still interacted closely in many parts of the world. As late as the end of the fourth century, the famous preacher John Chrysostom angrily condemned the many Antioch Christians who happily attended the synagogues and observed Jewish feasts and customs.[21]

A substantial middle ground of believers fitted entirely into neither of the new religious categories. These so-called Jewish Christians accepted Jesus as the Messiah but also obeyed Mosaic rules about Sabbath obedience, circumcision, and dietary laws. Church fathers often refer to sects in this mold called the Ebionites or Nazareans, who claimed to be heirs of the most ancient Jerusalem church. For centuries, indeed, a common academic mythology has portrayed the Ebionites as the authentic vessels of Jesus's true message, before it was betrayed by figures like Paul. That view is exaggerated, but Jewish Christians should be counted among the heirs of sectarian movements that had all but vanished in the mainstream Jewish tradition—groups like the Essenes, the Qumran sect, and the mysterious followers of Enoch.[22]

Before the 60s, such movements had exercised a potent influence in Jewish thought and culture. Presumably, the conflicts of those years did not annihilate each and every thinker of those movements or destroy all their texts; their flight from Palestine spread their ideas, although in new forms. The resulting exodus contributed to a widespread diaspora of alternative and sectarian forms of Judaism. Arguably, that alternative Judaism did not simply evaporate during the Jewish Revolt and its aftermath; rather, it relocated. Or as we might rather say, it returned to its spiritual home. So many of the innovations of the Crucible years had been influenced by Eastern cultures, both Persian and Mesopotamian, and we have seen the pervasive influence of Mesopotamian ideas in 1 Enoch. The revolution of the 60s CE forced many Jews to seek refuge in the East, ultimately in Mesopotamia itself.

Members of Jerusalem's Jesus movement now fled east across the Jordan, and so, almost certainly, did the followers of the Jewish baptist sects that looked to John rather than Jesus. Syriac Christian tradition reported the Jerusalem church's eastward migration into Mesopotamia. Reputedly, Christians reached Edessa very soon after the death of Jesus, with the earliest missionaries stemming from Antioch. These accounts point to a Christian presence based in

Seleucia-Ctesiphon from the early second century, which meshes well with the vigorous Jewish presence in that area. One of the most spectacular archaeological finds from late antiquity is the third-century CE city of Dura-Europos, on the Euphrates, which had both a lavishly decorated synagogue and an early church. Continuity from the Jewish sects is highly likely in Mesopotamia, the base of the great Church of the East (the later "Nestorian Church"), which in the Middle Ages spread its influence across much of Asia, reaching China, India, and Turkestan.[23]

Yet the closer we look at early Mesopotamian Christians, the more they resemble not just sectarian Judaism in general but specifically the world of the Dead Sea Scrolls. Like the people of Qumran, Eastern church thinkers used "holiness" as their technical term for the practice of celibacy. Ascetics also used the same term as the Qumran sect when they described themselves as sons (or daughters) of the Covenant, *qeiama*. Throughout the Middle Ages, the Mesopotamian church used in their worship and devotion a number of psalms over and above the familiar roster known in Europe, and only in modern times have those mysterious psalms also come to light in the Dead Sea Scrolls. Some kind of linkage from Qumran to Christian Mesopotamia seems likely, if by no means proved.[24]

Such a legacy might also be sought in early monasticism. In the first century CE, Egypt was the home of a still-mysterious group of ascetics called the Therapeutae, who were devoted to prayer, study, and spiritual reading. As described by Philo, they sound much like Essenes or the Qumran sect, and they seemingly prefigure the Christian monasticism that emerged in Egypt in the third century, though no modern historians draw neat linear connections between the movements. Monks also appear early in the historical record in eastern Syria, Mesopotamia, and Persia. Syrian monks were even fiercer than Egyptian in their asceticism and their contempt for the body. Taking the Egyptian and Syriac stories together, this history suggests at least the possibility of continuities from the sectarian Jewish world into early Christianity.[25]

TRACING THE GENEALOGIES of other once popular movements shows a similar inheritance. The early Christian centuries produced many communities and teachers that we now describe as Gnostic. That term has to be treated cautiously, because the believers themselves would usually have used some other word of self-description, commonly just "Christian." Moreover, the actual views that such groups held were so diverse that some scholars reject even the concept of Gnosticism as a myth that was invented in early church polemic and subsequently upheld by uncritical academics. Such a rejection goes too far, as many common threads of belief can indeed be found among the so-called Gnostics. Even so, only in retrospect were the Gnostics portrayed as a rogue Christian heresy rather than a distinctive form of that faith.[26]

Although Gnostics varied widely in their specific beliefs, most saw the universe in broadly dualist terms, seeing the material world not as fallen but rather as a flawed creation, beyond redemption. They taught a myth of Creation emanating from absolute perfection and descending to lower levels of reality. Commonly, Gnostic theorists identified the Creator of the material world with the Jewish God, as portrayed in the Old Testament, whom they saw as a lower-level divine being. Christ came from higher spiritual realms to redeem and reawaken the sparks of true divinity that survive within the pollutions of matter. Given its denigration of the Jewish God, it might at first sight seem futile to seek any connection between Gnosticism and any kind of Jewish tradition. Gnosticism is much more than just anti-Judaism, but without that element, it makes no sense. That would seem to put the Gnostic tradition at the opposite end of any intellectual spectrum from Judaism, but in fact continuities with sectarian Jewish movements can be traced.[27]

I have described the quandary faced by Jewish thinkers in the Hellenistic years, who had to reconcile their familiar beliefs with Platonism. Some, like Philo, argued that the absolute God might in fact have created the world on the lines portrayed in Genesis—but that was not the only possible interpretation. One might also view the material world as the work of an imperfect or even malevolent creator, a sinister Demiurge, who was at odds with the one true God. Such a conflict meshed well with the powerful drive in the Jewish world at exactly this time to imagine a powerful Devil who (by some accounts) was in fact Lord of this world. If that Satan is identified with the Demiurge, then this really would constitute full-scale cosmic dualism. On the available evidence, no group moved toward such despairing conclusions before the first century CE, but some assuredly did thereafter.[28]

Scholars have long debated the exact relationship between Gnosticism and Christianity, and the hypothetical existence of a "pre-Christian Gnosticism." I make no claims whatever for the existence of such a phenomenon, for any actual schools, sects, or movements during the pre-Christian era. Even so, much of Gnosticism could have been constructed without wandering too far outside Judaism as it existed, in its very diverse forms, in the Crucible years.

BEYOND MERELY CITING parallels, direct linkages can be drawn between the old Jewish world and the newer Gnostic sects. Taken together, these continuities help answer the question of how some of the most radical insights of the Crucible years actually developed when they were excluded from Jewish and Christian orthodoxies.[29]

Because of the means by which documents have been preserved, and particularly the dry climate, the vast majority of textual discoveries have been made in Egypt, most famously the Nag Hammadi library discovered in 1945. That emphasis does not mean that Egypt was the sole home of the movement, which had at least as firm a foundation to the east, in Syria and Mesopotamia. Throughout the early Christian centuries, much of the spiritual ferment occurred in the borderlands between the Roman and Persian empires. The earliest Gnostic thinker who can be identified with any confidence is Menander of Antioch, who taught in the last quarter of the first century CE. He was regarded as the Syrian founder of the movement, while Basilides was the pioneer in Egypt.[30]

The doctrines of both movements, Syrian and Egyptian, were absolutely rooted in the Crucible years. According to the orthodox church father Irenaeus, the mysterious Gnostic thinker Simon Magus claimed to have been incarnated because the angels ruling the world exercised their power badly, with each struggling for supremacy. His pupil Menander believed that the world was in subjection to angels, from whom believers needed to be liberated. In turn, Menander's successor, Saturninus (ca. 110 CE), taught that the world was the creation of seven angels. Angels created humanity, making man "a shining image bursting forth below from the presence of the supreme power." Saturninus was "the first to affirm that two kinds of men were formed by the angels, the one wicked, and the other good. And since the demons assist the most wicked, the Savior came for the destruction of evil men and of the demons, but for the salvation of the good."[31]

At so many points, those words carry a powerful sense of déjà vu. The division into evil and good races would have been thoroughly familiar to Jewish groups of the second and first centuries BCE, especially those at Qumran. So would the focus on angels, astrology, and the emphasis on determinism and predestination. Gnostic mythologies also gave a prominent role to the figure of Wisdom, Sophia, who was so central to Crucible-era speculations. In seeking an explanation for the sinful world they contemplated, many Gnostics turned to the Creation story. God himself could not have fallen into sin or darkness, but perhaps his handmaiden did. In one common system, Sophia had fallen from the dominions of Light to become entrapped in material darkness, from which she must be redeemed. Wisdom is thus the possession of the spiritual elite, and it distinguishes them from the gullible herd of humans mired in the material, the victims of cosmic deception.[32]

No less important than the ideas are the setting in which they first appeared. Antioch—which played a pivotal role in nascent Gnosticism—was a junction for many different groups and influences, including Jews, Samaritans, Christians, and pagan Greeks. As a former capital of the Seleucid kingdom, it was a center of Hellenistic learning, and its role in the spice routes and the Silk Road meant that its connections stretched deep into Asia. Already in the first century, Antioch had become one of the great centers of the eastern Mediterranean, surpassed only by Alexandria. Demonstrating the city's close link to Palestine, Antioch was the stronghold watching over Judea after the first Jewish War, the base from which future risings could be prevented. Antioch stands about three hundred miles from Jerusalem. Naturally, it had a thriving Jewish population in its *Kerateion* quarter, and it was, famously, the place where Jesus's disciples were first called Christians. As we have seen, this was one of the centers where Jews and Christians remained closely intertwined at least through the fourth century.[33]

With those parallels and potential points of contact, how plausible is it that the new Gnostic synthesis might have drawn on the Jewish sectarian world and even on Qumran itself? The chronology is suggestive. The Qumran settlement ceased to function around 70 CE, when the Dead Sea Scrolls were concealed. If (we might speculate) at least a few of the sectaries retained their ideas and sought to reconstruct something of what they had lost, then the natural setting for such activity would have been in Antioch during the 80s and 90s CE. That was the same time and place as the historical Menander and the Gnostic theorizing with which he is credited. Shortly after that, at the opening of the second century, a comparable Gnostic school emerged in Alexandria.

This is not to imply that Menander himself was a veteran of Qumran. For one thing, he was by origin a Samaritan rather than a Jew. But individuals who had known the Essene or Qumran worlds could have found their way directly to Antioch. We know that people circulated between the different schools of Jewish thought, and some seekers might well have made the transition to versions of Jewish Christianity. Defections and ideological shifts were particularly likely in a crisis atmosphere like that of the 70s, when even the revolutionary nationalist Josephus defected to the Romans. Even if not through actual individuals, older ideas could have migrated to Antioch through imported texts.

Menander's Samaritan background points to other dimensions of the problem of origins. I have repeatedly mentioned the size and influence of the Samaritan population in Palestine in these centuries, and Samaritans, like Jews, spread widely in their own Diaspora. At least some of the first Christians also had a Samaritan background, probably including the Stephen recorded in the book of Acts, the faith's very first martyr. (Stephen's last speech, a pioneering example of Christian biblical exegesis, repeatedly draws on Samaritan readings and interpretations.) That context is important because early Christian commentators consistently described the first-century Gnostic pioneers as Samaritans, or else they were based in that region. That includes Simon Magus himself, and the shadowy Dosithean sect from which Simon supposedly drew his ideas. Can we assume that first-century Samaritans shared many of the sectarian Jewish beliefs we have traced? Perhaps they had evolved a parallel esoteric tradition, which has otherwise been lost to history.[34]

Such a Samaritan angle would also explain why ideas that grew out of sectarian Judaism assumed such a radically anti-Judaic guise. Jewish-Samaritan relations degenerated during the first century CE, with intercommunal violence and raiding. Samaritans were also much less supportive of the anti-Roman revolt of the 60s than were the Jews, although some at least supported the revolutionary cause. The ethnic division was still greater during the Bar-Kokhba revolt, in which Samaritans remained neutral. In consequence, Jewish attitudes toward Samaritans hardened between 70 and 130, to the point that Jewish scholars and rabbis usually dismissed them as no different from Gentiles. Samaritan thinkers had little reason to praise "the God of the Jews."[35]

That trajectory closely recalls the patterns of Christian-Jewish relations in these same years. During the first century, members of the mainstream Jesus movement hoped to remain within the larger Jewish world, until they were forcibly expelled from synagogues and the larger community. Each side in the schism claimed to have a true understanding of God, rejecting the deformed version preached by its rival. Adding to the hostility were the successive political crises between 70 and 135 CE. Basilides, Carpocrates, and other Alexandrian Gnostics were working only a very few years after the suppression of the bloody Jewish insurgency in that city. No more than a decade following the failure of the Bar-Kokhba movement of the 130s CE, Marcion of Pontus became one of the most significant Christian thinkers of the whole century. He taught a radical separation between the Old and New Testaments, with only the latter portraying divine truth. The God of the Jews was a sinister being, quite distinct from the true God revealed in the New Testament, with his son, Jesus. Although Marcion was denounced as a heretic and (sometimes) a Gnostic, his anti-Judaic ideas survived for centuries.[36]

HOWEVER THEY ARE defined, Gnostics are today celebrated in popular history and religious writing, but Syria and Iraq both produced other important movements and thinkers who could with equal legitimacy claim an inheritance from the Crucible years.[37]

One intriguing current runs from the followers of John the Baptist. Usually, John is regarded as a precursor of Jesus, and the literature has assimilated him into the narrative as his cousin. The movement largely vanished as it was absorbed into mainstream Christianity, but that was a lengthy process. In fact, his movement had a very long afterlife as an independent group or denomination. Even today, the tiny Gnostic-dualist sect of the Mandaeans, which still survives in southern Iraq, claims a special inheritance from John the Baptist.[38]

Another pivotal movement was the Elchasaites, the so-called "Babylonian Baptists," who take us back to archaic forms of Jewish Christian belief. Western church writers report a heretical Parthian thinker called Elchasai, who lived in the early second century CE. He reported a vision he had experienced of the Son of God, a titanic being many miles tall, who had revealed to him a heavenly book. Elchasai advocated a special baptism for the remission of sins, but also urged full obedience to the Mosaic Law. This sounds like a standard Jewish Christian package of beliefs, but just where had Elchasai found his ideas? The fourth-century Christian writer Epiphanius places Elchasai in the context of a group of Jewish and Jewish Christian sects, including the Nazareans, but also a group he calls the "Ossaeans." That is a suggestive name, and the Ossaeans might be identical with the Essenes. Epiphanius is by no means the world's most reliable writer, but if he is correct in this instance, then Elchasai was an adherent of an Ossaean/Essene sect, which still lived around the Dead Sea at the end of the first century CE.[39]

Like that other sectarian Jewish movement, the mainstream Christians, the Elchasaites originated in Palestine, but during the era of political turmoil, they moved eastward into Syria and later established their major center of activity in Mesopotamia. And in this region, they created an enduring legacy.

In the third century CE, the prophet Mani founded a dualistic-Gnostic movement that drew on Christianity but was also influenced by Zoroastrianism and Buddhism. Mani taught an eternal struggle between two forces, God and Satan, who were identified with Light and Darkness, and the flawed material creation represented a mixture of Light and Dark forces. As in Gnostic thought, Jesus is the redeemer figure, who restores the fallen Adam. In its day, Manichaeanism was a great world religion, with influence stretching from France to the Pacific, and in various forms its manifestations appeared in Byzantium and Bulgaria, China and Turkestan. Even Augustine belonged to the sect for some years. Not until the seventeenth century did Mani's movement finally vanish from its last Chinese fastnesses. Manichaeans created a substantial body of scriptures and commentaries, most of which are now lost.[40]

This faith is the only example of a world religion that has arisen and then vanished entirely, seemingly without trace. The fact that it disappeared should not be taken to indicate any inherent weakness or failing of the movement, in comparison to (say) mainstream Christianity. The most important difference was that while Christianity acquired the support of states, Manichaeanism did not, and it was swept away by centuries of wars and persecutions.

Manichaean origins are today an exciting area of research in Jewish and early Christian history, particularly following the discovery of major collections of early documents, chiefly in Egypt. Mani, we now know, was born near Seleucia-Ctesiphon around 216 CE. He had many dealings with the Persian royal court, before his eventual martyrdom in 270. His mother was Parthian, and his father belonged to the Elchasaites. Mani himself was an Elchasaite in his youth, before deserting that sect to explore the revelations he had received from an angelic mentor. That would make his movement a lineal heir of Jewish dualist thinking.[41]

Mani also drew heavily on Enochic traditions, including some not recorded by Christian churches, even in Ethiopia. His elaborate Creation myth makes much use of great spiritual beings, rulers or archons, who recall the angels of the Enochic writings. Manichaeans venerated the book of the Giants, as rewritten by Mani to express his own distinctive doctrines. In that form, the Manichaeans treated the work as canonical, and through them it circulated in multiple languages, including Syriac, Greek, Latin, Middle Persian, Parthian, Old Turkic, Coptic, Sogdian, Uyghur, and Arabic. It was an international best seller.[42]

The Manichaeans drew on other movements that likewise combined Jewish sectarian and baptist ideas with Gnostic trappings. The most important of these was the Sethians, who venerated Adam's son Seth. Several major Sethian works have been rediscovered in modern times, including their alternative gospels. Early Jewish sects had a special interest in pre-Flood patriarchs like Adam and Seth, who were the common ancestors of all humanity, not just Jews alone. Beyond framing a classic Gnostic myth of Creation and Fall, Sethian writings describe practical means of responding to such a universe. They offer techniques for traveling to heavenly realms and sharing in the angelic liturgy and even rising to the status of divine beings. At so many points, Sethian thought harks back to Enochic mystical themes and the world of Qumran. Much of the sect's literature took apocalyptic forms, especially the Apocalypse of Adam found at Nag Hammadi. The work may derive from a baptist sect like the Elchasaites, and it speaks often of the water of life and "the holy baptism and the living water."[43]

ULTIMATELY, EVEN THE Manichaeans were consigned to the distant margins of historical development. However, another faith rising during these years was no less fully an heir of the Crucible years.

Western historians would say that the religion of Islam emerged in the Arabian peninsula during the early seventh century. In Muslim eyes, such a statement is incorrect, in that Islam actually originated with Adam and was subsequently upheld by the prophets and patriarchs extolled by Judaism, as well as by John the Baptist and Jesus. Muhammad merely restated the primeval truth. Islam grounded itself entirely in Jewish and Christian traditions, as these faiths existed in the early centuries of the Common Era.

At every stage, Islamic beliefs were products of the Crucible. Prophecy offers one example, and Muhammad's own revelation began when he first heard words uttered by the angel Gabriel. Muslims hold that revelation, the Qur'an, not just to be sacred but to preexist Creation itself, much like the images of cosmic Wisdom, and like later Jewish concepts of the Torah. The idea of the Day of Judgment dominates every part of the Qur'an, usually accompanied by florid descriptions of Heaven and Hell. Islamic eschatology would have been thoroughly familiar to Jews from the time of the Enochic writings onward or to early Christians. Under the name Idris, Enoch is a celebrated prophet of Islam and the focus of many tales. Appropriately, his Arabic name may reflect his role as "interpreter."[44]

Islam and its scriptures drew massively on Jewish and Christian precedents and by no means only from strictly orthodox models. The Qur'an often uses Old and New Testament stories, but commonly views them through later apocryphal lenses. The Qur'anic story of

Adam and his Fall, for instance, is taken from the tradition found in the Life of Adam and Eve, which also provides the story of Satan's own rebellion and Fall. Islam teaches nothing like dualism, and Jesus's messianic role is denied. Even so, there are plenty of survivals from the older movements, including Jewish Christians and Gnostics. Following early Gnostic writings, the Qur'an portrays a Jesus who escaped an illusory Crucifixion.[45]

But Islamic thought continued to develop long after the completion of the Qur'an. By the mid-seventh century, most of the Middle East was under the political power of Islamic regimes, which ultimately ruled from the Atlantic to the borders of China. The Hellenistic Triangle now became the central core of the Islamic world, although the older cities were by now replaced by more modern successors—respectively Baghdad, Cairo, and Damascus. In those areas, Muslims encountered thriving Christian, Jewish, and Zoroastrian cultures and acquired many of their beliefs, often from new converts to Islam. During the early eighth century, Islamic writers developed apocalyptic beliefs that focused on the imminent return of "Jesus the Messiah." However marked the differences between Judaism, Islam, and Christianity, the three faiths shared a pronounced family resemblance and common heritage in the Crucible era.[46]

THE GEOGRAPHIC SCALE of these developments is stunning. In the third and second centuries BCE, new ideas and themes emerged chiefly in Palestine and also in Diaspora territories such as Egypt. In the first centuries of the Common Era, the dispersal of Jewish derived movements brought the insights of the Crucible era to a much larger canvas. By around 100 CE, Christian writings are known from believers in Anatolia and Egypt, Greece and Italy, and soon, such texts would appear throughout the Roman and Persian empires. By 800 the Church of the East was establishing itself in China and Tibet. Emerging rabbinic Judaism found its most congenial home in Mesopotamia. But that was only part of a vast and indeed transcontinental story. Quite apart from mainstream Christianity and

Judaism, the Jewish Christian and dualist sects carried these spiritual motifs throughout the Middle East and North Africa, indeed deep into central Asia and ultimately China. And that was accomplished even before the rise of Islam, which dominated a realm ranging from Spain to China. The revolution spanned the known world.

Conclusion

CLOSED HISTORIES

_____

All scripture is inspired by God.

2 TIMOTHY 3:16

THE TWO OR three centuries before Jesus's time witnessed an extraordinary cultural and religious revolution, but that transformation is still barely acknowledged in historical writing, still less in popular perceptions. That lack of recognition tells us much about how we write the history of religions. We are not dealing with anything like a conspiracy of silence; rather, we face the difficulty of giving proper treatment to alternative historical paths, to historical might-have-beens.

That Crucible era thoroughly shaped the ways in which early Christians thought and acted. Contrary to many Christian assumptions, Jesus was rarely "telling the old, old story," that is, grounding himself entirely in the Hebrew Bible. Historically, few nonspecialists have paid much attention to that period, which is so difficult even to name accurately. The "intertestamental period" sounds hopelessly arcane and academic. Partly, that lack of attention results from our inevitable reliance on scriptural sources, which for centuries were by far the most easily accessible and which largely created the standard narrative. In Protestant Bibles at least, Deuterocanonical sources were long relegated to the inferior category of apocrypha, while recent Bible versions exclude them altogether. In consequence, many Christians encountered what seemed like a gap in the centuries before Jesus's time, a lengthy era consigned to an "age of expectation" and effectively a hole in the historical map.

Nor could that gap in continuity easily be filled by noncanonical sources, many of which have been discovered and made freely available only in quite recent times. That includes the Qumran materials as well as a wide range of Old Testament pseudepigrapha. And although scholars have long known critical texts like 1 Enoch, not until recently have its dating and context been well understood. Not only were the writings and ideas of the Crucible era neglected, but they were often treated with suspicion or hostility. The strict Protestant definition of the Old Testament follows that of rabbinic Judaism, which had little time for sources it deemed noncanonical. The consequence is a rather circular argument: by assumption, such scriptures have no place in the proper development of faith; therefore, they are not included in the familiar Bible, and therefore we exclude them from historical faith as we understand it. But to assert that ideas are not acceptable in faiths as they developed in later times does not mean that they were never significant or might not have become so given the appropriate circumstances.

I have remarked that using words like "sectarian" or "marginal" distorts our perception of historical development. In many religious contexts, and certainly not just in Judaism, we naturally speak of "mainstream" faith, which is often buttressed by terms such as "historic," "traditional," "orthodox," or even "normal." By definition, then, expressions of a religion that vary from the norm must be marginal, heterodox, or even abnormal. When considering such labels, though, we have to be conscious of multiple competing agendas. At any given time, any group wishes to portray its own ideas as authentic and mainstream and to dismiss its enemies as deviant. That temptation is all the greater when looking backward in time, after rival and "sectarian" ideas have withered or vanished utterly. Of course, claim the historians, what we have today is the norm, and it was always intended to be so. Alternative paths were historical blind alleys.

Religious groups in particular have an added agenda for making such boasts, with the claim that God actively intended the faith in question to follow one direction rather than another. That is how Christians treat rival currents such as Gnosticism, and it is how Jews view many of the "sectarian" ideas and scriptures of the Second Temple era. When encountering a word like "mainstream," then, the questions should be "Whose mainstream? And when?"

If Second Temple Jews agreed on common core ideas, a great many aspects of faith and practice were contested at least by some faction or group. Indeed, some of the nonmainstream ideas and writings are difficult to fit into even a broad understanding of historical Judaism or its companion religions. Some of those ancient motifs survived; others did not. The existence of Satan and Hell endured, albeit in a much more nuanced form than in mainstream Christianity. The theory that Satan created or ruled the material world vanished, as did movements holding that view. Nor did groups succeed in maintaining the once popular view that it was possible to worship Jesus as Christ while also following Jewish ritual and dietary laws, including the practice of circumcision. Jewish Christians, like dualists, failed to survive. And once something no longer exists, there is little point in remembering it or indeed treating its achievements with any fairness or objectivity. In many cases, lost movements can be used as object lessons, painted as failed spiritual experiments or even sinister heresies, all consigned firmly to the margins of memory. Without actual believers, who is left to complain about such unfairness?

To illustrate this point, think about how we commonly visualize the development of the "Judeo-Christian" tradition. One familiar metaphor imagines Judaism as the tree or trunk of which Christianity is an offshoot, and such botanical metaphors date back to early Christian times. Paul portrayed Gentile converts as being grafted onto the older and more cultivated tree or vine. But the tree-trunk image is problematic in suggesting solidity and uniformity, in a way that poorly fits the very diverse world of Judaism in the early

Common Era. Other analogies include the crucible in which identities and beliefs are dissolved, until they are reshaped into any number of new forms. Or we can vary the biological metaphor to speak of multiple green shoots, each in its time growing successfully, although some would eventually overshadow the others.

To RETURN TO Jesus's parable of the man sowing wheat while his enemy scatters bad seeds, different beliefs grew together side by side, until it eventually became apparent which of them would flourish as wheat and which were doomed to perish as historical weeds.

A comparable historical hindsight shapes our approach to scripture. Jews and Christians alike base their faith in a venerated body of scriptures, which they believe to hold a consistent and coherent body of teachings, and these writings justify later doctrines and practices. In actuality, a sizable gulf separates the thought-world of the Hebrew Bible from historic Judaism and Christianity. However, religions are well accustomed to absorbing and accommodating such inconsistencies.

They also adapt their understandings to take account of evolving doctrines and insights. However explicit a scripture might be on its surface, believers read it through the eyes of faith and through understandings that emerged after the actual time of composition. Christians, for instance, tend to read every gospel as if it contains the fully developed doctrines of the Virgin Birth and resurrection, even when the text in question might have little or nothing to say on that particular subject. On a larger canvas, Christians and Jews daily mine the Old Testament for doctrines that the text does not contain or at least not in any developed form. This is a legitimate strategy for believers or faith communities seeking spiritual enrichment, but one that has to be used with great care in any kind of historical approach.

Anyone interested in those scriptures, in the Bible broadly defined, should also be interested in the substantial body of writings that survive from the Crucible years, which provide the critical transition between the cultural and spiritual worlds of the Old and New Testaments. Without suggesting that apocryphal and alternative texts should be granted canonical status today, their historical importance is great, and in the case of the Enochic writings, it is overwhelming. Virtually all these texts are now easily available in readable versions, mainly on the Internet, but they are also accessible in published collections.

Rich resources are now available for anyone who wishes to see how ideas such as angels and Satan appeared or who seeks to explore such once popular writings as the book of Jubilees, the Psalms of Solomon, the Assumption of Moses, or the Testaments of the Twelve Patriarchs. For Christians, these are the lively voices breaking through the supposed divine silence of the intertestamental period. Quite apart from any literary merits they might possess, their historical appeal for both faiths should be irresistible.

I HAVE SPOKEN of forgotten movements and lost scriptures. Equally consigned to oblivion are the eras that produced them. Nonspecialists know that mighty cultures flourished in Greek and Roman times, but few could say much about what happened to those societies during the long centuries that separated Alexander the Great from the emperor Augustus, roughly from 323 BCE through the time of Christ. To put that in context, that 350 years is the time span that separates us today from, say, the English conquest of New Amsterdam from the Dutch or the final Ottoman Turkish efforts to overrun central Europe. The Roman Empire is a familiar historical reality, and anyone interested in the world of the New Testament realizes that that entity provides the essential political context for the beginnings of Christianity. Yet very few nonacademics have even heard of the once sprawling and wildly creative Seleucid or Ptolemaic empire. If asked to name a specific historical event from this era, Jews and Christians alike might well name the Maccabean revolt against an evil king, although few could likely pinpoint the actual state that he ruled.

Yet those centuries created the ideas, assumptions, and writings that shaped later faiths. This epoch gave us the kings and priests who determined later concepts of religious heroism and villainy: they were the originals from which were drawn so many images of messiahs and devils, martyrs and antichrists. Without knowing that Crucible era, any exploration of Jewish or Christian origins is a journey without maps. Or to change the metaphor, historical Christianity and Judaism seem to spring out of nowhere, worlds without roots.

Without knowing those roots, Christians and Jews are destined to endless misunderstandings and suspicions about their origins. Christians will continue to frame the Jews of Jesus's time according to the narrowest stereotypes of the Old Testament world, without seeing the true range of ideas and beliefs, so many of which were held by the primitive church. Jews and secular scholars alike will exaggerate the Gentile and Greek quality of so much of early Christianity and underplay its thoroughly Jewish quality. Without those roots, we can comprehend neither the Bible nor the faiths that grew from it.

The Crucible age is the indispensable past of the religious worlds we know.

ACKNOWLEDGMENTS

I HAVE BENEFITED from exchanges and conversations with many knowledgeable scholars and friends, none of whom should of course be blamed for any errors, misinterpretations, or misstatements in this book. These friends include Alan Benjamin, Christian Brady, Daniel Falk, Baruch Halpern, Ann Killebrew, Gary Knoppers, Gonzalo Rubio, and Ben Witherington.

Yet again, warm thanks to my colleagues at Baylor University, especially those in the Institute for Studies of Religion: David Jeffrey, Byron Johnson, Thomas Kidd, Jeff Levin, Gordon Melton, and Rodney Stark.

Many thanks also to my superb editor at Basic Books, Lara Heimert, and to my excellent agent, Adam Eaglin.

And above all, thanks to my wife, Liz Jenkins.

NOTES

INTRODUCTION

1. For present purposes, it does not matter whether Jesus himself actually told this story. It was credited to him and reflected the views of at least some early Christians.

2. Robert N. Bellah and Hans Joas, eds., *The Axial Age and Its Consequences* (Cambridge, MA. Belknap Press, 2012). The term "Axial Age" was coined by Karl Jaspers in 1949.

3. Shaul Shaked, ed., *Irano-Judaica* (Jerusalem: Ben-Zvi Institute for the Study of Jewish Communities in the East, 1982); Shaul Shaked, "Iranian Influence on Judaism," in *The Cambridge History of Judaism*, vol. 1, *The Persian Period*, edited by W. D. Davies and Louis Finkelstein (New York: Cambridge University Press, 1984), 308–325.

4. Baruch Halpern, *From Gods to God*, edited by M. J. Adams (Tübingen, Germany: Mohr Siebeck, 2009); Jerry L. Walls, ed., *The Oxford Handbook of Eschatology* (New York: Oxford University Press, 2008).

5. Terence L. Donaldson, *Judaism and the Gentiles* (Waco, TX: Baylor University Press, 2007).

6. For the pre-Flood figures, see Philip Jenkins, *The Many Faces of Christ* (New York: Basic Books, 2015).

7. Paine is quoted in Isaac Kramnick, "Reflections on Revolution," *History and Theory* 11, no. 1 (1972): 62.

8. For similar language in a messianic context, see the Aramaic Levi Document, in *The Dead Sea Scrolls*, edited by Michael Wise, Martin Abegg Jr., and Edward Cook (San Francisco: HarperSanFrancisco, 1996), 259. For Simon, see 3 Macc. 2 (3 Maccabees is found in Greek and Slavonic versions of the Bible). For the *Pirkei Avot*, see Moshe Schapiro and David Rottenberg, eds., *Midrash Shmuel* (Jerusalem: HaKtav Institute, 1994).

9. From Saki's story "The Jesting of Arlington Stringham," in *The Chronicles of Clovis* (London: John Lane, 1911), 86–92.

10. Lester L. Grabbe, Gabriele Boccaccini, and Jason M. Zurawski, eds., *The Seleucid and Hasmonean Periods and the Apocalyptic Worldview* (London: T. & T. Clark 2016).

11. Josephus, *Jewish Antiquities*, 13.13.5; Josephus, *Jewish War*, 1.4.3. Throughout, except where otherwise stated, I have used the translation of Josephus by William Whiston, at http://sacred-texts.com/jud/josephus/. See also Joshua Efron, *Studies on the Hasmonean Period* (Leiden, Netherlands: Brill, 1987).

12. Timothy H. Lim, *The Formation of the Jewish Canon* (New Haven, CT: Yale University Press, 2013).

13. Mathias Delcor, "The Apocrypha and Pseudepigrapha of the Hellenistic Period," in *Cambridge History of Judaism*, vol. 2, *The Hellenistic Age*, edited by W. D. Davies and Louis Finkelstein (New York: Cambridge University Press, 1990), 409–503; James L. Kugel, *Traditions of the Bible* (Cambridge, MA: Harvard University Press, 1998); George W. E. Nickelsburg, *Jewish Literature Between the Bible and the Mishnah*, 2nd ed. (Minneapolis: Fortress Press, 2005).

14. I am drawing here on David deSilva, *The Jewish Teachers of Jesus, James, and Jude* (New York: Oxford University Press, 2012). DeSilva argues powerfully that Jesus and his immediate circle would assuredly have known most of the key intertestamental works and been influenced by them in different ways. Gerbern S. Oegema and James H. Charlesworth, eds., *The Pseudepigrapha and Christian Origins* (New York: T. & T. Clark, 2008). Major collections and editions of such literature include James H. Charlesworth, ed., *The Old Testament Pseudepigrapha*, 2 vols. (Garden City, NY: Doubleday, 1983–1985); Louis H. Feldman, James L. Kugel, and Lawrence H. Schiffman, eds., *Outside the Bible*, 3 vols. (Philadelphia: Jewish Publication Society, 2013); and Richard Bauckham, James R. Davila, and Alex Panayotov, eds., *Old Testament Pseudepigrapha: More Noncanonical Scriptures*, 2 vols. (Grand Rapids, MI: Eerdmans, 2013–?). For earlier collections of these documents, see R. H. Charles, *The Apocrypha and Pseudepigrapha of the Old Testament* (Oxford: Clarendon Press, 1913); and M. R. James, *The Lost Apocrypha of the Old Testament* (London: Society for Promoting Christian Knowledge, 1920).

15. Alan F. Segal, *Rebecca's Children* (Cambridge, MA: Harvard University Press, 1986); Moshe Weinfeld, *Normative and Sectarian Judaism in the Second Temple Period* (New York: T. & T. Clark International, 2005).

16. Philo, "Of the Contemplative Life," http://www.earlychristianwritings.com/yonge/book34.html.

CHAPTER 1

1. Mark S. Smith, *The Early History of God* (Grand Rapids, MI: Eerdmans, 2002); Thomas Römer, *The Invention of God* (Cambridge, MA: Harvard University Press,

2015). Throughout this chapter, I have used Jan Christian Gertz, ed., *T&T Clark Handbook of the Old Testament* (London: T. & T. Clark, 2012).

2. Beate Pongratz-Leisten, ed., *Reconsidering the Concept of Revolutionary Monotheism* (Winona Lake, IN: Eisenbrauns, 2011).

3. *Jewish Encyclopedia*, s.v. "angelology," http://www.jewishencyclopedia.com /articles/1521-angelology; *Catholic Encyclopedia*, s.v. "angels," http://www.new advent.org/cathen/01476d.htm.

4. William M. Schniedewind, *How the Bible Became a Book* (New York: Cambridge University Press, 2004); Douglas A. Knight and Amy-Jill Levine, *The Meaning of the Bible* (New York: HarperOne, 2011).

5. Philip Jenkins, *Laying Down the Sword* (San Francisco: HarperOne, 2011).

6. George J. Brooke, Hindy Najman, and Loren T. Stuckenbruck, eds., *The Significance of Sinai* (Leiden, Netherlands: Brill, 2008).

7. Diana Vikander Edelman, ed., *The Triumph of Elohim* (Grand Rapids, MI: Eerdmans, 1996); Baruch Halpern, *From Gods to God*, edited by M. J. Adams (Tübingen, Germany: Mohr Siebeck, 2009); *Jewish Encyclopedia*, s.v. "monotheism," http://www.jewishencyclopedia.com/articles/10950-monotheism.

8. Some scholars would put the shift to pure monotheism still later, into the early sixth century. See Römer, *The Invention of God*; and Francesca Stavrakopoulou and John Barton, eds., *Religious Diversity in Ancient Israel and Judah* (New York: Continuum, 2010).

9. Judith M. Hadley, *The Cult of Asherah in Ancient Israel and Judah* (New York: Cambridge University Press, 2000).

10. See, for example, Linda S. Schearing and Steven L. McKenzie, eds., *Those Elusive Deuteronomists* (Sheffield, England: Sheffield Academic Press, 1999); Antony F. Campbell and Mark A. O'Brien, *Unfolding the Deuteronomistic History* (Minneapolis: Fortress Press, 2000); Thomas Römer, ed., *The Future of the Deuteronomistic History* (Leuven, Belgium: Leuven University Press, 2000); Schniedewind, *How the Bible Became a Book*; Jeffrey C. Geoghegan, *The Time, Place, and Purpose of the Deuteronomistic History* (Atlanta: Society of Biblical Literature, 2006); and Thomas C. Römer, *The So-Called Deuteronomistic History* (London: T. & T. Clark 2006).

11. Jenkins, *Laying Down the Sword*.

12. Oded Lipschits and Joseph Blenkinsopp, eds., *Judah and the Judeans in the Neo-Babylonian Period* (Winona Lake, IN: Eisenbrauns, 2003); Stephen L. Cook, *The Social Roots of Biblical Yahwism* (Leiden, Netherlands: Brill, 2004); Richard E. Rubenstein, *Thus Saith the Lord* (New York: Harcourt, 2006); Jonathan Stökl and Caroline Waerzeggers, eds., *Exile and Return* (Boston: De Gruyter, 2015).

13. Lawrence H. Schiffman, *From Text to Tradition* (Jersey City, NJ: KTAV, 1991); Lawrence H. Schiffman, *Understanding Second Temple and Rabbinic Judaism* (Jersey City, NJ: KTAV, 2003); Gabriele Boccaccini, *Roots of Rabbinic Judaism* (Grand Rapids, MI: Eerdmans, 2002); Shaye J. D. Cohen, *From the Maccabees to the Mishnah*, 2nd ed. (Louisville, KY: Westminster John Knox Press, 2006); Lester L. Grabbe, *Judaic*

Religion in the Second Temple Period (London: Routledge, 2000); Lester L. Grabbe, *An Introduction to Second Temple Judaism* (New York: Bloomsbury T. & T. Clark, 2010). Throughout this book, I have used Lester L. Grabbe, *A History of the Jews and Judaism in the Second Temple Period*, 2 vols. (London: T. & T. Clark, 2004).

14. For the aniconic tradition, see Halpern, *From Gods to God.*

15. George W. Savran, *Encountering the Divine* (New York: T. & T. Clark International, 2005); James L. Kugel, *The God of Old* (New York: Free Press, 2003).

16. Valery Rees, *From Gabriel to Lucifer* (New York: I. B. Tauris, 2013).

17. Reinhard G. Kratz, *The Prophets of Israel* (Winona Lake, IN: Eisenbrauns, 2015).

18. L. Stephen Cook, *On the Question of the "Cessation of Prophecy" in Ancient Judaism* (Tübingen, Germany: Mohr Siebeck, 2011). For Josephus, see Louis Feldman, "Josephus," in *The Cambridge History of Judaism*, vol. 3, *The Early Roman Period*, edited by William Horbury, W. D. Davies, and John Sturdy (New York: Cambridge University Press, 1999), 901–921; Jack Pastor, Pnina Stern, and Menahem Mor, eds., *Flavius Josephus* (Boston: Brill, 2011); and Michael Tuval, *From Jerusalem Priest to Roman Jew* (Tübingen, Germany: Mohr Siebeck, 2013).

19. These issues are discussed in multiple contributions in John J. Collins, ed., *The Oxford Handbook of Apocalyptic Literature* (New York: Oxford University Press, 2014): see, for instance, Stephen L. Cook, "Apocalyptic Prophecy"; and Hindy Najman, "The Inheritance of Prophecy in Apocalypse." See also Michael H. Floyd and Robert D. Haak, eds., *Prophets, Prophecy, and Prophetic Texts in Second Temple Judaism* (New York: T. & T. Clark, 2006); and John J. Collins, *The Apocalyptic Imagination*, 3rd ed. (Grand Rapids, MI: Eerdmans, 2016). For prophecy among the Qumran sect, see Kristin de Troyer and Armin Lange, eds., *Prophecy after the Prophets?* (Leuven, Belgium: Peeters, 2009).

20. Lester L. Grabbe and Robert D. Haak, eds., *Knowing the End from the Beginning* (London: T. & T. Clark, 2003).

21. Paul D. Hanson, *The Dawn of Apocalyptic* (Philadelphia: Fortress Press, 1975); E. J. C. Tigchelaar, *Prophets of Old and the Day of the End* (Leiden, Netherlands: Brill, 1996); David P. Melvin, *The Interpreting Angel Motif in Prophetic and Apocalyptic Literature* (Minneapolis: Fortress Press, 2013).

22. Antti Laato and Johannes C. De Moor, eds., *Theodicy in the World of the Bible* (Leiden, Netherlands: Brill, 2003); Joel S. Burnett, *Where Is God?* (Minneapolis: Fortress Press, 2010).

23. Adam Kotsko, *The Prince of This World* (Stanford, CA: Stanford University Press, 2016).

24. Philip Johnston, *Shades of Sheol* (Downers Grove, IL: InterVarsity Press, 2002); Alan F. Segal, *Life After Death* (New York: Doubleday, 2004); Philip C. Almond, *Afterlife* (Ithaca, NY: Cornell University Press, 2016).

25. For some incidental statements suggesting an afterlife, see, for instance, Isaiah 26:19: "Thy dead shall live, their bodies shall rise."

26. Mark Larrimore, *The Book of Job* (Princeton, NJ: Princeton University Press, 2013).

27. Samuel L. Adams, *Wisdom in Transition* (Leiden, Netherlands: Brill, 2008).

28. Mishnah Sanhedrin 10:1, http://www.sefaria.org/Mishnah_Sanhedrin .10.1?lang=en&layout=lines&sidebarLang=all.

29. Jerry L. Walls, ed., *The Oxford Handbook of Eschatology* (New York: Oxford University Press, 2008), especially the essays by Bill T. Arnold, "Old Testament Eschatology and the Rise of Apocalypticism"; and John J. Collins, "Apocalyptic Eschatology in the Ancient World."

30. Francis I. Andersen and David Noel Freedman, *Amos* (New Haven, CT: Yale University Press, 2007).

31. Bernard M. Levinson, *Legal Revision and Religious Renewal in Ancient Israel* (New York: Cambridge University Press, 2008); Adams, *Wisdom in Transition*; Halpern, *From Gods to God*; Miryam T. Brand, *Evil Within and Without* (Göttingen, Germany: Vandenhoeck & Ruprecht, 2013).

32. Shaye J. D. Cohen, *From the Maccabees to the Mishnah*, 2nd ed. (Louisville, KY: Westminster John Knox Press, 2006); Grabbe, *Judaic Religion in the Second Temple Period*; Grabbe, *Introduction to Second Temple Judaism*; Gertz, *T&T Clark Handbook of the Old Testament*.

33. Josephus, *Against Apion*, 1:37–43, http://penelope.uchicago.edu/josephus /apion-1.html; John M. G. Barclay, "*Against Apion*," in *Outside the Bible*, edited by Louis H. Feldman, James L. Kugel, and Lawrence H. Schiffman, 3 vols. (Philadelphia: Jewish Publication Society, 2013), 3:2898–2923.

34. Erich S. Gruen, "The Letter of Aristeas," in *Outside the Bible*, edited by Feldman, Kugel, and Schiffman, 3:2711–2769; Benjamin G. Wright III, *The Letter of Aristeas* (Boston: De Gruyter, 2015); Mladen Popović, ed., *Authoritative Scriptures in Ancient Judaism* (Leiden, Netherlands: Brill, 2010); Timothy H. Lim, *The Formation of the Jewish Canon* (New Haven, CT: Yale University Press, 2013).

35. John Kampen, *The Hasideans and the Origin of Pharisaism* (Atlanta: Scholars Press, 1988).

36. Ronald Hendel, "Isaiah and the Transition from Prophecy to Apocalyptic," https://www.academia.edu/821243/Isaiah_and_the_Transition_from_Prophecy _to_Apocalyptic.

37. Mark R. Sneed, *The Social World of the Sages* (Minneapolis: Fortress Press, 2015). Of course, the proliferation of texts did not suggest anything like a modern market or business in books. See Karel van der Toorn, *Scribal Culture and the Making of the Hebrew Bible* (Cambridge, MA: Harvard University Press, 2007).

38. R. H. Charles, *The Apocrypha and Pseudepigrapha of the Old Testament* (Oxford: Clarendon Press, 1913), cited at http://wesley.nnu.edu/sermons-essays-books/ noncanonical-literature/noncanonical-literature-ot-pseudepigrapha/the-book-of -jubilees/. The Terah story is also found in Genesis Rabbah 38:13, http://www .sefaria.org/Bereishit_Rabbah.38.13?lang=he-en&layout=heLeft&sidebarLang=all.

39. Melvin, *Interpreting Angel Motif.*

40. Gary N. Knoppers, *Jews and Samaritans* (New York: Oxford University Press, 2013).

41. Ibid.; Menachem Mor and Friedrich V. Reiterer, eds., *Samaritans* (New York: De Gruyter, 2010); Reinhard Pummer, *The Samaritans* (Grand Rapids, MI: Eerdmans, 2016).

42. Jörg Frey, Daniel R. Schwartz, and Stephanie Gripentrog, eds., *Jewish Identity in the Greco-Roman World* (Leiden, Netherlands: Brill, 2007); Oded Lipschits, Gary N. Knoppers, and Manfred Oeming, eds., *Judah and the Judeans in the Achaemenid Period* (Winona Lake, IN: Eisenbrauns, 2011).

CHAPTER 2

1. Lester L. Grabbe, *A History of the Jews and Judaism in the Second Temple Period,* 2 vols. (London: T. & T. Clark, 2006–2011), vol. 2, *The Coming of the Greeks: The Early Hellenistic Period.*

2. Throughout the chapter, I have used F. W. Walbank et al., eds., *The Cambridge Ancient History*, vol. 7, pt. 1, *The Hellenistic World*, 2nd ed. (New York: Cambridge University Press, 2008).

3. Graham Shipley, *The Greek World After Alexander* (New York: Routledge, 2000); Peter Thonemann, *The Hellenistic Age* (New York: Oxford University Press, 2016).

4. Paul J. Kosmin, *The Land of the Elephant Kings* (Cambridge, MA: Harvard University Press, 2014).

5. Domenico Musti, "Syria and the East," in *Cambridge Ancient History*, edited by Walbank et al., 175–220.

6. Günther Hölbl, *A History of the Ptolemaic Empire* (New York: Routledge, 2001); Eric Turner, "Ptolemaic Egypt," in *Cambridge Ancient History*, edited by Walbank et al., 118–174; "Translation of the Rosetta Stone," http://www.sacred -texts.com/egy/trs/trs07.htm.

7. Dee L. Clayman, *Berenice II and the Golden Age of Ptolemaic Egypt* (New York: Oxford University Press, 2014).

8. H. Heinen, "The Syrian-Egyptian Wars and the New Kingdoms of Asia Minor," in *Cambridge Ancient History*, edited by Walbank et al., 412–445.

9. Christoph Baumer, *The Church of the East* (New York: I. B. Tauris, 2006); Wolfram Gajetzki, *Greeks and Parthians in Mesopotamia and Beyond* (London: Bristol Classical Press, 2011); Rachel Mairs, *The Hellenistic Far East* (Berkeley: University of California Press, 2014); Kosmin, *Land of the Elephant Kings.*

10. This section is drawn from Glenn R. Bugh, ed., *The Cambridge Companion to the Hellenistic World* (New York: Cambridge University Press, 2006); and James J. Clauss and Martine Cuypers, eds., *A Companion to Hellenistic Literature* (Malden, MA: Wiley-Blackwell, 2010).

11. G. E. R. Lloyd, "Hellenistic Science," in *Cambridge Ancient History*, edited by Walbank et al., 321–347.

12. Nicola Denzey Lewis, *Cosmology and Fate in Gnosticism and Graeco-Roman Antiquity* (Leiden, Netherlands: Brill, 2013); Helen R. Jacobus, *Zodiac Calendars in the Dead Sea Scrolls and Their Reception* (Leiden, Netherlands: Brill, 2015). For the Seleucid use of Mesopotamian royal ideologies, see Eva Anagnostou-Laoutides, *In the Garden of the Gods* (New York: Routledge, 2017).

13. Jian-Liang Lin and Hong-Sen Yan, *Decoding the Mechanisms of Antikythera Astronomical Device* (Berlin: Springer, 2016).

14. Peter Adamson, *Philosophy in the Hellenistic and Roman Worlds* (Oxford: Oxford University Press, 2015).

15. John Donne, "An Anatomy of the World," http://www.bartleby.com/357/169.html.

16. Ian S. Moyer, *Egypt and the Limits of Hellenism* (New York: Cambridge University Press, 2011); Johannes Haubold et al., eds., *The World of Berossos* (Wiesbaden: Harrassowitz, 2013); John Dillery, *Clio's Other Sons* (Ann Arbor: University of Michigan Press, 2015).

17. Gregory E. Sterling, "Eupolemus," in *Outside the Bible*, edited by Louis H. Feldman, James L. Kugel, and Lawrence H. Schiffman, 3 vols. (Philadelphia: Jewish Publication Society, 2013), 1:686–704; Gregory E. Sterling, "Pseudo-Eupolemus," in ibid., 705–713 (the claims about Abraham can be found at 708–710). For the penetration of Greek language and culture into Jewish society, see the essays collected in Pieter W. van der Horst, *Japheth in the Tents of Shem* (Leuven, Belgium: Peeters, 2002); and James L. Kugel, ed., *Shem in the Tents of Japhet* (Leiden, Netherlands: Brill, 2002). For cosmopolitanism as an imperial ideology, see Myles Lavan, Richard E. Payne, and John Weisweiler, eds., *Cosmopolitanism and Empire* (New York: Oxford University Press, 2016).

18. Milton S. Terry, ed., *The Sibylline Oracles* (New York: Eaton and Mains, 1899), 84, bk. 3, 724–726, http://www.sacred-texts.com/cla/sib/sib05.htm.

19. M. Dandamayev, "The Diaspora," in *The Cambridge History of Judaism*, vol. 1, *Introduction: The Persian Period*, edited by W. D. Davies and Louis Finkelstein (New York: Cambridge University Press, 1984), 326–400; Harald Hegermann, "The Diaspora in the Hellenistic Age," in *The Cambridge History of Judaism*, vol. 2, *The Hellenistic Age*, edited by W. D. Davies and Louis Finkelstein (New York: Cambridge University Press, 1990), 115–166; Erich S. Gruen, *Diaspora: Jews Amidst Greeks and Romans* (Cambridge, MA: Harvard University Press, 2002).

20. Justin Pollard and Howard Reid, *The Rise and Fall of Alexandria* (New York: Penguin Books, 2007); Sheila L. Ager and Riemer A. Faber, eds., *Belonging and Isolation in the Hellenistic World* (Toronto: University of Toronto Press, 2013).

21. Sara Raup Johnson, *Historical Fictions and Hellenistic Jewish Identity* (Berkeley: University of California Press, 2004).

22. Josephus, *Jewish War*, 7.10.2–3; Josephus, *Jewish Antiquities*, 13.3.4.

23. "Since so excellent" is from the Letter of Aristeas, 310–311, http://www .ccel.org/c/charles/otpseudepig/aristeas.htm; Erich S. Gruen, "The Letter of Aristeas," in *Outside the Bible*, edited by Feldman, Kugel, and Schiffman, 3:2711–2769; Benjamin G. Wright III, *The Letter of Aristeas* (Boston: De Gruyter, 2015); Harry M. Orlinsky, "The Septuagint and its Hebrew Text," in *Cambridge History of Judaism*, edited by Davies and Finkelstein, 2:534–562; Tessa Rajak, *Translation and Survival* (Oxford: Oxford University Press, 2009); Timothy M. Law, *When God Spoke Greek* (New York: Oxford University Press, 2013); James K. Aitken and James N. Carleton Paget, *The Jewish-Greek Tradition in Antiquity and the Byzantine Empire* (New York: Cambridge University Press, 2014). Some scholars go much further in suggesting Hellenistic influence to the point of suggesting that much of the Bible as we have it was written in this period. See the debate in Lester L. Grabbe, ed., *Did Moses Speak Attic?* (Sheffield, England: Sheffield Academic Press, 2001).

24. Howard Jacobson, "Ezekiel the Tragedian," in *Outside the Bible*, edited by Feldman, Kugel, and Schiffman, 1:730–742. For Jewish culture in Egypt, see Anthony Hilhorst and George H. van Kooten, eds., *The Wisdom of Egypt* (Leiden, Netherlands: Brill, 2005).

25. Benjamin G. Wright III, "Wisdom of Ben Sira," in *Outside the Bible*, edited by Feldman, Kugel, and Schiffman, 3:2208–2353.

26. Jacob Neusner, *A History of the Jews in Babylonia* (Leiden, Netherlands: Brill, 1969); M. Rahim Shayegan, *Arsacids and Sasanians* (New York: Cambridge University Press, 2011); Seth Sanders, *From Adapa to Enoch* (Tübingen, Germany: Mohr Siebeck, 2017).

27. Yigal Levin, ed., *A Time of Change* (New York: T. & T. Clark, 2007).

28. Josephus, *Jewish Antiquities*, 13.6.

29. Iain Browning, *Jerash and the Decapolis* (London: Chatto & Windus, 1982); David Kennedy, *Gerasa and the Decapolis* (London: Duckworth, 2007); Jodi Magness, *The Archaeology of the Holy Land* (New York: Cambridge University Press, 2012).

30. John J. Collins, *Between Athens and Jerusalem*, 2nd ed. (Grand Rapids, MI: Eerdmans, 2000).

31. Madeleine Hallade, *Gandharan Art of North India* (New York: H. N. Abrams, 1968); Jeffrey D. Lerner, *The Impact of Seleucid Decline on the Eastern Iranian Plateau* (Stuttgart: Franz Steiner Verlag, 1999); Ladislav Stančo, *Greek Gods in the East* (Prague: Charles University in Prague, Karolinum Press, 2012); Rachel Mairs, *The Hellenistic Far East* (Berkeley: University of California Press, 2014); Christopher I. Beckwith, *Greek Buddha* (Princeton, NJ: Princeton University Press, 2015).

32. F. W. Walbank, "Monarchies and Monarchic Ideas," in *Cambridge Ancient History*, edited by Walbank et al., 62–100; Tessa Rajak et al., eds., *Jewish Perspectives on Hellenistic Rulers* (Berkeley: University of California Press, 2007); Rolf Strootman, *Courts and Elites in the Hellenistic Empires* (Edinburgh: Edinburgh University Press, 2014).

33. Ted Kaizer, ed., *The Variety of Local Religious Life in the Near East* (Leiden, Netherlands: Brill, 2008); Esther Eidinow and Julia Kindt, eds., *The Oxford Handbook of Ancient Greek Religion* (Oxford: Oxford University Press, 2016).

34. Martin Hengel, *Judaism and Hellenism* (Philadelphia: Fortress Press, 1974); Martin Hengel, *Jews, Greeks, and Barbarians* (Philadelphia: Fortress Press, 1980).

35. John J. Collins and Gregory E. Sterling, eds., *Hellenism in the Land of Israel* (Notre Dame, IN: University of Notre Dame Press, 2001); Jodi Magness, *The Archaeology of the Holy Land* (New York: Cambridge University Press, 2012); Regev Eyal, *The Hasmoneans* (Göttingen, Germany: Vandenhoeck & Ruprecht, 2013).

36. David deSilva, *The Jewish Teachers of Jesus, James, and Jude* (New York: Oxford University Press, 2012).

CHAPTER 3

1. *Jewish Encyclopedia*, s.v. "Hellenism," http://www.jewishencyclopedia.com/articles/7535-hellenism.

2. Josephus, *Jewish Antiquities*, bk. 12, http://penelope.uchicago.edu/josephus/ant-12.html.

3. Lester L. Grabbe and Oded Lipschits, eds., *Judah Between East and West* (New York: T. & T. Clark, 2011).

4. William Linn Westermann and Elizabeth Sayre Hasenoehrl, eds., *Zenon Papyri* (New York: Columbia University Press, 1934–1940); R. S. Bagnall, *The Administration of the Ptolemaic Possessions Outside Egypt* (Leiden, Netherlands: Brill, 1976); Lee Levine, *Jerusalem* (Philadelphia: Jewish Publication Society, 2002).

5. Martin Hengel, "The Political and Social History of Palestine from Alexander to Antiochus III," in *The Cambridge History of Judaism*, vol. 2, *The Hellenistic Age*, edited by W. D. Davies and Louis Finkelstein (New York: Cambridge University Press, 1990), 35–78.

6. For the "messenger," see Patrick Tiller, "The Sociological Settings of the Components of 1 Enoch," in *The Early Enoch Literature*, edited by Gabriele Boccaccini and John J. Collins (Leiden, Netherlands: Brill, 2007), 238. The description of John Hyrcanus is from Josephus, *Jewish Antiquities*, 13.10.7. See Michael Wise, Martin Abegg Jr. and Edward Cook, eds., *The Dead Sea Scrolls* (San Francisco: HarperSanFrancisco, 1996), 178, for the tongues of fire. For the Persian era, see Jeremiah W. Cataldo, *A Theocratic Yehud?* (New York: T. & T. Clark, 2009).

7. James C. VanderKam, *From Joshua to Caiaphas* (Minneapolis: Fortress Press, 2004).

8. Vasile Babota, ed., *The Institution of the Hasmonean High Priesthood* (Boston: Brill, 2013).

9. Joseph Blenkinsopp, *Judaism: The First Phase* (Grand Rapids, MI: Eerdmans, 2009); Oded Lipschits, Gary N. Knoppers, and Manfred Oeming, eds., *Judah and the Judeans in the Achaemenid Period* (Winona Lake, IN: Eisenbrauns, 2011).

10. George W. E. Nickelsburg, "Tobit," in *Outside the Bible*, edited by Louis H. Feldman, James L. Kugel, and Lawrence H. Schiffman, 3 vols. (Philadelphia: Jewish Publication Society, 2013), 3:2631–2662.

11. Christine E. Hayes, *Gentile Impurities and Jewish Identities* (Oxford: Oxford University Press, 2002).

12. Deborah W. Rooke, *Zadok's Heirs* (Oxford: Oxford University Press, 2000).

13. Lawrence M. Wills, ed., *Ancient Jewish Novels* (New York: Oxford University Press, 2002).

14. Hengel, "Political and Social History of Palestine," 35–78; Lester L. Grabbe, *A History of the Jews and Judaism in the Second Temple Period*, 2 vols. (London: T. & T. Clark, 2004), vol. 2. This section draws heavily on Josephus, *Jewish Antiquities*, bk. 12.

15. Josephus, *Jewish Antiquities*, bk. 12, chap. 4; 12.4.9 for the joke about stripping Syria to the bone.

16. The Damascus Document includes a specific prohibition of this kind of marriage, possibly with Tobiad behavior in mind: Joseph L. Angel, "Damascus Document," in *Outside the Bible*, edited by Feldman, Kugel, and Schiffman, 3:2991.

17. H. Heinen, "The Syrian-Egyptian Wars and the New Kingdoms of Asia Minor," in *The Cambridge Ancient History*, vol. 7, pt. 1, *The Hellenistic World*, edited by F. W. Walbank et al., 2nd ed. (New York: Cambridge University Press, 2008), 412–445.

18. Aryeh Kasher, *Jews, Idumaeans, and Ancient Arabs* (Tübingen, Germany: Mohr Siebeck, 1988). For the struggles of Hyrcanus, see Josephus, *Jewish Antiquities*, 12.4.11.

19. Josephus, *Jewish Antiquities*, 12.5.

20. H. Heinen, "The Syrian-Egyptian Wars and the New Kingdoms of Asia Minor," in *Cambridge Ancient History*, edited by Walbank et al., 412–445.

21. Christopher Tuckett, *The Book of Zechariah and Its Influence* (Burlington, VT: Ashgate, 2003).

22. Marko Jauhiainen, *The Use of Zechariah in Revelation* (Tübingen, Germany: Mohr Siebeck, 2005); Charlene McAfee Moss, *The Zechariah Tradition and the Gospel of Matthew* (Berlin: Walter de Gruyter, 2008). For the use of these texts at Qumran, see Wise, Abegg, and Cook, *The Dead Sea Scrolls*, 58.

23. Lena-Sofia Tiemeyer, "Will the Prophetic Texts from the Hellenistic Period Stand Up, Please?" in *Judah Between East and West*, edited by Grabbe and Lipschits, 255–279. For a Hellenistic context for the work, see, for instance, Hervé Gonzalez, "Zechariah 9–14 and the Continuation of Zechariah During the Ptolemaic Period," *Journal of Hebrew Scriptures* 13 (2013). Such arguments are of course anything but new. For a Hellenistic date, see Hinckley G. Mitchell, John Merlin Powis Smith, and Julius August Bewer, *A Critical and Exegetical Commentary on Haggai, Zechariah, Malachi and Jonah* (New York: Charles Scribner's Sons, 1912), 218–259.

A Hellenistic date is also followed in Hengel, "Political and Social History of Palestine," 51–52.

CHAPTER 4

1. E. Isaac, "1 (Ethiopian Apocalypse of) Enoch," in *The Old Testament Pseudepigrapha*, edited by James H. Charlesworth, 2 vols. (Garden City, NY: Doubleday, 1983–1985), 1:5–90; Miryam T. Brand, "1 Enoch," in *Outside the Bible*, edited by Louis H. Feldman, James L. Kugel, and Lawrence H. Schiffman, 3 vols. (Philadelphia: Jewish Publication Society, 2013), 2:1359–1452; George W. E. Nickelsburg and James C. VanderKam, *1 Enoch* (Minneapolis: Fortress Press, 2004).

2. The literature on 1 Enoch in recent decades includes multiple contributions to conferences as well as a great many books and scholarly articles. Some key works include Annette Yoshiko Reed and James C. VanderKam, *Enoch, a Man for All Generations* (Columbia: University of South Carolina Press, 1995); Nickelsburg and VanderKam, *1 Enoch*; Gabriele Boccaccini, ed., *Enoch and Qumran Origins* (Grand Rapids, MI: Eerdmans, 2005); Gabriele Boccaccini and John J. Collins, eds., *The Early Enoch Literature* (Leiden, Netherlands: Brill, 2007); Michael A. Knibb, *Essays on the Book of Enoch and Other Early Jewish Texts and Traditions* (Leiden, Netherlands: Brill, 2009); and Loren T. Stuckenbruck, *The Myth of Rebellious Angels* (Tübingen, Germany: Mohr Siebeck, 2014).

3. R. Doran, "Pseudo-Eupolemus," in *The Old Testament Pseudepigrapha*, edited by Charlesworth, 2:881.

4. Philip Jenkins, *The Many Faces of Christ* (New York: Basic Books, 2015).

5. David R. Jackson, *Enochic Judaism* (New York: A&C Black, 2004).

6. George W. E. Nickelsburg, *1 Enoch 1* (Minneapolis: Fortress Press, 2001); George W. E. Nickelsburg and James C. VanderKam, *1 Enoch 2* (Minneapolis: Fortress Press, 2011); Brand, "1 Enoch."

7. Knibb, *Essays on the Book of Enoch*, 197. The most comprehensive recent reading of the text is Daniel C. Olson, *A New Reading of the Animal Apocalypse of 1 Enoch* (Boston: Brill, 2013).

8. Boccaccini, *Enoch and Qumran Origins*.

9. Gabriele Boccaccini and Jason von Ehrenkrook, eds., *Enoch and the Messiah Son of Man* (Grand Rapids, MI: Eerdmans, 2007); Darrell L. Bock and James H. Charlesworth, eds., *Parables of Enoch* (London: Bloomsbury, 2013).

10. 1 Enoch 1. 8–9, from R. H. Charles, ed., *The Book of Enoch* (London: SPCK, 1917), http://www.sacred-texts.com/bib/boe/boe004.htm.

11. 1 Enoch 91. 9, http://www.sacred-texts.com/bib/boe/boe095.htm.

12. James C. Vanderkam, *An Introduction to Early Judaism* (Grand Rapids, MI: Eerdmans, 2001), 103. This apocalypse includes 1 Enoch 93:1–10 and 91:11–17. "All the works" is from 91:14–17, http://www.sacred-texts.com/bib/boe/boe097.htm.

13. 1 Enoch 21, http://www.sacred-texts.com/bib/bep/bep03.htm.

14. 1 Enoch 22, http://www.sacred-texts.com/bib/boe/boe025.htm.

15. 1 Enoch 54:6, http://www.sacred-texts.com/bib/boe/boe057.htm.

16. 1 Enoch 51:1–2, http://www.sacred-texts.com/bib/boe/boe054.htm.

17. 1 Enoch. 8, http://www.sacred-texts.com/bib/boe/boe011.htm; Annette Yoshiko Reed, *Fallen Angels and the History of Judaism and Christianity* (New York: Cambridge University Press, 2005); Angela Kim Harkins, Kelley Coblentz Bautch, and John C. Endres, eds., *The Watchers in Jewish and Christian Traditions* (Augsburg, Germany: Fortress Press, 2014); Archie T. Wright, *The Origin of Evil Spirits* (Minneapolis: Fortress Press, 2015).

18. Compare the treatment of the Noah story in the Genesis Apocryphon found in the Dead Sea Scrolls: Matthew J. Morgenstern and Michael Segal, "The Genesis Apocryphon," in *Outside the Bible*, edited by Feldman, Kugel, and Schiffman, 1:237–262; and Michael E. Stone, Aryeh Amihay, and Vered Hillel, eds., *Noah and His Book(s)* (Atlanta: Society of Biblical Literature, 2010). For other traditions, see Dorothy M. Peters, *Noah Traditions in the Dead Sea Scrolls* (Atlanta: Society of Biblical Literature, 2008).

19. Wise, Abegg, and Cook, *The Dead Sea Scrolls*, 246–25; Loren T. Stuckenbruck, "The Book of Giants," in *Outside the Bible*, edited by Feldman, Kugel, and Schiffman, 1:221–236.

20. John C. Reeves, *Jewish Lore in Manichaean Cosmogony* (Jerusalem: Hebrew Union College, 1992).

21. O. S. Wintermute, "Jubilees," in *The Old Testament Pseudepigrapha*, edited by Charlesworth; James L. Kugel, "Jubilees," in *Outside the Bible*, edited by Feldman, Kugel, and Schiffman, 1:272–466; James L. Kugel, *A Walk Through Jubilees* (Leiden, Netherlands: Brill, 2012).

22. "The first among men" is from Jubilees 4:16–19, in R. H. Charles, *The Apocrypha and Pseudepigrapha of the Old Testament* (Oxford: Clarendon Press, 1913), http://www.pseudepigrapha.com/jubilees/4.htm; Gabriele Boccaccini and Giovanni Ibba, eds., *Enoch and the Mosaic Torah* (Grand Rapids, MI: Eerdmans, 2009).

23. Mark Bredin, ed., *Studies in the Book of Tobit* (New York: T. & T. Clark, 2006); Athalya Brenner-Idan and Helen Efthimiadis-Keith, eds., *Tobit and Judith* (London: Bloomsbury T. & T. Clark, 2015).

24. The Qumran group also cited the Watchers: Wise, Abegg, and Cook, *The Dead Sea Scrolls*, 53.

25. Randal A. Argall, *1 Enoch and Sirach* (Atlanta: Scholars Press, 1995).

26. "Observe, Enoch, these heavenly tablets," is from 1 Enoch 8:1–3, http://www.sacred-texts.com/bib/boe/boe084.htm.

27. The sayings to Methuselah are from 1 Enoch 82:1, http://www.sacred-texts.com/bib/boe/boe085.htm; "according to that which appeared" is from 1 Enoch 93:1–2, http://www.sacred-texts.com/bib/boe/boe096.htm; Leslie Baynes, *The Heavenly Book Motif in Judeo-Christian Apocalypses 200 B.C.E.–200 C.E.* (Leiden,

Netherlands: Brill: 2012); Seth Sanders, *From Adapa to Enoch* (Tübingen, Germany: Mohr Siebeck, 2017).

28. Jubilees 8:3, http://www.pseudepigrapha.com/jubilees/8.htm.

29. Paul J. Kosmin, *The Land of the Elephant Kings* (Cambridge, MA: Harvard University Press, 2014), 102. For the Astronomical Book, I have benefited from a presentation by Elena Dugan of Princeton University at the Sixth Enoch Graduate Seminar held in Austin, Texas, in May 2016.

30. Leslie Baynes, *The Heavenly Book Motif in Judeo-Christian Apocalypses, 200 BCE–200 CE* (Boston: Brill, 2012).

31. Helge S. Kvanvig, *Roots of Apocalyptic* (Neukirchen-Vluyn, Germany: Neukirchener Verlag, 1988); Helge S. Kvanvig, *Primeval History* (Leiden, Netherlands: Brill, 2011); Ida Fröhlich, "Enmeduranki and Gilgamesh," in *A Teacher for All Generations*, edited by Eric F. Mason et al. (Leiden, Netherlands: Brill, 2012); Sanders, *From Adapa to Enoch*; James VanderKam, *Enoch and the Growth of an Apocalyptic Tradition* (Washington, DC: Catholic Biblical Association, 1984); Marc Van De Mieroop, *Philosophy Before the Greeks* (Princeton, NJ: Princeton University Press, 2016); Eva Anagnostou-Laoutides, *In the Garden of the Gods* (New York: Routledge, 2017).

32. Kvanvig, *Roots of Apocalyptic*; Matthew Neujahr, *Predicting the Past in the Ancient Near East* (Atlanta: Society of Biblical Literature, 2012); Robert P. Gordon and Hans M. Barstad, eds., *Thus Speaks Ishtar of Arbela* (Winona Lake, IN: Eisenbrauns, 2013).

33. Jeremy Black and Anthony Green, *Gods, Demons, and Symbols of Ancient Mesopotamia* (Austin: University of Texas Press, 1992); R. Doran, "Pseudo-Eupolemus," in *The Old Testament Pseudepigrapha*, edited by Charlesworth, 2:880; Gregory E. Sterling, "Pseudo-Eupolemus," *Outside the Bible*, edited by Feldman, Kugel, and Schiffman, 1:708, 712.

34. Sterling, "Pseudo Eupolemus," 712. For "Antediluvian Knowledge," see Pieter W. van der Horst, *Japheth in the Tents of Shem* (Leuven, Belgium: Peeters, 2002), 140–158.

35. Jackson, *Enochic Judaism*; John C. Reeves, "Complicating the Notion of an Enochic Judaism," in *Enoch and the Mosaic Torah*, edited by Boccaccini and Ibba, 373–383.

36. Boccaccini and Ibba, *Enoch and the Mosaic Torah*.

37. "Reared up that tower" is from 1 Enoch 89:73, http://www.sacred-texts.com/bib/boe/boe092.htm.

38. For a critique of many current theories on these issues, see Paul Heger, *Challenges to Conventional Opinions on Qumran and Enoch Issues* (Leiden, Netherlands: Brill, 2012).

39. Philip R. Davies, "Sects from Texts," in *New Directions in Qumran Studies*, edited by Jonathan G. Campbell, William John Lyons, and Lloyd K. Pietersen (New York: T. & T. Clark International, 2005), 69–82.

40. Boccaccini, *Enoch and Qumran Origins*; Joan E. Taylor, *The Essenes, the Scrolls, and the Dead Sea* (Oxford: Oxford University Press, 2012); Otto Betz, "The Essenes," in *The Cambridge History of Judaism*, vol. 3, *The Early Roman Period*, edited by William Horbury, W. D. Davies, and John Sturdy (New York: Cambridge University Press, 1999), 444–470; Joseph L. Angel, "Damascus Document," in *Outside the Bible*, edited by Feldman, Kugel, and Schiffman, 3:2975–3035.

41. Gabriele Boccaccini, *Beyond the Essene Hypothesis* (Grand Rapids, MI: Eerdmans, 1998).

42. "Destined to be destroyed" is from Jubilees 15:26, http://www.pseudepigrapha.com/jubilees/15.htm.

43. "This Law is for all the generations for ever" is from Jubilees 15:25–26, http://www.pseudepigrapha.com/jubilees/15.htm.

CHAPTER 5

1. John Grainger, *The Rise of the Seleukid Empire* (Barnsley, England: Pen and Sword, 2014); John Grainger, *The Seleukid Empire of Antiochus III* (Barnsley, England: Pen and Sword, 2015); John Grainger, *The Fall of the Seleukid Empire* (Barnsley, England: Pen and Sword, 2015).

2. Polybius 29.27.4, http://penelope.uchicago.edu/Thayer/E/Roman/Texts/Polybius/29*.html; H. Heinen, "The Syrian-Egyptian Wars and the New Kingdoms of Asia Minor," in *The Cambridge Ancient History*, vol. 7, pt. 1, *The Hellenistic World*, edited by F. W. Walbank et al., 2nd ed. (New York: Cambridge University Press, 2008), 412–445.

3. "Those that were of dignity" is from Josephus, *Jewish War*, 1.1.1, http://www.sacred-texts.com/jud/josephus/war-1.htm; Josephus, *Jewish Antiquities*, 12.4–5; 2 Macc. 2–6; Otto Mørkholm, "Antiochus IV," in *The Cambridge History of Judaism*, vol. 2, *The Hellenistic Age*, edited by W. D. Davies and Louis Finkelstein (New York: Cambridge University Press, 1990), 278–291.

4. Jonathan A. Goldstein, "The Hasmonean Revolt and the Hasmonean Dynasty," in *Cambridge History of Judaism*, edited by Davies and Finkelstein, 2:292–351; Sylvie Honigman, *Tales of High Priests and Taxes* (Berkeley: University of California Press, 2014); Seth Schwartz, *The Ancient Jews from Alexander to Muhammad* (New York: Cambridge University Press, 2014).

5. Honigman, *Tales of High Priests and Taxes*.

6. For Phinehas, see Philip Jenkins, *Laying Down the Sword* (San Francisco: HarperOne, 2011).

7. D. T. Potts, *Mesopotamia, Iran and Arabia from the Seleucids to the Sasanians* (Farnham, England: Ashgate Variorum, 2010); D. T. Potts, ed., *The Oxford Handbook of Ancient Iran* (New York: Oxford University Press, 2013); Rolf Strootman, *Courts and Elites in the Hellenistic Empires* (Edinburgh: Edinburgh University Press, 2014); Boris Chrubasik, *Kings and Usurpers in the Seleukid Empire* (Oxford: Oxford University Press, 2016).

8. Josephus, *Jewish Antiquities*, 13.

9. Vasile Babota, ed., *The Institution of the Hasmonean High Priesthood* (Boston: Brill, 2013).

10. Josephus, *Jewish War*, 1.2.5; Diodorus Siculus, xxxiv–xxxv, https://www.loebclassics.com/view/diodorus_siculus-library_history/1933/pb_LCL423.53.xml; Peter Schäfer, *Judeophobia* (Cambridge, MA: Harvard University Press, 2009).

11. The major original sources here are Josephus, *Jewish Antiquities*, bk. 13 (covering the years 160 BC—67 BC); and Josephus, *Jewish War*, bk. 1.

12. Regev Eyal, *The Hasmoneans* (Göttingen, Germany: Vandenhoeck & Ruprecht, 2013), 175–223.

13. For Mithridates, see Adrienne Mayor, *The Poison King* (Princeton, NJ: Princeton University Press, 2010).

14. Aryeh Kasher, *Jews, Idumaeans, and Ancient Arabs* (Tübingen, Germany: Mohr Siebeck, 1988).

15. Josephus, *Jewish Antiquities*, 13.9.1; James D. Purvis, "The Samaritans," in *Cambridge History of Judaism*, edited by Davies and Finkelstein, 2:591–613.

16. Louis H. Feldman, *Jew and Gentile in the Ancient World* (Princeton, NJ: Princeton University Press, 1996), 288–340.

17. Josephus, *Jewish Antiquities*, 13.11.

18. Ibid., 13.5.9; Joachim Schaper, "The Pharisees," in *The Cambridge History of Judaism*, vol. 3, *The Early Roman Period*, edited by William Horbury, W. D. Davies, and John Sturdy (New York: Cambridge University Press, 1999), 402–427; Günter Stemberger, "The Sadducees," in ibid., 428–443; Albert I. Baumgarten, "Jewish War: Excursus on Jewish Groups," in *Outside the Bible*, edited by Louis H. Feldman, James L. Kugel, and Lawrence H. Schiffman, 3 vols. (Philadelphia: Jewish Publication Society, 2013), 3:2888–2897.

19. Josephus, *Jewish Antiquities*, 13.10.5–6; Jacob Neusner and Bruce Chilton, eds., *In Quest of the Historical Pharisees* (Waco, TX: Baylor University Press, 2007). For Common Judaism, see E. P. Sanders, *Judaism* (London: SCM, 1992); and Wayne O. McCready and Adele Reinhartz, eds. *Common Judaism* (Minneapolis: Fortress Press, 2008).

20. Josephus *Jewish Antiquities*, 13.10.

21. Ibid., 13.14.2.

22. Ibid., 13.16.1.

23. Kenneth Atkinson, *Queen Salome* (Jefferson, NC: McFarland, 2012).

CHAPTER 6

1. See the excellent range of essays on these issues in Lester L. Grabbe, Gabriele Boccaccini, and Jason M. Zurawski, eds., *The Seleucid and Hasmonean Periods and the Apocalyptic Worldview* (London: T. & T. Clark, 2016). For Yose's title, see Mishnah Chagigah 2.7, http://www.sefaria.org/Mishnah_Chagigah.2.1-7?lang=en&layout=lines&sidebarLang=all.

2. Joshua Efron, *Studies on the Hasmonean Period* (Leiden, Netherlands: Brill, 1987); H. L. Ginsberg, "The Book of Daniel," in *The Cambridge History of Judaism*, vol. 2, *The Hellenistic Age*, edited by W. D. Davies and Louis Finkelstein (New York: Cambridge University Press, 1990), 504–523; Martha Himmelfarb, *The Apocalypse* (Malden, MA: Wiley-Blackwell, 2010); John J. Collins, ed., *The Oxford Handbook of Apocalyptic Literature* (New York: Oxford University Press, 2014); John J. Collins, *The Apocalyptic Imagination*, 3rd ed. (Grand Rapids, MI: Eerdmans, 2016).

3. Dean R. Ulrich, *The Antiochene Crisis and Jubilee Theology in Daniel's Seventy Sevens* (Leiden, Netherlands: Brill, 2015).

4. Andy M. Reimer, "Probing the Possibilities and Pitfalls of Post-colonial Approaches to the Dead Sea Scrolls," in *New Directions in Qumran Studies*, edited by Jonathan G. Campbell, William John Lyons, and Lloyd K. Pietersen (New York: T. & T. Clark International, 2005); Anathea Portier-Young, *Apocalypse Against Empire* (Grand Rapids, MI: Eerdmans, 2011); Daniel L. Smith-Christopher, "A Post-colonial Reading of Apocalyptic Literature," in *The Oxford Handbook of Apocalyptic Literature*, edited by John J. Collins (New York: Oxford University Press, 2014).

5. For Bel, see Lawrence M. Wills, ed., *Ancient Jewish Novels* (New York: Oxford University Press, 2002); Matthias Henze, "Additions to Daniel," in *Outside the Bible*, edited by Louis H. Feldman, James L. Kugel, and Lawrence H. Schiffman, 3 vols. (Philadelphia: Jewish Publication Society, 2013), 1:122–139.

6. John J. Collins, "Sibylline Oracles," in *The Old Testament Pseudepigrapha*, edited by James H. Charlesworth, 2 vols. (Garden City, NY: Doubleday, 1983–1985), 1:317–472; John J. Collins, *Seers, Sybils and Sages in Hellenistic-Roman Judaism* (Leiden, Netherlands: Brill, 1997).

7. Milton S. Terry, ed., *The Sibylline Oracles* (New York: Eaton and Mains, 1899), 88, bk. 3, lines 830–843, http://www.sacred-texts.com/cla/sib/sib05.htm.

8. Ibid., 89, bk. 3, lines 861–871.

9. Joshua Efron, *Studies on the Hasmonean Period* (Leiden, Netherlands: Brill, 1987).

10. Jubilees 32:1–2, http://www.pseudepigrapha.com/jubilees/32.htm; "Kings bearing rule": Testament of Moses/Assumption of Moses, 6, http://wesley.nnu.edu/index.php?id=2124.

11. H. C. Kee, "Testaments of the Twelve Patriarchs," in *The Old Testament Pseudepigrapha*, edited by Charlesworth, 1:775–828; James L. Kugel, "Testaments of the Twelve Patriarchs," in *Outside the Bible*, edited by Feldman, Kugel, and Schiffman, 2:1697–1855.

12. "And ye shall be puffed up" is from the Testament of Levi 4:16, http://www.sacred-texts.com/bib/fbe/fbe275.htm.

13. Testament of Levi 2:2, http://www.sacred-texts.com/bib/fbe/fbe273.htm.

14. Frank Moore Cross, *The Ancient Library of Qumran* (Minneapolis: Fortress Press, 1995), 98; Hanan Eshel, *The Dead Sea Scrolls and the Hasmonean State* (Grand Rapids, MI: Eerdmans, 2008).

15. George W. E. Nickelsburg, *Resurrection, Immortality, and Eternal Life in Intertestamental Judaism*, rev. ed. (Cambridge, MA: Harvard University Press, 2006); Alan F. Segal, *Life After Death* (New York: Doubleday, 2004); Jon D. Levenson, *Resurrection and the Restoration of Israel* (New Haven, CT: Yale University Press, 2006); Kevin J. Madigan and Jon D. Levenson, *Resurrection* (New Haven, CT: Yale University Press, 2008); Philip C. Almond, *Afterlife* (Ithaca, NY: Cornell University Press, 2016).

16. Daniel R. Schwartz, "2 Maccabees," in *Outside the Bible*, edited by Feldman, Kugel, and Schiffman, 3:2832–2888.

17. Martha Himmelfarb, "Afterlife and Resurrection," in *The Jewish Annotated New Testament*, edited by Amy-Jill Levine and Marc Zvi Brettler (New York: Oxford University Press, 2011).

18. Josephus, *Jewish War*, 2.8.10–11; Almond, *Afterlife*.

19. Josephus, *Jewish War*, 2.8.14; Acts 23.8.

CHAPTER 7

1. Michael Wise, Martin Abegg Jr., and Edward Cook, eds., *The Dead Sea Scrolls* (San Francisco: HarperSanFrancisco, 1996), 150–172; Gabriele Boccaccini, ed., *Enoch and Qumran Origins* (Grand Rapids, MI: Eerdmans, 2005); Géza G. Xeravits, ed., *Dualism in Qumran* (New York: T. & T. Clark, 2010); Jean Duhaime, "War Scroll," in *Outside the Bible*, edited by Louis H. Feldman, James L. Kugel and Lawrence H. Schiffman, 3 vols. (Philadelphia: Jewish Publication Society, 2013), 3:3116–3151; Kipp Davis et al., eds., *The War Scroll: Violence, War and Peace in the Dead Sea Scrolls and Related Literature* (Leiden, Netherlands: Brill, 2015).

2. I have throughout this chapter used Jonathan G. Campbell, William John Lyons, and Lloyd K. Pietersen, eds., *New Directions in Qumran Studies* (New York: T. & T. Clark International, 2005); Timothy H. Lim and John J. Collins, *The Oxford Handbook of the Dead Sea Scrolls* (New York: Oxford University Press, 2010); James C. VanderKam, *The Dead Sea Scrolls Today*, rev. ed. (Grand Rapids, MI: Eerdmans, 2010); Devorah Dimant, ed., *The Dead Sea Scrolls in Scholarly Perspective* (Leiden, Netherlands: Brill, 2012); and John J. Collins, *The Dead Sea Scrolls* (Princeton, NJ: Princeton University Press, 2013).

3. John J. Collins and Robert A. Kugler, eds., *Religion in the Dead Sea Scrolls* (Grand Rapids, MI: Eerdmans, 2000).

4. Joan E. Taylor, *The Essenes, the Scrolls, and the Dead Sea* (Oxford: Oxford University Press, 2012). Josephus's account of the Essenes is in his *Jewish War*,

2.8.2–14. Otto Betz, "The Essenes," in *The Cambridge History of Judaism*, vol. 3, *The Early Roman Period*, edited by William Horbury, W. D. Davies, and John Sturdy (New York: Cambridge University Press, 1999), 444–470. A minority view held by some distinguished scholars associates the sect with the Sadducees.

5. Modern scholars disagree about the identity of the Teacher and other figures in the story, with likely dates for the action ranging from the early second century into the mid-first century BCE. Wise, Abegg, and Cook, *The Dead Sea Scrolls*, 52; Joseph L. Angel, "Damascus Document," in *Outside the Bible*, edited by Feldman, Kugel, and Schiffman, 3:2975–3035. The relationship between Teacher and Priest is told at length in the Pesher (commentary) on Habbakkuk found at Qumran: Bilhah Nitzan, "Pesher Habakkuk," in ibid., 1:636–666.

6. Hanan Eshel, *The Dead Sea Scrolls and the Hasmonean State* (Grand Rapids, MI: Eerdmans, 2008).

7. "To whom God had made known": Nitzan, "Pesher Habakkuk," 1:648; Sacha Stern, ed., *Sects and Sectarianism in Jewish History* (Leiden, Netherlands: Brill, 2011).

8. Timothy H. Lim et al., eds., *The Dead Sea Scrolls in Their Historical Context* (Edinburgh: T. & T. Clark, 2000).

9. "On the day of Judgment": Nitzan, "Pesher Habakkuk," 1:662.

10. "Brutal men seek': Wise, Abegg, and Cook, *The Dead Sea Scrolls*, 93; "my office is among the gods," is from ibid., 113. Compare Angela Kim Harkins, "Thanksgiving Hymns (*Hodayot*)," in *Outside the Bible*, edited by Feldman, Kugel, and Schiffman, 2:2018–2094.

11. "You appointed the Prince": Wise, Abegg, and Cook, *The Dead Sea Scrolls*, 162–163; Jean Duhaime, "War Scroll," in *Outside the Bible*, edited by Feldman, Kugel, and Schiffman, 3:3140.

12. "Now, this God created man" quoted in Theodor H. Gaster, *The Dead Sea Scriptures*, 3rd ed. (Garden City, NY: Anchor Press, 1976), 48–49; Alex P. Jassen, "Rule of the Community," in *Outside the Bible*, edited by Feldman, Kugel, and Schiffman, 3:2923–2974. The Treatise on the Two Spirits is found at 2935–2940.

13. Wise, Abegg, and Cook, *The Dead Sea Scrolls*, 433–36; Andrew D. Gross, "Visions of Amram," in *Outside the Bible*, edited by Feldman, Kugel, and Schiffman, 2:1507–1510.

14. Wise, Abegg, and Cook, *The Dead Sea Scrolls*, 84–114.

15. Daniel J. Harrington, *Wisdom Texts from Qumran* (New York: Routledge, 1996); Matthew J. Goff, *The Worldly and Heavenly Wisdom of 4QInstruction* (Leiden, Netherlands: Brill, 2003); Matthew J. Goff, *Discerning Wisdom* (Leiden, Netherlands: Brill, 2007); Samuel L. Adams, *Wisdom in Transition* (Leiden, Netherlands: Brill, 2008); Florentino García Martínez, eds., *Echoes from the Caves* (Leiden, Netherlands: Brill, 2009); Armin Lange, "Wisdom Literature from the Qumran Library," in *Outside the Bible*, edited by Feldman, Kugel, and Schiffman, 3:2399–2443. For 4QInstruction, *Musar leMevin*, see 2418–2440; the passage quoted is on

2423–2424. The other translation cited is Wise, Abegg, and Cook, *The Dead Sea Scrolls*, 381. The legend about Seth is recorded in Josephus, *Jewish Antiquities*, 1.2.3.

16. F. I. Anderson, "2 (Slavonic Apocalypse of) Enoch," in *The Old Testament Pseudepigrapha*, edited by James H. Charlesworth, 2 vols. (Garden City, NY: Doubleday, 1983–1985), 1:91–221; Andrei A. Orlov and Gabriele Boccaccini, eds., *New Perspectives on 2 Enoch* (Leiden, Netherlands: Brill, 2012); Andrei A. Orlov, *Divine Scapegoats* (Albany: SUNY Press, 2015).

17. H. C. Kee, "Testaments of the Twelve Patriarchs," in *The Old Testament Pseudepigrapha*, edited by Charlesworth, 1:775–828; James L. Kugel, "Testaments of the Twelve Patriarchs," in *Outside the Bible*, edited by Feldman, Kugel, and Schiffman, 2:1697–1855.

18. Testament of Asher is quoted in http://www.tertullian.org/fathers2/ANF-08/anf08-14.htm. "Choose therefore for yourselves" is from the Testament of Levi, http://www.ccel.org/ccel/schaff/anf08.iii.v.html. The Testament of Issachar is in http://www.sacred-texts.com/bib/fbe/fbe281.htm. Naphtali is quoted in http://www.sacred-texts.com/bib/fbe/fbe287.htm.

19. Kugel, "Testaments of the Twelve Patriarchs," in *Outside the Bible*, edited by Feldman, Kugel, and Schiffman, 2:1709. Despite the resemblance, the medieval list of deadly sins does not derive from the Testaments but rather looked to a passage in the book of Proverbs, 6:16–19. William Loader, *Philo, Josephus, and the Testaments on Sexuality* (Grand Rapids, MI: Eerdmans, 2011); Miryam T. Brand, *Evil Within and Without* (Göttingen, Germany: Vandenhoeck & Ruprecht, 2013). The Testament of Dan is quoted in http://www.sacred-texts.com/bib/fbe/fbe285.htm. Reuben is quoted in http://www.newadvent.org/fathers/0801.htm.

20. Eugene H. Merrill, *Qumran and Predestination* (Leiden, Netherlands: Brill, 1975); James C. VanderKam, *The Dead Sea Scrolls Today*, rev. ed. (Grand Rapids, MI: Eerdmans, 2010).

21. Bilhah Nitzan, "Pesher Habakkuk," in *Outside the Bible*, edited by Feldman, Kugel, and Schiffman, 1:637; "From the God of knowledge" is from Florentino García Martínez and Eibert J. C. Tigchelaar, eds., *The Dead Sea Scrolls Study Edition* (Grand Rapids, MI: Eerdmans, 1999), 75.

22. For "But the wicked you created," see Wise, Abegg, and Cook, *The Dead Sea Scrolls*, 89. Compare Angela Kim Harkins, "Thanksgiving Hymns (*Hodayot*)," in *Outside the Bible*, edited by Feldman, Kugel, and Schiffman, 2:2033.

23. "Read the book of all the deeds of mankind" is from 1 Enoch 81:1–3, http://www.sacred-texts.com/bib/boe/boe084.htm.

24. Josephus, *Jewish War*, 2.8.7.

25. Alex P. Jassen, "Rule of the Community," in *Outside the Bible*, edited by Feldman, Kugel, and Schiffman, 3:2934. For the baptismal liturgy, 4Q414, see Wise, Abegg, and Cook, *The Dead Sea Scrolls*, 390–391; Jonathan David Lawrence, *Washing in Water* (Atlanta: Society of Biblical Literature, 2006).

26. Jason M. Silverman, *Persepolis and Jerusalem* (New York: T. & T. Clark International, 2012).

27. Mary Boyce, *A History of Zoroastrianism*, 3 vols. (Leiden, Netherlands: Brill, 1975–1991); Mary Boyce, "Persian Religion in the Achemenid Age," in *The Cambridge History of Judaism*, vol. 1, *Introduction: The Persian Period*, edited by W. D. Davies and Louis Finkelstein (New York: Cambridge University Press, 1984), 279–307; Mary Boyce, ed., *Textual Sources for the Study of Zoroastrianism* (Chicago: University of Chicago Press, 1990). See also Shaul Shaked, ed., *Irano-Judaica* (Jerusalem: Ben-Zvi Institute for the Study of Jewish Communities in the East, 1982); Shaul Shaked, "Iranian Influence on Judaism," in *Cambridge History of Judaism*, edited by Davies and Finkelstein, 1:308–325; and Anthony J. Tomasino, *Judaism Before Jesus* (Downers Grove, IL: InterVarsity Press, 2003).

28. Quoted in Boyce, "Persian Religion in the Achemenid Age," in *Cambridge History of Judaism*, edited by Davies and Finkelstein, 1:283–284.

29. Bilhah Nitzan, "Pesher Habakkuk," in *Outside the Bible*, edited by Feldman, Kugel, and Schiffman, 1:636–666. For Herodotus, see William Stearns Davis, *Readings in Ancient History* (Boston: Allyn and Bacon, 1912), 2:58–61.

30. *Amesha Spentas*, or Bounteous Immortals: "Amesha Spentas," http://www.iranicaonline.org/articles/amesa-spenta-beneficent-divinity.

CHAPTER 8

1. Stephen D. Moore, *Empire and Apocalypse* (Sheffield, England: Sheffield Phoenix, 2006); Nienke Vos and Willemien Otten, eds., *Demons and the Devil in Ancient and Medieval Christianity* (Leiden, Netherlands: Brill, 2011).

2. *Jewish Encyclopedia*, s.v. "angelology," http://www.jewishencyclopedia.com/articles/1521-angelology; *Catholic Encyclopedia*, s.v. "angels," http://www.newadvent.org/cathen/01476d.htm; Anthony J. Tomasino, *Judaism Before Jesus* (Downers Grove, IL: InterVarsity Press, 2003); Loren T. Stuckenbruck, *The Myth of Rebellious Angels* (Tübingen, Germany: Mohr Siebeck, 2014).

3. Saul M. Olyan, *A Thousand Thousands Served Him* (Tübingen, Germany: Mohr Siebeck, 1993); Kevin P. Sullivan, *Wrestling with Angels* (Leiden, Netherlands: Brill, 2004).

4. These calculations are based on http://www.biblegateway.com/.

5. "Raphael, one of the holy angels" is from 1 Enoch 20, http://www.sacred-texts.com/bib/boe/boe023.htm. Other translations replace Raphael with Suriel: Miryam T. Brand, "1 Enoch," in *Outside the Bible*, edited by Louis H. Feldman, James L. Kugel, and Lawrence H. Schiffman, 3 vols. (Philadelphia: Jewish Publication Society, 2013), 2:1359–1452.

6. James L. Kugel, "Testaments of the Twelve Patriarchs," in *Outside the Bible*, edited by Feldman, Kugel, and Schiffman, 2:1792–1793; *Catholic Encyclopedia*, s.v. "guardian angel," http://www.newadvent.org/cathen/07049c.htm.

7. Olyan, *Thousand Thousands Served Him.*

8. Andrei A. Orlov, *Divine Scapegoats* (Albany: SUNY Press, 2015).

9. *Jewish Encyclopedia,* s.v. "Gabriel," http://www.jewishencyclopedia.com/articles/6450-gabriel.

10. "For on the first day" is quoted from Jubilees 2:2, http://www.pseud epigrapha.com/jubilees/2.htm.

11. "The lowest is, for this cause, more gloomy" is from the Testament of Levi, 3, http://www.tertullian.org/fathers2/ANF-08/anf08-07.htm.

12. Aleksander R. Michalak, *Angels as Warriors in Late Second Temple Jewish Literature* (Tübingen, Germany: Mohr Siebeck, 2012). "Today is [God's] appointed time" is quoted in Kipp Davis, "There and Back Again," in *The War Scroll: Violence, War and Peace in the Dead Sea Scrolls and Related Literature,* edited by Kipp Davis et al. (Leiden, Netherlands: Brill, 2015), 143–44. Michael Wise, Martin Abegg Jr., and Edward Cook, eds., *The Dead Sea Scrolls* (San Francisco: HarperSanFrancisco, 1996), 159.

13. "And [they] will equally preserve" is from Josephus, *Jewish War,* 2.8.7.

14. For the Aramaic Levi Document, see Wise, Abegg, and Cook, *The Dead Sea Scrolls,* 252–253; Michael E. Stone and Esther Eshel, "Aramaic Levi Document," in *Outside the Bible,* edited by Feldman, Kugel, and Schiffman, 2:1490–1506; Jonas C. Greenfield, Michael E. Stone, and Ester Eshel, eds., *The Aramaic Levi Document* (Leiden, Netherlands: Brill, 2004). For the seven angels ordaining Levi, see the Testament of Levi, 8, http://www.tertullian.org/fathers2/ANF-08/anf08-07 .htm. "The angel opened" is from James L. Kugel, "Testaments of the Twelve Patriarchs," in *Outside the Bible,* edited by Feldman, Kugel, and Schiffman, 2:1729; Michael D. Swartz, "Angelic Liturgy," in ibid., 1985–2017.

15. For the Qumran text about Michael, see Wise, Abegg, and Cook, *The Dead Sea Scrolls,* 426–427; for the Zedekiah story, ibid., 402–403; Maxwell Davidson, *Angels at Qumran* (New York: Bloomsbury: T. & T. Clark, 1992).

16. Deut. 32:8, Septuagint, http://www.ellopos.net/elpenor/greek-texts/septuagint/chapter.asp?book=5&page=32.

17. "There are many nations" is from Jubilees 15:31–32, http://www.pseud epigrapha.com/jubilees/15.htm.

18. Josephus, *Jewish War,* 2.16.4.

19. Jeffrey Burton Russell, *Devil* (Ithaca, NY: Cornell University Press, 1977); Harry A. Kelly, *Satan: A Biography* (New York: Cambridge University Press, 2006); Philip C. Almond, *The Devil* (Ithaca, NY: Cornell University Press, 2014); Adam Kotsko, *The Prince of This World* (Stanford, CA: Stanford University Press, 2016).

20. Hector M. Patmore, *Adam, Satan, and the King of Tyre* (Leiden, Netherlands: Brill, 2012).

21. "In the present age" is from Wise, Abegg, and Cook, *The Dead Sea Scrolls,* 55. "And create in them an upright spirit": Jubilees 1:19, http://www.pseudepigrapha .com/jubilees/1.htm.

22. Wise, Abegg, and Cook, *The Dead Sea Scrolls*, 240–241.

23. Michael E. Stone, *A History of the Literature of Adam and Eve* (Atlanta: Scholars Press, 1992); Michael E. Stone, *Apocryphal Adam Books* (Leiden, Netherlands: Brill, 1996); Gary A. Anderson, Michael Stone, and Johannes Tromp, *Literature on Adam and Eve* (Leiden, Netherlands: Brill, 2000); Gary A. Anderson and Michael E. Stone, *A Synopsis of the Books of Adam and Eve*, 2nd ed. (Atlanta: Society of Biblical Literature, 2001); Philip Jenkins, *The Many Faces of Christ* (New York: Basic Books, 2015). "The Watchers, who with" is from 2 Enoch 18:3, http://www .sacred-texts.com/bib/fbe/fbe125.htm. F. I. Andersen, "2 (Slavonic Apocalypse of) Enoch," in *The Old Testament Pseudepigrapha*, edited by James H. Charlesworth, 2 vols. (Garden City, NY: Doubleday, 1983–1985), 1:91–222; Kenneth Atkinson, "Testament of Moses?," in *Outside the Bible*, edited by Feldman, Kugel, and Schiffman, 2:1856–1868.

24. M. A. Knibb, "Martyrdom and Ascension of Isaiah," in *The Old Testament Pseudepigrapha*, edited by Charlesworth, 2:143–176; J. N. Bremmer, T. R. Karmann, and T. Nicklas, eds., *The Ascension of Isaiah* (Leuven, Belgium: Peeters, 2016). "The angel of lawlessness" is from Martyrdom and Ascension 2:4–5, http://www.earlychristianwritings.com/text/ascension.html; Harold W. Attridge, "Testament of Job," in *Outside the Bible*, edited by Feldman, Kugel, and Schiffman, 2:1872–1899.

25. Jubilees 17 for Abraham and Isaac; chap. 48 for Pharaoh and Egypt, http:// wesley.nnu.edu/sermons-essays-books/noncanonical-literature/noncanonical -literature-ot-pseudepigrapha/the-book-of-jubilees/.

26. "And I heard the fourth voice," 1 Enoch 40:7, http://www.sacred-texts. com/bib/boe/boe043.htm; James L. Kugel, "Testaments of the Twelve Patriarchs," in *Outside the Bible*, edited by Feldman, Kugel, and Schiffman, 2:1707.

27. "The demons are the spirits" is from R. H. Charles, *The Apocrypha and Pseudepigrapha of the Old Testament* (Oxford: Clarendon Press, 1913), introduction, http:// wesley.nnu.edu/sermons-essays-books/noncanonical-literature/noncanonical -literature-ot-pseudepigrapha/the-book-of-jubilees/.

28. Gideon Bohak, *Ancient Jewish Magic* (New York: Cambridge University Press, 2008); Shaul Shaked, James Nathan Ford, and Siam Bhayro, *Aramaic Bowl Spells* (Leiden, Netherlands: Brill, 2013–); Yuval Harari, *Jewish Magic Before the Rise of Kabbalah* (Detroit: Wayne State University Press, 2017).

29. The Qumran text cited is the Song of the Sage, 4Q510–11: see Wise, Abegg, and Cook, *The Dead Sea Scrolls*, 415. The prayer is from Michael E. Stone and Esther Eshel, "Aramaic Levi Document," in *Outside the Bible*, edited by Feldman, Kugel, and Schiffman, 2:1495.

30. For the blurry lines separating "high" and "low" traditions, see April D. DeConick, Gregory Shaw, and John D. Turner, eds., *Practicing Gnosis* (Leiden, Netherlands: Brill, 2013).

31. Bohak, *Ancient Jewish Magic*.

32. "And we explained to Noah," Jubilees 10:12–13, http://wesley.nnu.edu/sermons-essays-books/noncanonical-literature/noncanonical-literature-ot-pseudepigrapha/the-book-of-jubilees/.

33. Stanley E. Porter, ed., *The Messiah in the Old and New Testaments* (Grand Rapids, MI: Eerdmans, 2007).

34. Sigmund Mowinckel, *He That Cometh* (Grand Rapids, MI: Eerdmans, 2005); Shirley Lucass, *The Concept of the Messiah in the Scriptures of Judaism and Christianity* (New York: T. & T. Clark International, 2011). The *Encyclopedia Judaica* reference is quoted in Joseph A. Fitzmyer, *The Dead Sea Scrolls and Christian Origins* (Grand Rapids, MI: Eerdmans, 2000), 81.

35. Gerbern S. Oegema, *The Anointed and His People* (Sheffield, England: Sheffield Academic Press, 1998).

36. Gabriele Boccaccini and Jason von Ehrenkrook, eds., *Enoch and the Messiah Son of Man* (Grand Rapids, MI: Eerdmans, 2007).

37. Craig A. Evans, "Messiahs," in *Encyclopedia of the Dead Sea Scrolls*, edited by Lawrence H. Schiffman and James C. Vanderkam (Oxford: Oxford University Press, 2000), 537–542.

38. John J. Collins, *The Scepter and the Star*, 2nd ed. (Grand Rapids, MI: Eerdmans, 2010).

39. "Until the Messiah of Righteousness comes": Genesis Pesher, 4Q252; cf. Wise, Abegg, and Cook, *The Dead Sea Scrolls*, 277. "The messiahs of Aaron" is from ibid., 139. Jesper Høgenhaven, "The Book of Zechariah at Qumran," *Scandinavian Journal of the Old Testament* 27 (2013): 107–117.

40. "He will be called" is from 4Q246, in Wise, Abegg, and Cook, *The Dead Sea Scrolls*, 268–270; "First Born Son" text is 4Q369 in ibid., 328–330; John J. Collins, "Son of God," in *Outside the Bible*, edited by Feldman, Kugel, and Schiffman, 1:620–622.

41. 4Q521 is in Wise, Abegg, and Cook, *The Dead Sea Scrolls*, 420–422; "War of the Messiah," 4Q285, is in ibid., 291–294.

CHAPTER 9

1. Benjamin G. Wright and Lawrence M. Wills, eds., *Conflicted Boundaries in Wisdom and Apocalypticism* (Atlanta: Society of Biblical Literature, 2005); Matthew J. Goff, *Discerning Wisdom* (Leiden, Netherlands: Brill, 2007); Samuel L. Adams, *Wisdom in Transition* (Leiden, Netherlands: Brill, 2008).

2. Martin Hengel, *Judaism and Hellenism* (Philadelphia: Fortress Press, 1974); Martin Hengel, *Jews, Greeks, and Barbarians* (Philadelphia: Fortress Press, 1980).

3. Lloyd P. Gerson, *From Plato to Platonism* (Ithaca, NY: Cornell University Press, 2013).

4. Peter Adamson, *Philosophy in the Hellenistic and Roman Worlds* (Oxford: Oxford University Press, 2015).

5. Martin Hengel, "The Interpenetration of Judaism and Hellenism in the Pre-Maccabean Period," in *The Cambridge History of Judaism*, vol. 2, *The Hellenistic Age*, edited by W. D. Davies and Louis Finkelstein (New York: Cambridge University Press, 1990), 2:167–228.

6. Hartmut Gese, "Wisdom Literature in the Persian Period," in *The Cambridge History of Judaism*, vol. 1, *Introduction: The Persian Period*, edited by W. D. Davies and Louis Finkelstein (New York: Cambridge University Press, 1984), 1:189–218; John Day, Robert P. Gordon, and H. G. M. Williamson, eds., *Wisdom in Ancient Israel* (New York: Cambridge University Press, 1998); Alice M. Sinnott, *The Personification of Wisdom* (Burlington, VT: Ashgate, 2005); John Jarick, ed., *Perspectives on Israelite Wisdom* (New York: Bloomsbury T. & T. Clark, 2016).

7. Ian S. Moyer, *Egypt and the Limits of Hellenism* (New York: Cambridge University Press, 2011).

8. Benjamin G. Wright III, "Wisdom of Ben Sira," in *Outside the Bible*, edited by Louis H. Feldman, James L. Kugel, and Lawrence H. Schiffman, 3 vols. (Philadelphia: Jewish Publication Society, 2013), 3:2208–2353; Adams, *Wisdom in Transition*; Othmar Keel and Silvia Schroer, *Creation* (Winona Lake, IN: Eisenbrauns, 2015); Mark R. Sneed, *The Social World of the Sages* (Minneapolis: Fortress Press, 2015).

9. Peter Enns, "Wisdom of Solomon," in *Outside the Bible*, edited by Feldman, Kugel, and Schiffman, 3:2155–2208.

10. David Winston, "Philo and the Wisdom of Solomon on Creation, Revelation and Providence," in *Shem in the Tents of Japhet*, edited by James L. Kugel (Leiden, Netherlands: Brill, 2002), 109–130.

11. Rebecca Lesses, "Divine Beings," in *The Jewish Annotated New Testament*, edited by Amy-Jill Levine and Marc Zvi Brettler (New York: Oxford University Press, 2011).

12. Adam Kamesar, ed., *The Cambridge Companion to Philo* (New York: Cambridge University Press, 2009); Mireille Hadas-Lebel, *Philo of Alexandria* (Leiden, Netherlands: Brill, 2012).

13. David T. Runia, "On the Creation of the World," in *Outside the Bible*, edited by Feldman, Kugel, and Schiffman, 1:882–901. "According to the image of God" Gen. 1:27, Septuagint, http://www.ellopos.net/elpenor/physis/septuagint -genesis/1.asp?pg=3;. Psalm 82, Septuagint, http://www.ellopos.net/elpenor/ greek-texts/septuagint/chapter.asp?book=24&page=82; Thomas H. Tobin, *The Creation of Man* (Washington, DC: Catholic Biblical Association of America, 1983).

14. Hadas-Lebel, *Philo of Alexandria*; Carl Séan O'Brien, *The Demiurge in Ancient Thought* (New York: Cambridge University Press, 2015).

15. James H. Charlesworth, *The Old Testament Pseudepigrapha and the New Testament* (New York: Cambridge University Press, 1985), 66; Daniel Boyarin, "Logos, a Jewish Word," in *Jewish Annotated New Testament*, edited by Levine and Brettler.

16. Alan F. Segal, *Two Powers in Heaven* (Leiden, Netherlands: Brill, 1977); Peter Schäfer, *The Jewish Jesus* (Princeton, NJ: Princeton University Press, 2012); Daniel Boyarin, *The Jewish Gospels* (New York: New Press, 2012).

17. Peter Thacher Lanfer, *Remembering Eden* (New York: Oxford University Press, 2012). Several biblical books, including Ezekiel, might well have allusions to Eden, although they are not explicit: Martha Himmelfarb, *Between Temple and Torah* (Tübingen, Germany: Mohr Siebeck, 2013), 11–23.

18. Michael Wise, Martin Abegg Jr., and Edward Cook, eds., *The Dead Sea Scrolls* (San Francisco: HarperSanFrancisco, 1996), 53.

19. Michael E. Stone, *A History of the Literature of Adam and Eve* (Atlanta: Society of Biblical Literature, 1992); Michael E. Stone, *Apocryphal Adam Books* (Leiden, Netherlands: Brill, 1996); Gary A. Anderson, Michael Stone, and Johannes Tromp, eds., *Literature on Adam and Eve* (Leiden, Netherlands: Brill, 2000); Gary A. Anderson and Michael E. Stone, *A Synopsis of the Books of Adam and Eve*, 2nd ed. (Atlanta: Society of Biblical Literature, 2001); Gary A. Anderson, *The Genesis of Perfection* (Louisville, KY: Westminster John Knox, 2001); Philip Jenkins, *The Many Faces of Christ* (New York: Basic Books, 2015).

20. John R. Levison, *Portraits of Adam in Early Judaism* (Sheffield: JSOT Press, 1988).

21. Jubilees 3–4, http://wesley.nnu.edu/sermons-essays-books/noncanonical-literature/noncanonical-literature-ot-pseudepigrapha/the-book-of-jubilees/.

22. "In the image of your glory," Wise, Abegg, and Cook, *The Dead Sea Scrolls*, 414. The eschatological text is 4QFlorilegium, and it is variously translated. See ibid., 225–228.

23. M. D. Johnson, "Life of Adam and Eve," in *The Old Testament Pseudepigrapha*, edited by James H. Charlesworth, 2 vols. (Garden City, NY: Doubleday, 1983–1985), 2:249–296.

CHAPTER 10

1. This account is drawn from Josephus, *Jewish War*, 2.1–6. "It was a glorious thing" is from ibid., 1.33.2. Mladen Popović, ed., *The Jewish Revolt Against Rome* (Leiden, Netherlands: Brill, 2011); Honora Howell Chapman and Zuleika Rodgers, eds., *A Companion to Josephus in His World* (Malden, MA: John Wiley & Sons, 2016).

2. Josephus, *Jewish War*, 2.3.1, for the Galileans and Idumeans; 2.4.1 for the spreading disorder.

3. This account is drawn from Josephus, *Jewish Antiquities*, bk. 14; Emilio Gabba, "The Social, Economic and Political History of Palestine, 63 BCE–CE 70," in *The Cambridge History of Judaism*, vol. 3, *The Early Roman Period*, edited by William Horbury, W. D. Davies, and John Sturdy (New York: Cambridge University Press,

1999), 94–167; Anthony J. Tomasino, *Judaism Before Jesus* (Downers Grove, IL: InterVarsity Press, 2003).

4. Bieke Mahieu, *Between Rome and Jerusalem* (Leuven, Belgium: Peeters, 2012).

5. Adam K. Marshak, *The Many Faces of Herod the Great* (Grand Rapids, MI: Eerdmans, 2015).

6. E. Mary Smallwood, *The Jews Under Roman Rule* (Boston: Brill Academic, 2001).

7. Samuel Rocca, *Herod's Judaea* (Tübingen, Germany: Mohr Siebeck, 2008); Joseph Patrich, *Studies in the Archaeology and History of Caesarea Maritima* (Leiden, Netherlands: Brill, 2011); Norman Gelb, *Herod the Great* (Lanham, MD: Rowman & Littlefield, 2013).

8. James H. Charlesworth, *Jesus and Archaeology* (Grand Rapids, MI: Eerdmans, 2006).

9. The Assumption of Moses, 6, http://wesley.nnu.edu/index.php?id=2124; Kenneth Atkinson, "Testament of Moses," in *Outside the Bible*, edited by Louis H. Feldman, James L. Kugel, and Lawrence H. Schiffman, 3 vols. (Philadelphia: Jewish Publication Society, 2013), 2:1856–1868.

10. Benedikt Eckhardt, ed., *Jewish Identity and Politics Between the Maccabees and Bar Kokhba* (Leiden; Boston: Brill, 2012).

11. Douglas R. Edwards, *Religion and Society in Roman Palestine* (New York: Routledge, 2004); Zeev Weiss, *The Sepphoris Synagogue* (Jerusalem: Israel Exploration Society, 2005).

12. Smallwood, *Jews Under Roman Rule*.

13. Rocca, *Herod's Judaea*; Andreas J. M. Kropp, *Images and Monuments of Near Eastern Dynasts, 100 BC–AD 100* (Oxford: Oxford University Press, 2013).

14. R. B. Wright, "Psalms of Solomon," in *The Old Testament Pseudepigrapha*, edited by James H. Charlesworth, 2 vols. (Garden City, NY: Doubleday, 1983–1985), 2:639–670; David deSilva, *The Jewish Teachers of Jesus, James, and Jude* (New York: Oxford University Press, 2012), 144–146.

15. DeSilva, *Jewish Teachers*, 165–174; D. R. A. Hare, "The Lives of the Prophets," in *The Old Testament Pseudepigrapha*, edited by Charlesworth, 2:379–400.

16. Mark A. Chancey, *The Myth of a Gentile Galilee* (New York: Cambridge University Press, 2002).

17. Martin Hengel, *The Zealots* (Edinburgh: T. & T. Clark, 1997); Mark A. Brighton, *The Sicarii in Josephus's Judean War* (Leiden, Netherlands: Brill, 2009).

18. Josephus, *Jewish War*, 2.13.4–5. The term for "divine inspiration" here is *proschemati theiasmou* (Acts 21:38); David B. Levenson, "Messianic Movements," in *The Jewish Annotated New Testament*, edited by Amy-Jill Levine and Marc Zvi Brettler (New York: Oxford University Press, 2011).

19. Lester L. Grabbe, Gabriele Boccaccini, and Jason M. Zurawski, eds., *The Seleucid and Hasmonean Periods and the Apocalyptic Worldview* (London: T. & T. Clark, 2016).

20. Lee I. Levine, *The Ancient Synagogue* (New Haven, CT: Yale University Press, 2000); Wayne O. McCready and Adele Reinhartz, eds., *Common Judaism* (Minneapolis: Fortress Press, 2008); Rina Talgam, *Mosaics of Faith* (University Park: Pennsylvania State University Press, 2014).

21. Daniel K. Falk, "Words of the Luminaries," in *Outside the Bible*, edited by Feldman, Kugel, and Schiffman, 2:1960–1984; Arnaldo Momigliano, *On Pagans, Jews, and Christians* (Middletown, CT: Wesleyan University Press, 1987).

22. Anders Runesson, "The Nature and Origins of the 1st Century Synagogue," http://www.bibleinterp.com/articles/Runesson-1st-Century_Synagogue_1.shtml.

23. Daniel R. Schwartz and Zeev Weiss, eds., *Was 70 CE a Watershed in Jewish History?* (Leiden, Netherlands: Brill, 2012).

24. Annette Yoshiko Reed, "Testament of Abraham," in *Outside the Bible*, edited by Feldman, Kugel, and Schiffman, 2:1671–1696; http://www.newadvent.org/fathers/1007.htm; https://en.wikipedia.org/wiki/Testament_of_Abraham.

25. Lawrence M. Wills, ed., *Ancient Jewish Novels* (New York: Oxford University Press, 2002). C. Burchard, "Joseph and Aseneth," in *The Old Testament Pseudepigrapha*, edited by Charlesworth, 2:177–248; Ross S. Kraemer, *When Aseneth Met Joseph* (New York: Oxford University Press, 1998); Patricia Ahearne Kroll, "Joseph and Asenath," in *Outside the Bible*, edited by Feldman, Kugel, and Schiffman, 3:2525–2590.

26. Louis H. Feldman, *Jew and Gentile in the Ancient World* (Princeton, NJ: Princeton University Press, 1996); E. Mary Smallwood, "The Diaspora in the Roman Period Before CE 70," in *Cambridge History of Judaism*, edited by Horbury, Davies, and Sturdy, 168–191; Morton Smith, "The Gentiles in Judaism, 125 BCE–CE 66," in ibid., 192–249; Erich S. Gruen, *Diaspora* (Cambridge, MA: Harvard University Press, 2002); Christine E. Hayes, *Gentile Impurities and Jewish Identities* (Oxford: Oxford University Press, 2002); Charlotte Elisheva Fonrobert, "Judaizers, Jewish Christians, and Others," in *Jewish Annotated New Testament*, edited by Levine and Brettler. For Adiabene, see Eric Maroney, *The Other Zions* (Lanham, MD: Rowman & Littlefield, 2010).

27. Levine, *The Ancient Synagogue.*

28. Geza Vermes, *Jesus the Jew* (Minneapolis: Fortress Press, 1981).

29. J. B. Lightfoot, "On Some Points Connected with the Essenes," in *Dissertations on the Apostolic Age* (London: Macmillan, 1892), 323–407, http://philologos.org/__eb-jbl/essenes.htm; Geza Vermes, *Scrolls, Scriptures, and Early Christianity* (New York: T. & T. Clark International, 2005); Florentino García Martínez, eds., *Echoes from the Caves* (Leiden, Netherlands: Brill, 2009).

30. Jaime Clark-Soles, *Death and the Afterlife in the New Testament* (New York: T. & T. Clark, 2006); Daniel R. Schwartz, "Jewish Movements of the New Testament Period," in *Jewish Annotated New Testament*, edited by Levine and Brettler.

31. F. Segal, *The Other Judaisms of Late Antiquity* (Atlanta: Scholars Press, 1987).

32. Geza Vermes, "Jewish Miracle Workers in the Late Second Temple Period," in *Jewish Annotated New Testament*, edited by Levine and Brettler.

33. Geza Vermes, *Jesus in His Jewish Context* (Minneapolis: Fortress Press, 2003).

34. For the influence of the Psalms of Solomon on messianic ideas, see deSilva, *Jewish Teachers*.

35. For Caesarea, see Josephus, *Jewish War*, 2.13.7, 2.14.5; Mladen Popović, ed., *The Jewish Revolt Against Rome* (Leiden, Netherlands: Brill, 2011); Steve Mason, *A History of the Jewish War* (New York: Cambridge University Press, 2016).

36. For the inscription to Titus, see Mason, *History of the Jewish War*.

37. Josephus, *Jewish War*, 2.18.

38. Josephus, *Jewish War*, 2.18.2.

CHAPTER 11

1. Irenaeus Against Heresies, 24.4, http://www.newadvent.org/fathers/0103124.htm.

2. For "inverted Judaism," see Lester L. Grabbe, *An Introduction to Second Temple Judaism* (New York: T. & T. Clark, 2010). See also Jaan Lahe, *Gnosis und Judentum* (Leiden, Netherlands: Brill, 2012).

3. Daniel R. Schwartz and Zeev Weiss, eds., *Was 70 CE a Watershed in Jewish History?* (Leiden, Netherlands: Brill, 2012).

4. *Jewish Encyclopedia*, s.v. "Fiscus Judaicus," http://www.jewishencyclopedia.com/articles/6157-fiscus-judaicus.

5. Gerbern S. Oegema, *The Anointed and His People* (Sheffield, England: Sheffield Academic Press, 1998); Carl B. Smith, *No Longer Jews* (Peabody, MA: Hendrickson, 2004); Miriam Pucci Ben Ze'ev, *Diaspora Judaism in Turmoil, 116/117 CE* (Leuven, Belgium: Peeters, 2005); Mireille Hadas-Lebel, *Jerusalem Against Rome* (Leuven, Belgium: Peeters 2006); James J. Bloom, *The Jewish Revolts Against Rome, A.D. 66–135* (Jefferson, NC: McFarland, 2010); Jodi Magness, *The Archaeology of the Holy Land* (New York: Cambridge University Press, 2012).

6. James C. VanderKam, *The Jewish Apocalyptic Heritage in Early Christianity* (The Hague: Van Gorcum, 1996); Marko Jauhiainen, *The Use of Zechariah in Revelation* (Tübingen, Germany: Mohr Siebeck, 2005).

7. Written around the same time as Revelation, the Christian liturgy found in the *Didache* (Teaching) ends with the apocalyptic words, "Let grace come and let this world pass away": http://www.earlychristianwritings.com/text/didache-lake.html.

8. Adam H. Becker, "2 Baruch," in *Outside the Bible*, edited by Louis H. Feldman, James L. Kugel, and Lawrence H. Schiffman, 3 vols. (Philadelphia: Jewish Publication Society, 2013), 2:1565–1585; Karina Martin Hogan, "4 Ezra," in ibid., 1607–1668.

9. Kenneth R. Jones, *Jewish Reactions to the Destruction of Jerusalem in A.D. 70* (Leiden, Netherlands: Brill, 2011); Matthias Henze and Gabriele Boccaccini, eds., *Fourth Ezra and Second Baruch* (Boston: Brill, 2013).

10. "What, therefore, will there be," 2 Baruch 3:5, http://wesley.nnu.edu/sermons-essays-books/noncanonical-literature/noncanonical-literature-ot-pseudepigrapha/the-book-of-the-apocalypse-of-baruch-the-son-of-neriah-or-2-baruch/.

11. Hindy Naiman, *Losing the Temple and Recovering the Future* (New York: Cambridge University Press, 2014).

12. Hayim Lapin, *Rabbis as Romans* (New York: Oxford University Press, 2012).

13. "The Holy One," is quoted in Jacob Neusner, *A History of the Jews in Babylonia* (Leiden, Netherlands: Brill, 1969), 74; Hayim Lapin, "The Origins and Development of the Rabbinic Movement in the Land of Israel," in *The Cambridge History of Judaism*, vol. 4, *The Late Roman-Rabbinic Period*, edited by Steven T. Katz (New York: Cambridge University Press, 2006), 206–229; Charlotte Elisheva Fonrobert and Martin S. Jaffee, eds., *The Cambridge Companion to the Talmud and Rabbinic Literature* (New York: Cambridge University Press, 2007); Seth Schwartz, *The Ancient Jews from Alexander to Muhammad* (New York: Cambridge University Press, 2014); Moulie Vidas, *Tradition and the Formation of the Talmud* (Princeton, NJ: Princeton University Press, 2014).

14. Alan F. Segal, *Rebecca's Children* (Cambridge, MA: Harvard University Press, 1986); Joshua E. Burns, *The Christian Schism in Jewish History and Jewish Memory* (New York: Cambridge University Press, 2016).

15. "Nay, even blasphemies": Justin Martyr, "Dialogue with Trypho," 79, http://www.earlychristianwritings.com/text/justinmartyr-dialoguetrypho.html; Steven T. Katz, "The Rabbinic Response to Christianity," in *Cambridge History of Judaism*, edited by Katz, 259–298.

16. Annette Yoshiko Reed, "Apocrypha, 'Outside Books,' and Pseudepigrapha: Ancient Categories and Modern Perceptions of Parabiblical Literature," handout from fortieth Philadelphia seminar titled "Christian Origins: Parabiblical Literature," October 10, 2002, http://ccat.sas.upenn.edu/psco/year40/areed2.html; Lorenzo DiTommaso and Christfried Böttrich, eds., *The Old Testament Apocrypha in the Slavonic Tradition* (Tübingen, Germany: Mohr Siebeck, 2011); Philip Jenkins, *The Many Faces of Christ* (New York: Basic Books, 2015); Andrei A. Orlov, *Divine Scapegoats* (Albany: SUNY Press, 2015).

17. Andrei A. Orlov, *The Enoch-Metatron Tradition* (Tübingen, Germany: Mohr Siebeck, 2005); April D. DeConick., ed., *Paradise Now* (Leiden, Netherlands: Brill, 2006); Andrei Orlov, *From Apocalypticism to Merkabah Mysticism* (Leiden, Netherlands: Brill, 2007); Martha Himmelfarb, *Between Temple and Torah* (Tübingen, Germany: Mohr Siebeck, 2013).

18. I am drawing heavily on the work of David deSilva, in *The Jewish Teachers of Jesus, James, and Jude* (New York: Oxford University Press, 2012). See also Marc Zvi Brettler, "The New Testament Between the Hebrew Bible (Tanakh) and Rabbinic Literature," in *The Jewish Annotated New Testament*, edited by Amy-Jill Levine and Marc Zvi Brettler (New York: Oxford University Press, 2011).

19. Epistle of Barnabas 18:1, translated by J. B. Lightfoot, http://www.early christianwritings.com/text/barnabas-lightfoot.html.

20. David Nirenberg, *Anti-Judaism* (New York: W. W. Norton, 2013). For the earlier background, see Emilio Gabba, "The Growth of Anti-Judaism; or, The Greek Attitude Towards the Jews," in *The Cambridge History of Judaism*, vol. 2, *The Hellenistic Age*, edited by W. D. Davies and Louis Finkelstein (New York: Cambridge University Press, 1990), 614–656; Peter Schäfer, *Judeophobia* (Cambridge, MA: Harvard University Press, 2009). Eusebius is quoted from the Ecclesiastical History 4:6, http://www.ccel.org/ccel/schaff/npnf201.iii.ix.vi.html.

21. Robert L. Wilken, *John Chrysostom and the Jews* (Berkeley: University of California Press, 1983); Adam H. Becker and Annette Yoshiko Reed, eds., *The Ways That Never Parted* (Tübingen, Germany: Mohr Siebeck, 2003); Dan Jaffé, ed., *Studies in Rabbinic Judaism and Early Christianity* (Leiden, Netherlands: Brill, 2010).

22. A. F. J. Klijn, *Jewish-Christian Gospel Tradition* (Leiden; New York: Brill, 1992); J. Carleton Paget, "Jewish Christianity," in *The Cambridge History of Judaism*, vol. 3, *The Early Roman Period*, edited by William Horbury, W. D. Davies, and John Sturdy (New York: Cambridge University Press, 1999), 731–775; David Frankfurter, "Beyond Jewish Christianity," in *Ways That Never Parted*, edited by Becker and Reed; Antti Marjanen and Petri Luomanen, eds., *A Companion to Second-Century Christian "Heretics"* (Leiden, Netherlands: Brill, 2008); Sacha Stern, ed., *Sects and Sectarianism in Jewish History* (Leiden, Netherlands: Brill, 2011); Petri Luomanen, *Recovering Jewish-Christian Sects and Gospels* (Leiden, Netherlands: Brill, 2012); Andrew Gregory et al., eds., *The Oxford Handbook of Early Christian Apocrypha* (Oxford: Oxford University Press, 2016).

23. Han J. W. Drijvers, *East of Antioch* (London: Variorum Reprints, 1984); Peter M. Edwell, *Between Rome and Persia* (New York: Routledge, 2008).

24. Joseph Amar, "A Shared Voice," *Times Literary Supplement*, October 3, 2014. For continuing Jewish-Christian contacts, see Michal Bar-Asher Siegal, *Early Christian Monastic Literature and the Babylonian Talmud* (New York: Cambridge University Press, 2013).

25. Philo, "On the Contemplative Life," http://www.earlychristianwritings .com/yonge/book34.html; Ross S. Kraemer, *Unreliable Witnesses* (New York: Oxford University Press, 2011); David M. Hay, "On the Contemplative Life," in *Outside the Bible*, edited by Feldman, Kugel, and Schiffman, 3:2481–2501.

26. Michael Allen Williams, *Rethinking "Gnosticism"* (Princeton, NJ: Princeton University Press, 1999); Karen King, *What Is Gnosticism?* (Cambridge, MA: Belknap Press of Harvard University Press, 2003); Jenkins, *Many Faces of Christ*.

27. Lahe, *Gnosis und Judentum*; Carl Séan O'Brien, *The Demiurge in Ancient Thought* (New York: Cambridge University Press, 2015).

28. John D. Turner and Ruth Majercik, eds., *Gnosticism and Later Platonism* (Atlanta: Society of Biblical Literature, 2000); Kevin Corrigan and Tuomas Rasimus, eds., *Gnosticism, Platonism and the Late Ancient World* (Leiden, Netherlands: Brill, 2013).

29. Birger A. Pearson, *Ancient Gnosticism* (Minneapolis: Fortress Press, 2007).

30. For Menander, see Irenaeus, "Against Heresies," http://www.newadvent.org/fathers/0103123.htm.

31. "The first to affirm": ibid., 24:2, http://www.newadvent.org/fathers/0103124.htm.

32. Nicola Denzey Lewis, *Cosmology and Fate in Gnosticism and Graeco-Roman Antiquity* (Leiden, Netherlands: Brill, 2013).

33. Isabella Sandwell, *Religious Identity In Late Antiquity* (New York: Cambridge University Press, 2007).

34. Stanley Jerome Isser, *The Dositheans* (Leiden, Netherlands: Brill, 1976).

35. Gary N. Knoppers, *Jews and Samaritans* (New York: Oxford University Press, 2013), 220–225.

36. Antti Marjanen and Petri Luomanen, eds., *A Companion to Second-Century Christian "Heretics"* (Leiden, Netherlands: Brill, 2008); Sebastian Moll, *The Arch-Heretic Marcion* (Tübingen, Germany: Mohr Siebeck, 2010); Nirenberg, *Anti-Judaism*; Judith M. Lieu, *Marcion and the Making of a Heretic* (New York: Cambridge University Press, 2015).

37. John C. Reeves, *Heralds of That Good Realm* (Leiden, Netherlands: Brill, 1996); Kurt Rudolf, "The Baptist Sects," in *Cambridge History of Judaism*, edited by Horbury, Davies, and Sturdy, 3:471–500.

38. Jorunn J. Buckley, *The Mandaeans* (New York: Oxford University Press, 2002); Birger A. Pearson, *Ancient Gnosticism* (Minneapolis: Fortress Press, 2007); Gerard Russell, *Heirs to Forgotten Kingdoms* (New York: Basic Books, 2014).

39. Gerard P. Luttikhuizen, *The Revelation of Elchasai* (Tübingen, Germany: Mohr Siebeck, 1985), 111–117; F. Stanley Jones, *Pseudoclementina Elchasaiticaque inter judaeochristiana* (Leuven, Belgium: Peeters, 2012).

40. This account of the Manichaeans is drawn from Samuel N. C. Lieu, *Manichaeism in Mesopotamia and the Roman East* (Leiden, Netherlands: Brill, 1994); Reeves, *Heralds of That Good Realm*; Andrew Welburn, ed., *Mani, the Angel and the Column of Glory* (Edinburgh: Floris Books 1998); J. Kevin Coyle, *Manichaeism and Its Legacy* (Leiden, Netherlands: Brill, 2009); and Nicholas J. Baker-Brian, *An Ancient Faith Rediscovered* (London: T. & T. Clark, 2011). For the tradition in central and East Asia, see Zsuzsanna Gulácsi, *Mani's Pictures* (Leiden, Netherlands: Brill, 2015).

41. Iain Gardner, Jason BeDuhn, and Paul Dilley, *Mani at the Court of the Persian Kings* (Leiden, Netherlands: Brill, 2015).

42. John C. Reeves, "Jewish Pseudepigrapha in Manichaean Literature," in *Tracing the Threads*, edited by John C. Reeves (Atlanta: Society of Biblical Literature, 1994), 173–203; April D. DeConick, Gregory Shaw, and John D. Turner, eds., *Practicing Gnosis* (Leiden, Netherlands: Brill, 2013).

43. Dylan M. Burns, *Apocalypse of the Alien God* (Philadelphia: University of Pennsylvania Press, 2014). For "The holy baptism and the living water," see the Apocalypse of Adam, http://gnosis.org/naghamm/adam.html. John D. Turner, *Sethian Gnosticism and the Platonic Tradition* (Quebec: Presses Université Laval, 2001).

44. Christian Lange, ed., *Locating Hell in Islamic Traditions* (Leiden, Netherlands: Brill, 2015); S. R. Burge, *Angels in Islam* (New York: Routledge, 2012).

45. Brian A. Brown, *Noah's Other Son* (New York: Continuum, 2007); Gabriel Said Reynolds, *The Qur'an and Its Biblical Subtext* (New York: Routledge, 2010). For possible links with Jewish Christianity, see John G. Gager, "Did Jewish Christians See the Rise of Islam?," in *Ways That Never Parted*, edited by Becker and Reed, 361–372; Jenkins, *Many Faces of Christ*.

46. Zeki Saritoprak, *Islam's Jesus* (Gainesville: University Press of Florida, 2014).

INDEX

PHILIP JENKINS is a distinguished professor of history at the Institute for Studies of Religion, Baylor University. The author of many books, Jenkins divides his time between Texas and Pennsylvania.

Photograph by James Rasp